EUROPE
AND CIVIL SOCIETY

Published in our
centenary year
～ **2004** ～
MANCHESTER
UNIVERSITY
PRESS

EUROPE IN CHANGE   SERIES EDITORS *Thomas Christiansen and Emil Kirchner*

Carlo Ruzza

EUROPE
AND CIVIL SOCIETY

Movement coalitions and European
governance

MANCHESTER UNIVERSITY PRESS
Manchester and New York

distributed exclusively in the USA by Palgrave

Published by Manchester University Press
Oxford Road, Manchester M13 9NR, UK
and Room 400, 175 Fifth Avenue, New York, NY 10010, USA
www.manchesteruniversitypress.co.uk

Distributed exclusively in the USA by
Palgrave, 175 Fifth Avenue, New York,
NY 10010, USA

Distributed exclusively in Canada by
UBC Press, University of British Columbia, 2029 West Mall,
Vancouver, BC, Canada V6T 1Z2

British Library Cataloguing-in-Publication Data
A catalogue record for this book is available from the British Library

Library of Congress Cataloging-in-Publication Data applied for

ISBN 0 7190 6177 6 *hardback*

First published 2004

13 12 11 10 09 08 07 06 05 04   10 9 8 7 6 5 4 3 2 1

Typeset in Minion with Lithos
by Northern Phototypesetting Co Ltd, Bolton
Printed in Great Britain
by CPI, Bath

CONTENTS

Tables and Figures

Tables

Figures

ACKNOWLEDGEMENTS

Too many people had a part in the making of this book to list them all. First I would like to thank the EU personnel and scores of activists who generously contributed time to be interviewed. Among the people working in EU institutions, in the Commission Angela Liberatore helped me with contacts, information and, as the civil servant administering two EU grants, also provided me with useful questions and suggestions on topics to pursue. Annette Bossher and Ludwig Kraemer helped me with materials, interviews and contacts. In the European Parliament special thanks to Michael Elliott, Glyn Ford, Bart Staes and Jose Luis Linazasoro. At the European Monitoring Centre against Racism (EUMC) I would like to thank Peter Fleissner and Birgitta Lowander. Thanks to Giampiero Alhadeff from Solidar and Nello Rubatto from EFA.

I would like to thank Bill Gamson, Orlando Patterson, Alessandro Pizzorno and Klaus Eder for many useful discussions. Thanks also to Susan Pedersen, and Tom Ertman, with whom I shared my office at Harvard for many useful discussions over the years, and Cheril Zollars. Thanks to Oliver Schmidtke, my co-author of several articles.

At Trento I would like to thank Fortunata Piselli, Stefano Fella and the team that helped me with frame analysis, particularly Emanuela Bozzini who helped to coordinate the team activities. My work on the anti-racist movement started with a McCarthur Foundation grant to study peace movements at the Center for International Affairs at Harvard. My work on environmental policy and the environmental movement was supported by two EU Commission grants (ENV4-CT96-0198, and EV5V-CT 94-0389). Special thanks to the Environmental Unit of DG Research, the Waste Management unit of DG Environment and the Anti-Racist unit of DG Social Affairs.

My heartfelt thanks to Lella without whom this book would not have been possible.

Abbreviations

ACF	Advocacy Coalition Framework
AEBR	Association of European Border Regions
AER	Assembly of European Regions
AFET	Committee on Foreign Affairs, Human Rights, Common Security and Defence
AP	Action Plan
CAF	Charities Aid Foundation
CAP	Common Agricultural Policy
CECODHAS	Comité Européen de Coordination de l'Habitat Social
CEFIC	European Confederation of Chemical Industries
CEMR	Council of European Municipalities and Regions
CLRAE	Congress of Local and Regional Authorities
CONECCS	Consultation, the European Commission and Civil Society
CoR	Committee of the Regions
DG	Directorate-General
EA	European Alliance
EAP	Environmental Action Programme
EB	Eurobarometer
EBLUL	European Bureau for Lesser Used Languages
Ebs	Eurobarometer Special Surveys
ECAS	European Citizen Action Service
ECJ	European Court of Justice
ECRE	European Council of Refugees and Exiles
EEA	European Economic Area
EEB	European Environmental Bureau
EFA	European Free Alliances
EHRF	European Human Rights Foundation
EMAS	Environmental Management and Audit Scheme
EMF	European Migrant Forum
ENAR	European Network against Racism
EP	European Parliament
EPE	European Partners for the Environment
ESC	European and Social Committee
ESPF	European Social Policy Forum
EU	European Union
EUMC	European Monitoring Centre against Racism and Xenophobia
EURAG	European Federation of the Elderly
EWL	European Women's Lobby
EYAR	European Year Against Racism
EYF	European Youth Forum
FEANTSA	European Federation of National Organisations Working with the Homeless
FOE	Friends of the Earth International
IGC	Intergovernmental Conference

ILGA	International Lesbian and Gay Association
IR	International Relations
LIBE	Committee on Citizens' Freedoms and Rights, Justice and Home Affairs
MAC	Movement-Inspired Advocacy Coalition
MEP	Member of the European Parliament
MF	Migrants' Forum
MO	Movement Organisation
MPG	Migration Policy Group
NGO	Non-Governmental Organisation
OCS	Organised Civil Society
POS	Political Opportunity Theory
R&D	Research and Development
RETT	Committee on Regional Policy, Transport and Tourism
RM	Resource Mobilisation Theory
SEA	Single European Act
SL	Starting Line
SMO	Social Movement Organisation
UNICE	Union of Industrial Employers' Confederations of Europe
WHO	World Health Organisation
WVS	World Value Survey
WWF	World Wide Fund for Nature

1

Introduction

The re-location of advocacy

Public-interest associations often find it difficult to gain access to the European Union (EU) institutions. It is expensive to set up offices in Brussels; activists require highly specialised legal and technical competence if they are to operate effectively; and organisations need sufficient personnel and resources to be able to address the different phases of the policy process. Nevertheless, over the years a large number of public-interest associations have opened offices in Brussels. Among them are representatives of an impressive array of social causes and political positions, including activist groups which not long ago were known only for their spectacular protest tactics. This has happened because as the centre of gravity of several policy areas has shifted to Brussels so too have lobbyists, political advisors and technical experts, and increasingly political activists and voluntary workers as well. The aim of this book is to examine the consequences of this re-location of advocacy. It will do so by looking at the interaction between campaigners and EU institutions in certain key areas of social activism: environmental policy, anti-racism and regionalism.

The re-location of aspects of social activism to the Community level is a complex process with manifold consequences for both the institutional sector and the civil society from which public interest groups arise. Viewed from the multifarious perspectives of different policy areas, evaluation of the reasons for, and the repercussions of, this re-location requires understanding of the consequences of the process of European integration for organised civil society (hereafter OCS) – a complex sector which includes non-governmental organisations (NGOs), social movements, advocacy groups, charities, representatives of self-help organisations and promotional groups.[1]

At member state level, but increasingly at the EU level as well, these diverse organisations are pressing for a greater voice in the policy process, for more resources and for greater visibility. This is a politically controversial phenomenon, for it touches upon such contentious issues as the role of expertise in the policy process, the proper functioning of the state and its relation to majoritarian processes. A range of attitudes is taken towards public interest groups and their attempts to exert more influence. Many of them have been helped by parts of the EU institutional framework. Indeed, commissioners, parliamentarians and other institutional actors sometimes welcome and even support their work. Their presence is seen as the voice of an emerging European civil society – a voice to be encouraged because it addresses a perceived isolation of the European level of governance – and as a potentially useful counterbalance against the power of organised private interests. However, other observers have grown weary of advocates without the legitimacy that springs from participation in electoral contests, and dispute the claim by public pressure groups that they represent public interests.

Often, their representativeness and their operating procedures – selection of issues, of leaders and their decision-making rules – are considered insufficiently transparent to warrant the public resources and the strong impact on the policy process that they seek. Their accountability is considered inadequate. However, even critics agree that the role of public interest groups cannot be ignored in a European decision-making structure traditionally very receptive to private interests and with limited capacity to utilise majoritarian rules. In recent years, scholars, NGO personnel and EU institutional actors have joined in a debate on what the proper role of the voluntary sector should be, on its financing structure and on its levels of access to the policy process. This book aims to contribute to this debate. The role of the voluntary sector is growing in several member states (Commission 1997b). Analysis of its impact and modes of operation at EU level is necessary both in relation to the ongoing debate on EU institutional change and in order to understand the important specific fields in which public interest groups operate – fields such as environmental policy, anti-racist policy and regional policy that this study will address.

The voluntary sector as a whole is now formed by a large and internally differentiated set of organisations, at both EU level and within member states. It comprises such diverse types of organisation as churches, charities and multi-faith groups, self-help groups, development organisations, poverty relief and institutionalised social movement organisations. These various types of organisations sometimes coexist in specific policy areas, forming broad advocacy coalitions with the help of institutional actors and member state-based organisations. A complex, expanding and still little known field of social interests has emerged, and it is this phenomenon that the book intends to examine. The context of study also raises broad issues of legitimacy and accountability in the EU which are as important as the workings of specific policy sectors. I shall focus on the advocacy coalitions in which institutionalised social movement organisations play a significant role. These are distinctive and socially significant phenomena because they import into the context of EU institutions the social activism, the innovative policy ideas and the media visibility that characterised the institutionalised social movements of the 1980s in several member states.

The umbrella groups of institutionalised social movements and the coalitions that they have formed in the EU reflect the transformation of important aspects of social idealism in Europe at the beginning of the twenty-first century. Although a large part of the social movement sector prominent in the last few decades has become substantially institutionalised (Eder 1996; Rootes 1997; Giugni and Passy 1998b), and increasingly coordinates efforts with a growing array of public-interest organisations, voluntary associations, advocacy groups and Non-Governmental Organisations (NGOs), it still retains certain features distinctive of protest organisations and its links with the social movement sector.[2] Yet for several of the activists of these movement-inspired advocacy coalitions (hereafter MACs), operating efficiently in Brussels has required them to acquire coalition-forming, legal, negotiating and technical skills not often found in the social movement sector.

In Brussels, and in the other locations of the EU institutions and agencies, activist-inspired advocacy coalitions have joined a host of associations of civil society in an expanding arena of public-interest representation and service delivery. Their EU dynamics reflect a general trend in the member state structure of organised civil society whereby a thriving third sector is gradually taking over some of the social functions of the state. Institutionalised social movements are performing some of the roles of political parties and the state, channelling policy advice, policy analysis and advocacy in a variety of political arenas. As different territorial levels of political authority become increasingly nested in the EU system, the European level is becoming a significant target of these advocacy coalitions. EU public-interest lobbying consequently acquires ever-greater importance in the multiple avenues of a dispersed political authority.

This new-found importance of public associations raises questions concerning the factors that make them worthy of support, and the mechanisms by which they conduct their operations in Brussels. It also raises the question of why public-interest associations participate in the EU policy process, especially considering that their presence may legitimate a system that they often claim is deaf to their demands and which they may oppose, identifying it with the harmful aspects of globalisation. The component of the social movement sector opposed to international and supranational organisations has grown considerably in recent years, compelling re-consideration of the strategies of those organisations that collaborate with EU institutions. Answering the above questions will require investigation into the role of public-interest associations at different stages of the policy process, the thinking of their cadres and policy analysts, their political values and strategies. In other words, it will be necessary to go beyond analysis of policy outcomes and broadly investigate the role of NGOs and related organisations in the policy process – the structures and processes in which they are involved. The purpose of this book, therefore, is to investigate these issues in certain policy areas where different kinds of public-interest association have established a presence in Brussels, comparing the way in which they operate, and not merely evaluating their strength or policy outcomes.

In this introductory chapter, the object of study– coalitions inspired by social movements – will be defined and a scheme proposed with which to investigate their modes of operation. In chapter 2, before analysis of the case studies, a scheme will be discussed for the study of their impact at different levels of governance. Focusing on movement coalitions – and not as frequently happens in policy analysis on specific policy events – is particularly useful because it affords better understanding of the interconnections that arise across levels of governance.

The fact that public-interest groups represent diffused interests and large constituencies, the importance of the issues that they raise for the media and public opinion and their multifarious connections with political institutions at various levels requires assessment of their impact throughout a set of broad networks of influence. Their weakness in addressing specific policy issues should not induce the observer to deny their importance, which should be evaluated in terms, for instance, of feeding ideas into the policy process, shaping the preferences of conventional political actors, providing normative anchors for a variety of policy actors and utilising the media effectively. In-depth interviews with diverse policy actors will permit assessment of the salience of other levels of European governance in actors' thinking – particularly the impact of national and regional politics, and of time dependent and path dependent constraints. It will also be possible to compare such impact with the impact of other interests, such as industrial lobbies, in a system that increasingly includes a multiplicity of actors in horizontal governance. All these actors have short-term and long-term interests that may not emerge from examination of specific policy events but are often clearly articulated by concerned actors. In particular, EU policy-makers have a long-term interest in legitimating their operations, and they can in part achieve this goal through the closer involvement of public pressure groups. The presence of OCS in Brussels could be encouraged as a way of injecting purpose into a project of 'EU construction' whose idealism seems to have gone astray. This connection between EU public pressure groups and EU legitimacy (see Greenwood 1997) has been evident in the recent debate on civil society and the centrality of public-interest associations in the debate on democratising the EU. For instance, an entire team was assembled to work on the role of NGOs and civil society for the preparation of the 2001 White Paper on Governance (Commission 2001c; Commission, Preston *et al.* 2001).

Before discussing the specific coalitions examined, it may be helpful to provide an introduction to the general role of lobbies and social movements in the EU, and to the re-emerging concern with civil society.

The field of EU functional representation

As a policy-making system, the EU is traditionally receptive to all sorts of interest groups, both private and public. Access is generally easier to EU institutions than to similar national ones, even if some areas are less permeable than others (Mazey and Richardson 1993). But access is not equally available to all types of actor. The European system of representation has always taken a pro-business stance – an ethos, as several Commission officials have stressed, still entrenched in EU institutions. Civil servants often maintain that business influence and competence should be enlisted to help the state run the economy. This is advocated, not through the integration of business organisations into the state but at the meso level (Lehnbruch and Schmitter 1982; Smith 1993) through a system of extensive consultation. Business organisations generally welcome this role – a role characterising a pluralist rather that corporatist set of relations.[3] All groups are able to find ways to exert influence in this system, but the amount of resources available to them largely determines their effectiveness as lobbyists. For this reason, public-interest groups, which typically suffer from Olson's (1965) diffuse-interests disadvantages, are in a weaker position.

Several scholars point to the weakness of public-interest associations and the obstacles that they encounter in a system oriented by a neo-liberal ethos at odds with the values of many of these groups, and in a policy environment for which they are ill prepared because they lack the necessary technical skills, resources, negotiating skills and sometimes the willingness to mediate on principled positions. These factors may undermine their importance in the policy process. For instance, Mazey and Richardson note that voluntary organisations, consumer associations and environmental groups often lack the political clout to influence EU-level policy (Mazey and Richardson 1994: 213), while Paterson points out their inability to retain an active involvement in their advocacy work throughout the policy process (Paterson 1991). Greenwood also notes their weakness in comparison with associational resources, although they now constitute over 20 per cent of EU groups (Greenwood 1997: 178). However, some scholars have also emphasised the largely favourable climate that general interest groups find in Brussels. For instance, Majone argues that diffused interests are better represented at EU level than in member states, citing factors such as the activism of the Court of Justice (ECJ), the desire of the European Parliament (EP) to find a distinctive role, and the isolation of the Commission from the political process (Majone 1996: 78). Similarly, Pollack underlines the special opportunities that diffused interests enjoy in Brussels on the basis of the multiplicity of points of access to the EU system (Pollack 1997).

Clearly, EU public interest groups can be stronger than they are in some member states, particularly because of the support of institutional actors, and yet relatively weak in the EU policy process compared to other interests. As Kirchner points out, lobbies at the EU level are effective when they have 'staying power', namely the ability to lobby in a policy process broadly and at all its stages

(Kirchner 1992). This is difficult to achieve with limited resources and amid substantial difficulties in aggregating preferences, these being well-known traits of diffused interests. Yet several factors additional to the ones just mentioned have recently altered this situation in favour of public interest groups, and made their study of particular importance. EU policy-making currently suffers from a general crisis of legitimacy, and from a crisis of integration as justified by the values of security and prosperity that sufficed for a previous generation of European elites.

EU public-interest associations

There are currently numerous European third-sector organisations and institutionalised representatives of social movements which deem it important to have a base in Brussels.[4] Some of them have an obvious connection to social movements, others have some such connection but it is less clearly defined and many others have no direct connection to a movement at all. Among the organisations for which a movement is important are the European Women's Lobby (EWL) related to the women's movement, the European Disability Forum linked with the disability rights movement, ILGA-Europe, an association of gay, lesbian, bisexual and transgender organisations (with around 300 members) linked to the gay rights movement. Eurolink Age (a network of 140 organisations and individuals) and the European Federation of the Elderly concentrate on policy issues of concern to the pensioners' movement. ENAR (European Network against Racism, a coalition of about 600 European NGOs) and the Migration Policy Group (MPG) work to combat racism and are related to the anti-racist movement. Active in the area of environmentalist concerns are such movement-related organisations as Greenpeace and Friends of the Earth. The field of regionalist associations comprises organisations for the protection of minority languages and cultures such as the European Bureau for Lesser Used Languages (EBLUL). Even more prominent in this field are small parties and EP committees closely linked with these associations and movements.[5]

Other organisations may espouse one or more movements at particular points in time, or as a secondary concern all the time. These include the Youth Forum, which has in the past worked on anti-racism, and Inclusion Europe (thirty-one members and networks in thirty countries), which is committed to advancing the human rights and defending the interests of people with intellectual disability and shares the concerns of disability rights movements. There are then organisations which belong to a broad pro-inclusion coalition but are more closely connected to churches or other NGOs than to social movements.[6] Their number has grown steadily over recent years (Commission 2000a). These groups engage in similar action to that of other interest groups: they lobby, they provide policy-makers with information, they accumulate resources and use them to promote policy change. For these reasons these groups can be viewed as generally belonging to the diversified universe of interest associations, although the wisdom of differentiating them has sometimes been questioned (Burstein, Eaton *et al.* 1997).

However, I intend to argue that public-interest groups differ in important respects. Even while undergoing a process of institutionalisation, public-interest groups, NGOs, social movement groups and the many advocacy groups that they inspire in Brussels are distinctly different from other forms of functional representation. They are based on the free donation of time and energy by dedicated groups of activists and, as will be seen later, they have a distinctive relation with political formations and with the media. This donation of resources by these groups and their importance for public opinion are rooted in their unusual ideological character. Their main identifying trait is a normative commitment which makes them viable despite their limited resources and motivates their endeavour to come to terms with institutional environments and cope with substantial opposition and practical difficulties. Their independence from vested interests gives them a distinctive level of credibility that relates to the issue of political legitimacy so increasingly crucial for the EU. The policy areas in which these groups have a substantial presence are therefore different – I shall argue for an exceptionalism of movement-related policy areas.

Public-interest advocacy coalitions must compete for influence with powerful adversaries – industrial lobbies and sectoral associations – whose view of the social arena is often very different from that of many public-interest associations, if not indeed opposed to it. They must also compete with the dominant ethos of the institutionalised European project as it has developed historically: an ethos that rewards cost-benefit analysis, the professionalism of lobbyists, the quality of the information that these provide to policy-makers and an ability to address policy issues systematically and technically. Many in the NGO sector see these skills as more compatible with the efforts of private lobbies than with competing alternatives. This factor may well impact on the agenda-setting strategies of advocacy coalitions and marginalise those groups less willing to reframe their message in economic terms and to acquire the necessary technical skills.

Yet their task has been facilitated by recent developments. The advocacy provided by associations of what is sometimes collectively referred to as 'organised civil society' (OCS)[7] is gradually becoming recognised as important. This is particularly the case in relation to advocacy coalitions whose impact is ensured by the importance for public opinion of the movements that they support.

Governance and civil society

There are several reasons why public-interest associations have recently acquired importance. These relate to the renewed emphasis on civil society's contribution to a decentralised, networked exercise of political authority, often referred to as governance.[8] In addition to specific EU-level reasons, which will be examined in detail in the following chapters, there are general ones that can only be briefly mentioned here.

In general, one should stress factors such as the so called 'crisis of politics', which refers to citizens' disenchantment with politics; the crisis of representation, which refers to issues such as the dominance of executives; the crisis of the party system as a vehicle for societal representation; and other connected processes that will be discussed in this chapter. These have undermined reliance on traditional forms of representation, which at the EU level translates into a widely discussed perception of crisis. Among historical factors that explain this crisis, generational differences, notably the end of the 'permissive consensus' which sustained European integration in the past, are important. Unlike the generation that witnessed the Second World War, more recent generations have not perceived the same threats to security, and have not therefore looked to European institutions as a shield from them. The collapse of the Soviet bloc has similarly contributed to a diminished perception of threat and related faith in integration for security purposes. With reference to political factors, it has been argued that support for integration was rooted in the low salience that EU affairs had in public opinion in conjunction with elite support for economic reasons. The protracted debate over the Maastricht agreements would have made 'Europe' salient at the popular level and created a generalised sense of disillusionment with the remoteness of the institutional apparatus which, starting in the 1990s, has been reflected in a sharp decline for approval for integration. In cultural terms, the literature has pointed to the generalised re-emergence of nationalist ideologies after the collapse of universalist world views such as Marxism and to an extent the advancement of certain processes of secularisation. This has determined a new localism with which EU integration sits uneasily. State elites, the paladins of integration but also the beneficiaries of the re-location of difficult policy choices and unpopular decisions to the EU level, have found themselves facing a crisis, in terms of their relationship to the supranational level and the degree of popular consensus for the European project.

At the same time, integration becomes increasingly necessary for a variety of reasons, among which defensive strategies against the economic impact of globalisation play an important role. In brief, there is a perception that faced with a crisis of legitimating ideologies, of economic margins of manoeuvre and of losses of sovereignty, states are losing power and are exposed to contradictory pressure to increase integration, though they may be penalised for it in electoral terms. Consequently, the function of governing has radically changed in the context of a political weakening of the traditional state.

This ambivalence at member state level has blocked the possibility of improving representation mechanisms at the EU level, accentuating their crisis and stimulating the consideration of alternative forms of representation to those based on electoral mechanisms. At supranational level, the acceleration of supranational integration with its multi-level governance structure, without a change in mechanisms of representation, has further undermined political legitimacy and exposed the limits of the current institutional set-up. Representation through the EP is problematic on several counts (Marsh and Norris 1997). The unfair and unsatisfactory character of the dominant States-based representation has been frequently observed (Weale and Nentwich 1998; Banchhoff and Smith 1999; Scharpf 1999).

Thus, functional representation remains as a potential alternative but at present it is also regarded as unsatisfactory on several accounts such as the dominance of private interests over diffused ones, and the weakness of institutions such as the Economic and Social Committee (ESC) specifically concerned with it. Yet it constitutes one of the few areas in which change appears more feasible and it is for this reason that the contours of an improved role for OCS in the decision-making system are frequently emphasised in EU documents.

The nexus among civil society, social movements, social capital and governance is being examined through a growing body of literature, and it recurs in the official documents of supranational and international institutions (Cohen and Arato 1999; Crook 2000; Commission, Preston *et al.* 2001; United Nations 2001). The concept of civil society, in particular, strikes many observers as warranting special interest as a construct that constitutes a third level of political action located between decreasing political interest, knowledge and commitment at the level of individuals, on the one hand, and the functions of the state, which are shrinking or at least being substantially redefined in economic terms, on the other (Weiss 1998). Various authors have proposed differing definitions of 'civil society' as a concept, and works on political theory have traced its changes of meaning over time and in different theories (Cohen and Arato 1999), highlighting the new importance of the concept, as well as of the related concept of social capital, in different European contexts (Putnam, Leonardi *et al.* 1993; Hirst and Khilnani 1996; Herrmann 1999; Eder and Giesen 2001; Keating and McGarry 2001). Here, it can merely be noted that civil society comprises sets of groups that connect the state institutional realm with the social realm. These groups, which include institutionalised social movements and small movement-parties, are semi-institutionalised formations that play a crucial role in representing diffused interests and act as important 'linking institutions'. Their importance has been repeatedly stressed in the literature. For instance, Kamrava (1996: 49) divides institutions into state and social ones, and sees certain social movements as components of civil society linking the two. His scheme stresses the role of 'linking institutions' (environmental groups, poverty-relief or women's rights groups) in connecting state institutions (i.e. legislatures, state bureaucracies, police) and social institutions (i.e. family, kin, education, economics). Powell and DiMaggio also point to the institutional status of social movements, noting that: 'The institutions of the modern polity, in our conceptualisation, include the state but are not limited to it. They also include, notably, a "public sphere" of collective discourse and social movements, and a rationalised or "civil" society of publicly chartered but formally "private" bodies and agents (e.g. corporations, enterprise managers, science, professions, and modern individuals)' (1991: 207). Cohen and Arato (1999) view social movements as performing the positive function of realising the potential of modern civil society. This book intends to clarify the dynamics of this linking function, and the obstacles to it, with particular reference to institutionalised social movements. However, it is not assumed that this is a positive function. The existence and nature of Michelsonian processes of elite formation and reproduction needs to be questioned in this respect.

Movements and EU institutions

The incorporation of social movements is facilitated by the increasing internal differentiation of the social movement sector. On the one hand, there is the revival of political protest movements, united in their opposition to the manner in which globalisation has impacted on the developing world and the environment – the 'no-global movement' so prominent in recent years at events staged by international organisations. On the other hand, many of the older social movements grow increasingly institutionalised, developing the technical skills and acquiring the political legitimacy necessary for acceptance as credible interlocutors in Brussels.

The idealism of many previously successful social movements – particularly the new movements of the 1980s – has been re-fashioned as they have acquired some of the skills that make them valuable to policy-makers and have learned to adapt to the Brussels institutional milieu. Movements have peaked and then demobilised. Conflicts that marked European societies in the post-war period – the labour–capital conflict and those carried forward by the many social movements that arose in the 1970s and 1980s – are being re-defined in the post-cold war neo-liberal climate. However, although these movements have disappeared from the streets, their energy, vision and resources have permeated regular politics to a significant extent, shaping the political and cultural agenda in important ways. Whilst the new protests mounted by anti-globalisation campaigners are gaining visibility, several movements that previously focused on protest have become institutionalised. Following the pattern of the institutionalisation of the labour–capital conflict, their goals and values are being increasingly expressed by a host of public-interest lobbies, small parties and voluntary organisations in a variety of institutional domains, including EU institutions.

Social movements embody utopias. The great idealisms of the twentieth century were rooted in powerful movements, notably Marxist, nationalist and trade unionist. As some movements grow less appealing, new ones emerge and gain popularity. At any point in time there exist a few distinct families of social movements reflecting political theories with varying degrees of coherence but with a central core that characterises them as political doctrines (Freeden 1995, 1996, 1998). Just as a language may have several local dialects, so movements take different forms in specific local contexts, for instance the EU and its member states. They react to different sets of problems and are shaped by different political contexts. Movement activists are generally organised into networks of individuals and organisations on the basis of shared collective identities. Around these networks arise broader advocacy coalitions with less cohesion in ideological and structural terms but which disseminate movements throughout the institutional realm.

Like political institutions in member states, EU institutions react to movements somewhat ambiguously. They may marginalise popular movements when they consider them to be disruptive, unrepresentative, extremist and lacking credibility; but the presence of these movements may also remedy the much-debated remoteness of the European institutions. Their grounding at EU level may also meet institutional desires for dialogue with civil society while at the same time addressing movement aspirations for policy relevance.

Environmental, anti-racist and regionalist movements have marked the political landscape of the generation of activists born after the Second World War and subsequently: their social and political importance is unquestionable, and their personnel no longer consists of politically naive young activists. Since the heyday of mass protest, activists have had to learn how to be effective in complex political environments. In order to do so, they have often had to learn the technical aspects of the policies they advocate, the workings of institutions and bureaucracies and the importance of successfully handling the media. They have also had to coordinate strategies at international and supranational levels, which has sometimes required them to open offices in Brussels and join the growing number of lobbying organisations, private firms and local authorities which have likewise entered the EU arena of interest representation.

The institutionalisation of movements is not confined to the EU environment, however. The social movements that emerged in Europe during the 1980s have undergone a transformation, acquiring a variety of new roles and re-defining some of their old features throughout Europe, so that they are now able to support their EU-level offices from relatively powerful bases in member states. They have professionalised their cadres and developed lobbying skills, which they seek to deploy where they can be most effective – addressing the likes of parliaments, local authorities, universities, regulating authorities, the media and churches. But the European level presents distinctive opportunities and a growing importance that parallels the increasing policy impact of the process of EU integration.

Given that EU institutions are a major source of decision-making power, social movements can more effectively lobby for the policies that they advocate from Brussels. As in several member states, so at the EU level they can also form small parties, sometimes referred to as 'movement-parties' (green and regionalist parties, for example) which, while retaining many features of the social movement that prompted them, are able to exert a stronger and lasting institutional impact (Müller-Rommel 1985, 1990). Movement activists can meet policy-makers and set out their positions. 'Movement-parties' are distinctively hybrid formations extending movement politics into institutional settings. In addition to policy impact, movements also see Brussels as a source of funding, and as a base from which triangulation between national movements can be facilitated and coordinated.

This expanded role of movement activists has required acquisition of a set of competences that exceed the skills utilised by most first-generation activists to deal with policy environments. These include legal knowledge, technical and scientific expertise, public relations skills, a detailed understanding of the policy process and the development of personal contacts with members of the civil service, elected representatives and the press. In developing and refining these competences, social movements have acquired many of the features of public-interest lobbies and are often virtually indistinguishable in their operations from other promotional groups. However, given the size of the body of public opinion that they often represent, and their potential threat of disruption, they have a visibility that makes them important and distinctive objects of study.

It is therefore of importance to examine which movements are present in Brussels and why, how effective they are, what they do, how successful they are and how their situation has changed in recent years, and why. This will be ascertained through in-depth analysis of a set of case studies, addressing such questions as the following. Do they differ across policy sectors, or are there similarities among them related to the fact that they are social movements? Are these similarities connected to specific characteristics of the EU policy environment? If policy sectors are rather different in the way they operate, how does this affect social movements?

By concentrating on movement-related activities, it is possible to refine the analysis of interest representation in Brussels, which is a highly diversified sector and allows only limited generalisations when studied in its entirety. In addition, focusing on social movements also makes it possible to address the topical link between EU institutions and European civil society. As will be discussed in detail below, movements and their various forms of representation in institutional settings have features that make them more influential than one would expect from their limited resources. They have a particular resonance in public opinion, an importance in civil society that strikes a sensitive chord in the European process of integration, a pool of activists ready to donate time and resources, and a number of sympathetic and committed insiders within the EU institutions.

Movements and NGOs

Direct social movement representation through social movement organisations in Brussels is only one avenue of representation for the sector. Movements could bring their protest to Brussels, but very seldom have the resources and skills to do so. It is too expensive to re-locate the activists that such actions would require, and given the opaque nature of the EU policy process it would be fairly ineffective and costly. Thus while on occasions there have been protest actions in Brussels – those of French farmers are a well-publicised example – direct action is generally not a viable or even desirable option, as several movement activists have pointed out. A second approach is to act through protest actions taking place in member states but with the EU level as the main reference point. This requires a synchronisation of protest activities to guarantee sufficient impact and presupposes a sensitivity of the EU governance system to such strategies. However, synchronisation is difficult to stimulate as it relies on reactions to political opportunities emerging cross-nationally and this only rarely takes place. It might take place as reactions to continent-wide crises such as episodes of transborder pollution or global security threats, but it is otherwise difficult to organise. In addition, the absence of a fully integrated media system connected to the EU governance system and therefore of an electorate sensitive to Brussels' protests makes EU-level mobilisation ineffective. For these reasons, movements are more effective in their role as policy advisers or information providers and accordingly as warning indicators of reactions in member states. Brussels can therefore be seen as a de-territorialised space upon which movement advocacy converges from several member states. In this role movement actions are best accomplished through broad advocacy coalitions of networks of movement organisations and like-minded institutional allies.

Movements, then, act through broader movement-inspired advocacy coalitions, which comprise movement activists as well as sympathisers, external supporters, instrumental and principled allies in a variety of organisations and institutions. Pro-movement sentiments can be expressed and represented in political arenas by civil society organisations either directly at the EU level or at member state level, with subsequent implications at EU level. The various organisations and individuals that seek to influence decision-making in Brussels can choose among several avenues for interest representation. Different institutions can be addressed at the same time or at different times; other strategies and other levels of governance can be utilised. This availability of multiple channels of representation in Brussels applies to all social interests. As mentioned, the latter can find receptive institutional channels in a variety of settings – parliamentary committees, specific units of Directorates-General (DGs), political parties, regional offices – and be embodied by a variety of organisations, such as trade unions, Commission-sponsored networks, churches and specific organisations in the voluntary sector. There is, in effect, a dialogue in progress between the main policy ideas of certain social movements and institutional frameworks. Movements can at times inspire institutional settings, but it would be excessive to claim that they have a direct impact on policy. Rather, negotiation takes place between the priorities of movements and the concerns of the organisations that 'host' them in the institutional realm. This is a process that can be defined as a sort of 'housing' of movements within institutions – a process which, I will argue, is based on a complex exchange of symbolic and material resources.[9]

One important category of organisations involved in this process of movement 'housing' comprises social-inclusion advocacy coalitions. Equally important are churches, left-wing parties and trade unions, and naturally for a different kind of movement, extreme-right parties. This plurality of collaborating organisations around key movement ideas requires the use of more inclusive terms to indicate the impact of movements in EU contexts. In much of the political science and sociological literature, the forms of functional representation of interests are clearly differentiated. In recent years, however, this clear demarcation has been called into question. Broader concepts like 'advocacy coalition' or 'epistemic community' have been proposed to bridge distinctions that in certain contexts appear too rigid and do not allow proper conceptualisation of the synergies among different but regularly collaborating organisational structures (Haas 1989; Sabatier and Jenkins-Smith 1993; Marks, Scharpf *et al.* 1996; Sabatier 1998). As I shall argue in greater detail in the following chapters, the distinctions drawn in the literature among movements, NGOs, church activist groups, etc. are important, but they should not obscure the commonality of intent that has developed around certain social-movement-inspired social controversies. As a more all-encompassing term, the concept of '*movement-related advocacy coalitions*' – or, more concisely, 'movement advocacy coalitions' and 'movement coalitions' will be used to denote the collaborating sets of individuals, networks and organisations which share a normative commitment to movement-inspired social change. These differ from social movements in that they are more all-encompassing, institutionalised, organisationally less stable and more fragmented.

Movement advocacy coalitions

Visions of social change circulate in society and are sometimes promoted and re-elaborated by social movements. They may also be embodied by a variety of organisations, institutions and individuals in different work roles, in addition to the designated representatives of movement organisations. This makes for a potentially varied composition of movement-related advocacy coalitions. Besides a variable core of movement representatives, advocacy coalitions may also include a number of movement activists whose commitment is private but who represent other organisations, such as bureaucracies or general-interest parties. Hence, for instance, the memberships of several European labour and social-democratic parties comprise anti-racist activists who have spent years promoting anti-racist legislation. At the EU level there are Members of the European Parliament (MEPs) who have spent over thirty years promoting anti-racism, and bureaucrats who in private are members of anti-racist organisations. These individuals are activists but they do not represent movement organisations. Then there are the sympathisers who identify with the goals of a movement but whose main loyalties lie with other organisations, examples being Labour Party MEPs specifically and consistently concerned with regionalist or green issues. To the extent that movements' goals are accepted by generalist organisations, one may also find institutional actors who support movements' policies as part of their support for other organisations, without their necessarily having a normative commitment to a movement. For instance, certain regional offices may be linked with regionalist parties and share the linguistic policies of regionalist movements. Their representatives may express support for these policies without individual normative commitment.

Thus, the number, work role, ethical commitment and influence of the activists and sympathisers supporting a movement in an advocacy coalition are variable. They range from movements with a small number of activists related to movement organisations, to movements with larger activist bases in Brussels, individuals who subscribe to a movement's objectives and attempt to promote them in their working lives without a specific mandate from the movement's organisation and individuals whose support for a movement's objectives is strong but accidental in that it derives from other commitments.

The movement coalitions that I studied were selected from among the most visible of their kind in Brussels. For in-depth understanding of these advocacy coalitions it was necessary to limit the choice; hence the coalitions examined include representatives of the main families of left-oriented movements active in Brussels. I omitted other families of social movements which may be equally important but are too diverse to be analysed within a common framework, such as farmers' movements, euro-sceptic and extreme-right movement coalitions.

Three families of movements

The coalitions that are considered in this study differ in terms of how established institutions have been prepared to incorporate them. Some coalitions have proved more 'usable' by institutions than others; and some have had a closer resonance with specific institutional discourses, or with popular culture at large. This, it is argued, is one important predictor of the specific institutionalisation trajectories of the movements that inspire these coalitions. The three movements and the multiplicity of promotional groups relating to them exemplify ideas and practices that have been institutionalised: the environmental movement, the anti-racist movement and the family of minority-nationalism movements have undertaken a variety of initiatives, including the sponsoring of items of legislation, research programmes, pilot projects and litigation in the ECJ.

Explaining the outcomes of these initiatives requires consideration of factors internal to advocacy coalitions, and of ones relating to the operations of the EU system of governance in general, and to the policy areas addressed by different advocacy coalitions in particular. Through this analysis, I aim to clarify such outcomes as the level of Europeanisation of the different policy areas and the timing of Europeanisation, the policy approach prevalent in different areas in terms of type of policy instruments, intensity and horizontal diffusion and the prevalent policy ideas that guide the policy process in the different sectors examined.

The EU system is highly fragmented, and power is unevenly distributed among policy sectors. It is difficult to generalise from one type of advocacy coalition to all of them, or from the role and impact of certain movement groups to others. Reviewing three of the important sectors for challenging groups will permit an investigation as to whether the various ways that EU institutions interact with advocacy coalitions have shared features, and to document the differences.

The main movement lobbies that are considered in their relation to EU institutions are examples of important movement families with different stances *vis-à-vis* the institutions. The relationship of these movements to institutions differs considerably because of various factors: the differing legal bases of the policies that they address, their differing historical relations with elected institutions and their differing degrees of internal cohesion. Environmentalism is a successful movement with a broad and deep resonance in a number of EU institutions. Anti-racism is a movement that until recently was markedly less successful within the EU institutional environment. Recent developments such as the introduction of article 13 in the Amsterdam treaty and the widespread reaction to Jorg Haider's inclusion in the Austrian government have improved its prospects. In the EU context, ethno-regionalism is a more fragmented movement. While this movement's demands for a radical re-allocation of power and/or political independence characterises a set of small regionalist parties united in the European Free Alliances and a number of other cultural and political formations, an emphasis on the devolution of decision-making power at the local level has been incorporated in the objectives of many European regions.

Common to all these advocacy coalitions, it is argued in this book, is the fact that they are expressions of social movements which also reflect wider sensibilities. They express cultural currents that have traversed Western societies in recent years and found embodiment in a variety of similar localised movements such as the ones analysed here. Their features in common are that they are universalist, that they seek to benefit wider society (see Gamson 1975: 61–63), and that they have survived for a significant amount of time. Duration is important; merely by virtue of their duration they differ from movements that have disappeared rapidly. Their roots in institutional environments are deeper than those of other, short-lived movements, in that they date back to at least the 1970s. The selection of case studies in this guide was guided by the criterion of importance in Europe in general, and specifically in the environment of EU institutions. Thus unsuccessful movements were ruled out from my analysis, since these would not survive long enough to become institutionalised. And specifically they would not be incorporated (or would be very weak) in the Brussels environment, which screens out marginal social concerns.

While it is difficult to establish the specific impact of movement advocacy coalitions on particular decisions involving a variety of actors at different levels of governance, it is possible to examine the reasons for the overall success (or lack of it) of different policy areas as perceived by policy actors. This, therefore, constitutes the dependent variable in this study, which will be articulated in terms of different types of outcomes: the structural features of the policy process and its discursive features – that is, the prevailing policy ideas of different sectors.[10] As Greenwood stresses, it is methodologically almost impossible to definitively prove the specific 'influence' of interests over policy outcomes (Greenwood 1997: 255). Thus, as Greenwood argues, one should focus as much on outputs as on outcomes (1997). As the role of these groups is as much one of general sensitising activities to complement their often modest role in specific policy events, one has to take a broad view of their impact. Through in-depth interviews with policy actors, it will be possible to document the scope and impact of this sensitising role and its impact on policy agendas. Analyses of case studies previously recorded in the literature and key-actor interviews point to differing levels of success by the three movement coalitions in Brussels, and they qualify the meaning of success. It is clear that success must be articulated along at least two main dimensions: one is the ability to achieve policy objectives; the other is the ability to be recognised as a legitimate policy actor (that is, a source of valid policy ideas) and consequently incorporated into decision-making. Secondly, success should be examined with reference to different types of institutions: representation in majoritarian institutions like the EP has causes and consequences that differ from those of success in the Commission environment or in the world of organised interest representation. The case studies were therefore selected in order to articulate these different dimensions of the variable 'success'. The case studies, which will now be briefly introduced, will examine the determinants of the global outcomes of the different coalitions.

Environmentalism

The first case concerns how the environmentalist ideal emerges and its impact on a political context – the European institutions in Brussels – which may use it for a variety of purposes.

In the years since the mid-1960s – this being the short history of environmental policy in EU institutions – environmental regulation has been successful. And success arrived relatively early for this movement. In 1967–87 the Commission introduced over 200 directives, regulations and decisions in a manner relatively unaffected by political events (Majone 1989: 165; Judge 1993: 114). This led early commentators to define this policy area as 'remarkable' (Hildebrand 1993: 23) and an undeniable success (Johnson and Corcelle 1989: 2). As Majone points out, environmental regulation significantly increased in a period of general de-regulation and profoundly shaped environmental policy in member states (Majone 1993). Environmentalism in some circumstances can advance careers, it can be used as a tool to re-define and win business competition and it can provide corporate identity. In other circumstances, environmentalism calls for direct action with protracted and disruptive protest.

Like the other cases, this one focuses on the institutionalised sector of the environmental movement. Arising largely from pressure applied by public opinion and environmental movements, environmental policy has grown into a comprehensive set of concerns marking out new problem areas like climate change, and it spreads across a variety of other policy areas, such as tourism, agriculture and transport. European institutions are crucial for environmental regulation, both because of the integrated character of European economies and because of the cross-border nature of many environmental threats. For this reason, institutions such as the European Commission and the EP have aroused substantial interest among national environmental movements, whose lobbying initiatives have attempted to offset the powerful influence of industrial lobbies and public pressure groups. Social movement groups like Greenpeace, Friends of the Earth and others have permanent representation in Brussels. This study will explore the nature of their interaction with the composite Brussels institutional environment, highlighting the gradual but undiminishing institutionalisation of this policy area and of its advocates. It is instructive that Wilson, writing in the late 1980s, noted, with others, that environmentalists were excluded from the policy process together with representatives of consumer groups and tax-payers (Wilson 1990: 71). Their disruption was then understood as a tactic of last resort. However, early in the twenty-first century, this is no longer the case. Many of the groups once excluded from regular consultation are now part of it in several countries, and this is certainly the case of environmentalists in Brussels, who are by no means marginal. Nonetheless, environmentalism as a cultural current remains a viable inspiration for newly emerging movements, such as anti-globalisation. This study will accordingly need to consider what has happened at a global political level to open the doors for these groups, and not just enquire as to how the movements have changed. In other words, how does their incorporation take place? And is their presence making a difference? If the incorporation of political outsiders is an important variable, what are the mechanisms that specify this openness? These questions will be considered in the light of the trajectory of a much less successful movement, anti-racism.

Anti-racism

The field of anti-racism is part of a broader field, preoccupied with preventing social exclusion, which includes related concerns such as poverty and gender discrimination, and which broadly belongs to social policy. As Geyer notes, despite the concerted efforts of many, social policy has always been hindered by resistance from member states, a variety of interest groups and notably capital, by institutional constraints in this area and by the limitations of social policy in member states. And this history of the sector is not set to be reversed in any major way in the near future (see Geyer 2000: 2). This also applies to the area of social exclusion, which emerged as a policy concern in the mid-1980s particularly in relation to the Social Charter and the Social Dimension. The history of social exclusion can be summarised as essentially an extended dispute between an interventionist Commission and Parliament and a much less enthusiastic Council. In relation to anti-poverty policy, this became apparent after the fourth anti-poverty programme of 1994, when a collapse of support for EU integration led to a curb on integrationist dynamics (Geyer 2000: 162). Racism as a form of discrimination can be connected with other forms of discrimination like gender discrimination, which was expressly mentioned in article 119, although the original treaties made no references to racism. The issue appeared prominently on the political agendas of member states in the 1970s, but at the EU level it became important only in the mid-1980s with a set of EP studies and declarations. But it was not until the Amsterdam Treaty of 1997 that a solid legal basis was provided by article 13, which outlaws racial discrimination. Since then, a set of initiatives has emerged at EU level, but this policy area remains weak, generally only trailing initiatives in member states (Geyer 2000: 171).

Anti-racism is part of a broad family of movements which combat various forms of social exclusion by addressing such issues as disability rights, women's social exclusion, gay rights, old-age issues and the more strictly related issue of migrants' social exclusion. Anti-racism is a movement that receives the oft-professed public support of EU institutions. However, it will be argued that this sector is weaker than environmentalism because of the weaker legal basis of the social policy area within which it has been framed. Moreover, it enjoys a widespread but less determined institutional activism within EU bodies; the issues that it raises are of more marginal concern to contemporary EU public opinion; and its constituency is highly fragmented in terms of the movement's goals and methods. Thus, anti-racism as a transnational norm enjoys broad and unquestioning support, but as a movement it suffers from its univocal leftist placement. This feature may guarantee support from the broad family of leftist movements but it hinders its appeal at a variety of other levels. The reasons why the anti-racist sector encounters difficulties in translating discursive support into policy initiatives will accordingly be a focus for this study.

Minority ethno-regionalism

Since the 1970s ethno-regionalist movements have re-emerged in Europe. The recent affluence of some of the regions in which these movements are prominent, such as Catalonia and the Basque country, has trickled down to the local ethno-territorial movements with cultural and media prominence. A cultural revival of local traditions as a reaction to globalisation has led to the re-discovery of political grievances against state capitals and their ruling elites in several member states. The process of regionalisation under way in all the large member states has given greater legitimacy to regionalism. Since the 1980s even newly minted movements like the Italian Lombard League/Northern League have found support among previously indifferent populations.

These processes cannot be understood in isolation from the challenges and opportunities that the process of European integration has brought to regions. For instance, access to a large market means that even small areas are potentially self-sufficient and able to benefit from economies of scale previously available only within the framework of nation-states. The funds made available for regional initiatives by the centre have given regions greater independence from member states. Policies discussed and coordinated with regional authorities empower European regions, and those with strong independentist movements can take advantage of these political opportunities, utilising them to promote those movements' objectives if this empowers local elites, or if these movements acquire electoral importance. In addition, they can form alliances with other peripheral regions and collaborate in resisting what they perceive as the state's internal colonialism.

However, the integration of Europe also entails a degree of cultural homogenisation that may be seen as further undermining aspirations to protect local cultures and traditions that many ethno-regionalist movements already believed to be threatened by nation building and state building. Movement supporters therefore consider a complex set of factors in defining their relation to the EU.

As will be argued here, these calculations differ somewhat according to the specific regionalist movement's political position along the right–left axis, the degree of power that it enjoys domestically and its political culture in relation to the process of EU integration. This creates a fragmented set of ethno-regionalist movements at EU level which find it impossible to collaborate on many issues. However, a general consensus on empowering regions has emerged – as distinct from a more radical emphasis on regionalism – and it chimes with the regionalisation project pursued by EU elites as part of a strategy to defuse the national–supranational conflict.

As will be clear from this short introduction to the case studies, the three families of advocacy coalitions differ greatly in terms of policy impact, this being determined by how policy fields operate – that is, by the typical dynamics of the complex recurrent interaction between organisations and the individuals that support each of the movement coalitions. This, together with the impact of other political channels of representation, has determined outcomes that differ in terms of the closeness to movements' positions, the policy content that was Europeanised, the policy instruments adopted, the policy ideas pursued and the timing of Europeanisation. These outcomes are different from the policy approach of member states and call for an understanding of the role of advocacy coalitions and other types of representation in determining outcomes. For instance, environmental policy is more stringent than in Southern Europe, but less effective in regulating agriculture – an area of powerful EU lobbies – than in areas of high environmental standards. Anti-racist policy joined multicultural and assimilationist principles prevalent in different parts of the continent, and it emerged much later than in all member states. Regionalist policies are characterised by a higher prevalence of functionalist modes of representation and their independentist aspirations are marginalised. To understand these outcomes one has to examine the role of different actors and, specifically, advocacy coalitions in the policy process.

An approach which concentrates on processes and not just on outcomes is what the new institutionalists term a 'process-approach'; it will be the guiding methodology of this book (Powell and DiMaggio 1991; Immergut 1998; Peters 2000).

Methodology

The methodology of this study, which is discussed in detail in appendix A, consists of an assessment of the impact of movement coalitions at three levels of governance through three separate approaches and integrating them with particular reference to EU-level dynamics. At the member state level, influence is examined through a consideration of public opinion dynamics as reflected in comparative European survey analyses. These data are interpreted in the light of the way institutional constraints at EU and domestic levels of governance filter the impact of voters' preferences and in the different traditions of impact of the voluntary sector on policy-making. Secondly, at the level of EU policy formation, policy documents and OCS documents were examined and assessed as to their consonance in terms of themes, policy approaches and normative orientations.

At the level of the specific operations of different policy communities, responses to a set of in-depth interviews collected in over ten years of fieldwork were examined and a content analysis undertaken, involving a comparison and search for regularities among types of actors. A record of when characteristic statements emerged was then compiled. About fifty in-depth interviews were formally conducted in each area and across EU institutions and diffuse interest groups in order to elucidate how actors perceived the role of other actors in the policy process, the role of historical changes over the last two decades, key events and crises and their impact on the different sectors, the impact of institutional changes and specifically the role of social movement organisations and institutional activists. Also examined were perceptions of EU legitimacy and the role of different policy areas in this respect, and of the role of public opinion. Several additional interviews on these themes collected in the context of other studies were also utilised. To the extent that they are unambiguous, only significant types of responses have been reported. The analysis cites, where appropriate, typical responses to illustrate typologies of respondents and of policy processes identified.

This ideal-typical approach is designed to identify the substantial differences that exist across roles of participants in the policy process whilst recognising that substantial differences also exist within each category of actors. It is often not possible to find substantial agreement in any institutional domain. For instance, EU elites speak with many voices, the Commission is not a unified actor and in many instances it is not possible to identify typical responses. However, not infrequently, the structural position of actors does lead to similar views, and it is in researching this that this work is concentrated. Nonetheless, when substantial differences emerge even within a specific category, a new concept can be formulated, an example being the concept of 'institutional activist'.

Thus, in identifying and summarising typical responses at different levels of governance, evidence is utilised based on different methods and involving various political actors, including respondents involved in different MACs.

Conclusions

In this chapter, the importance of the sector of public-interest associations at Community level has been stressed and a subset of these associations identified: those connected with a social movement. It has been argued that they are distinctive in terms of their special relationship to public communication, their ability to supplement their lobbying activities with the threat of protest and their ability to utilise a free and normatively driven donation of time and resources from their activist base in member states. There are indications that this sector stands in a symbiotic relation with EU institutions, particularly the Commission, Parliament (EP), Committee of the Regions (CoR) and ESC. By arguing that this symbiotic relation can be explained by these institutions' concerns for legitimacy and the controversial issue of the democratic deficit, this chapter has set out a research agenda. In brief, the crucial factual questions that need to be addressed are:

- What levels of access are available to movement advocacy coalitions, and what is their impact on policy-making?
- What resources can they deploy, and for what reasons do activists and institutional actors engage with each other?
- Are there key mechanisms that characterise the relationships between MACs and EU institutions? What impact do MACs have on policy-making?

These questions will be addressed in chapter 6 and 7, after the case studies have been presented and discussed. But there is a broader set of questions that must also be dealt with. Movement coalitions also have a symbiotic relationship with an increasingly institutionalised and weakly internationalised and interconnected European social movement sector. As is often the case, social movement groups with differing degrees of institutionalisation more or less intentionally support each other, as the extreme ones attract media attention and are instrumental in agenda-setting, and the institutionalised ones offer credible alternatives to the public and policy-makers (Gamson, Fireman *et al.* 1982; Gamson 1988). Unlike epistemic communities, their range of views is wide enough to accommodate different causal beliefs and knowledge bases (Haas 1992: 18), and their moral/social conscience sustains commitment and high-risk activities. Hence, social movements are differentiated from pressure groups, given that the former can often use the ultimate weapon of substantially disrupting public order and can rely on the free donation of time and energy by activists (see Walker 1991: 187). They also often have sufficient social importance to attract substantial albeit discontinuous media coverage (Eyerman and Jamison 1991). Also to be stressed is their role in the creation of new constituencies and new knowledge in the policy process. Social movements perform a special role that derives from processes of identity creation that exceed the boundaries of public interest groups (Diani 1992:14). Thus, they may well encompass epistemic communities, but possible recourse to violence and generalised identity creation make them more influential and give a special power to NGOs active in a social movement.

These considerations raise a set of questions concerning their claim to represent social groups and an associational sector which often considers itself in need of special attention at EU level because it feels marginalised in member states.

Are MACs experiencing collective action problems similar to those of private lobbies? Is their claim to represent member state associations grounded in fact?

These questions will be addressed in the concluding section of this book. Answering them will require broader reflection on how civil society represents itself at EU level, and on the role of social movements and the advocacy coalitions that they inspire. The emphasis in this book when answering these questions will be on the *framing of ideas*, the *institutional structure* of the respective policy area and the *interaction between movements and policy-makers*.

Summary

This chapter has introduced the main themes of the book. It started with the observation that as policy areas migrate to Brussels, important consequences arise for contentious politics, which is at least partially displaced from nation-states without easy access to its re-location at Community level. It is posited that at EU level contentious actors develop rather institutionalised features and become embedded in movement-inspired advocacy coalitions. These coalitions interact in a policy-making structure which is constrained by different institutional rules, prevalent policy orientations and the greatly different levels of access and resources of the actors involved. Institutional structures and policy discourses act as filters. They mediate the impact of advocacy coalitions producing distinctive results. The following chapters will identify and analyse the mechanisms that filter the input of advocacy coalitions.

Notes

1 EU documents and officials sometimes refer to the broad term of organised civil society (as in ESC 2000a, 2001a, 2001b). However, they also utilise the term 'associations' or NGOs for the same purpose.

2 Defining NGOs is a complex undertaking because they take a variety of forms and seek to accomplish a multiplicity of tasks. For a working definition which recognises the complexity of the sector I refer to a Commission document which describes NGOs thus: 'The term "NGO" can nevertheless be used as shorthand to refer to a range of organisations that share the following characteristics: NGOs are not created to generate personal profit. Although they may have paid employees and engage in revenue-generating activities they do not distribute profits or surpluses to members or management. NGOs are voluntary. This means that they are formed voluntarily and that there is usually an element of voluntary participation in the organisation; NGOs are distinguished from informal or ad hoc groups by having some degree of formal or institutional existence. Usually, NGOs have formal statutes or other governing documents setting out their mission, objectives and scope. They are accountable to their members and donors; NGOs are formally independent, in particular of government and other public authorities and of political or commercial organisations; NGOs are not self-serving in aims and related values. Their aim is to act in the public arena at large, on concerns and issues related to the well being of people, specific groups of people or society as a whole. They are not pursuing the commercial or professional interests of their members. Though these common characteristics can help describe the notion of the term "NGO", it must be borne in mind that their size as well as their scope of activities can vary considerably' Commission (2000a).

3 This is a model which Schmitter describes as based on a system of interest representation in which 'the constituent units are organised into an unspecified number of multiple, voluntary, competitive non-hierarchically ordered and self-determined categories which are not specifically licensed, recognised, subsidized, created or otherwise controlled in leadership selection or interest articulation by the state' (Schmitter 1974).

4 Their exact number is difficult to quantify as it varies rapidly over time and it includes well resourced and active organisations and dormant organisations with limited resources. As Greenwood showed, over one Euro group in five are public interest groups. Greenwood's sample study of these organisations indicates a population of either very small organisations with about two staff members (20 per cent) or larger ones with more than six–ten (20 per cent) or more than eleven (26 per cent) staff members; 64 per cent of these organisations have a budget size of over 100,000 Euro (Greenwood 1997).

5 The literature has examined these formations from a variety of perspectives and with varying degrees of empirical elaboration. Among significant contributions are Judge (1992); Rucht (1997); Smith, Chatfield and Pagnucco (1997); De Winter and Tursan (1998); Hubert (1998); Ruzza (2000a, 2000b); Delwit, Külahci *et al.* (2001); Mazey, (2001).

6 They include, for instance, the International Council on Social Welfare, which promote the cause of social welfare, social justice and social development; CECODHAS (Comité Européen de Coordination de l'Habitat Social) with forty-seven members, and FEANTSA (the European Federation of National Organisations Working with the Homeless) which brings together more than sixty NGOs and associations.

7 There are differing views of what civil society should include. For the purposes of this study a modified version of the view presented in the Commission White Paper on Governance will be adopted as a working definition of civil society: 'Civil society includes the following: trade unions and employers' organisations ("social partners");non-governmental organisations; professional associations; charities; grass-roots organisations;

organisations that involve citizens in local and municipal life with a particular contribution from churches and religious communities.' In the context of this work and in line with positions central to the literature and also with the definition of civil society posited by the report of group 2a of the White Paper on Governance (Commission, M. Preston, *et al.* 2001), the Commission.will not view organised economic interests as constitutive of civil society (Cohen and Arato 1999). See also ESC (1999b).

8 For a definition of governance see for instance the United Nations' Commission on Global Governance, whose well-known report *Our Global Neighbourhood* defined governance as the sum of the many ways individuals and institutions, public and private, manage their common affairs. It is a continuing process through which conflicting or diverse interests may be accommodated and cooperative action may be taken. It includes formal institutions and regimes empowered to enforce compliance, as well as informal arrangements that people and institutions either have agreed to or perceive to be in their interest (Commission on Global Governance 1995). The EU Commission frequently connects the focus on governance with the role of organised civil society. For instance the Forward Studies Unit utilises a definition that stresses organised civil society: 'Governance is the capacity of human societies to equip themselves with systems of representation, institutions, processes and intermediary bodies in order to manage themselves by intentional action. This capacity of conscience (the intentional action), of organisation (the institutions and intermediary bodies), of conceptualisation (the systems of representation), of adaptation to new situations is a characteristic of human societies' (Commission 2000b).

9 For the concept of 'movement hosting' and 'housing' see also Chapter 2 and Ruzza (1997).

10 Greenwood (1997).

2

The impact of movement coalitions on policy-making

Influences of movement coalitions

How far and where does one need to look to explain movement coalitions in Brussels? They deploy their influence in Brussels but they have roots in all member states and advocate issues that are debated internationally. Their EU personnel are limited but members and supporters supply advice and resources from all the EU countries. In those countries and in Brussels their views are echoed in the media, and activists are included in several decision-making fora. But other views and other interest representatives are also included, and are frequently more resourced and influential. This chapter will consider the mechanisms by which movement coalitions exert influence across levels of governance, and it will draw up a scheme with which to examine these mechanisms in the case studies.

The influence of social movements on EU policy-making operates directly through advocacy by national and EU-level activists, and indirectly through the impact of social movements on other political actors. Like other interest groups, social movement organisations engage in complex exchanges with policy-makers whereby influence and resources are traded for information, some control over their base and the avoidance of disruptive action. Pursued through their involvement are valuable shared objectives such as some aggregation of preferences, and an injection of potentially useful new ideas into the policy process (Ruzza 2002). However, while in the case of private-interest organisations these goals are largely confined to the economic sphere, in the case of social movements they concern complex cultural issues and the structure of civil society. One is obliged to acknowledge that public opinion dynamics and their political implications are central to their impact and that they operate across levels of governance.

It is helpful in this regard to consider a typology proposed by Weiler and his colleagues (Weiler, Haltern *et al.* 1995: 28) which distinguishes among three levels of political decision-making, which involve different actors, arenas and processes. Weiler *et al.* note that EU decision-making involves an international, a supranational and an infranational arena in which different actors predominate and act according to different rules. This distinction identifies a sphere where the principal actors are governments acting in an international arena on the basis of a scarcely institutionalised set of rules. Secondly the authors identify a supranational arena in which Community institutions together with governments interact on the basis of clearly defined norms. At this level policy is formulated by the interaction of the institutions – Council, Commission and Parliament in particular. In this context EU institutional architects are important players. However, other actors particularly relevant in this context are NGOs and their agenda-setting strategies. Thirdly they point to an arena defined by the interaction of member state administrations, public and private associations and EU institutions interacting in EU policy communities on the basis of scarcely institutionalised rules. At this level policy is elaborated by second level organs of governance – Commission directorates, Committees, NGOs and private interests. This inter–supra–infra trichotomy then conceptualises the role of the same actors but in functions in which one or the other is more prominent.

This classification can be usefully applied to conceptualise the influences of movement coalitions. Their influence takes place at all three levels. The exercise of these influences is made possible by fundamental decisions taken in an intergovernmental framework where history-making decisions can be taken, but also by the strategies of EU architects acting in relation to the constraints of the system of governance at the EU level and the ideas that it produces, and by the operating procedures and norms of policy communities. The classification by Weiler *et al.* enables account to be taken of the fact that, on the one hand, movement coalitions relate to international- and national-level dynamics which generate social movements and give them prominence in public opinion while, on the other, they respond to supranational dynamics which orient their incorporation into EU institutions. At EU level they are active in policy communities, but also aspire to a more fundamental role than the mere representation of functional interests, advocating a re-interpretation of norms and institutions – a role that pertains to the strategies of EU institutional architects (Bellamy 2001: 63). Thus, although both intergovernmental and EU institutional approaches are important in framing the role of movement coalitions, for each level one must identify the key factors that affect the impact of movement coalitions, and the impact of specific coalitions. The interaction between movement coalitions and governments and their possible institutionalisation responds to events in member states. It also responds to agenda-setting strategies and institutional dynamics at EU level and to the values and operating procedures of policy communities, indicating a complex but necessary research agenda. The EU-level outcomes of particular coalitions are determined by the specific interaction that takes place between various arenas over time. Analysis of this interaction will be the purpose of my case studies.

In brief, we can conceptualise the theoretical task at hand as one of identifying a set of filters that are interposed between issues as they emerge in society and their politicisation and regulation. OCS is a first filter which includes mechanisms of agenda-setting, transferral to EU level and interventions in a set of arenas where other actors are prominent. In these arenas – and as an analytical tool those described by Weiler *et al.* will be referred to – they have to come to terms with structural constraints and discursive priorities, which also constitute a set of filters to be identified and examined. These filters are what determine the characteristics of policy processes and the policy outcomes that prevail in different policy areas and distinguish the EU level from the way issues are treated by different member states.

This chapter will thus concentrate on the arenas and processes identified by Weiler *et al.*, and which reflect the emphases of particular approaches to the study of EU dynamics. In considering the different types of influence, some of the findings in the literature will be re-formulated into a set of hypotheses. In addition, the most distinctive features of diffused interests at the EU level and their relations with EU institutions in recent years will be introduced.

Given the focus of this study, and space constraints, the impact of advocacy coalitions in member states will not be examined in any detail. However, the reasons why they have become prominent in certain types of states will be indicated, as will the main public opinion dynamics, events that have accompanied their trajectory and the manner in which crucial domestic constraints were reflected in Brussels, for instance in relation to intentions to Europeanise specific policies. A more detailed analysis will be conducted on the other two arenas – particularly the policy-community arena, which is of specific relevance here.

Perspectives on advocacy coalitions

As mentioned, the concept of advocacy coalition is useful in indicating the collaboration that takes place among like-minded individuals, even if based in different organisations. At times an entire organisation might support an advocacy coalition, but the existence of cohesive organisational support is not necessary for the formation of a viable advocacy coalition. However, to study movement-related advocacy coalitions, we can take for granted the presence of movement organisations, which are those organisations that most specifically embed movements as bodies of opinions diffused in society.[1] As already mentioned, the movements that are represented in Brussels by organisations are institutionalised entities. That is, these organisations have distinctive features. They rely on a more or less formalised internal division of labour, on formal (or semi-formal) rules, on professionalisation and also on a degree of normative and cognitive diffusion of their views that embed them with stability in European societies (Ruzza 1997; Seippel 2001). Thus they often work in association with established channels of political representation such as parties and churches. However, such heterogeneous entities are rarely able to produce coherent demands unless facing stark choices such as those posed by crisis situations, and their message is also often internally nuanced. These characteristics have been usefully examined by social movement research.

Perspectives from social movements research

The literature on social movements is an important referent for the study of advocacy coalitions. A variety of key concepts in the social movement literature can be employed to assess the impact of social advocates in Brussels. Movements perform two roles: on the one hand they feed ideas into the policy process; on the other, they act as political forces – networks of activists and sympathisers – organised into structures and committed to effecting social and political change. This dual role has been central to works in the 'Framing' tradition which, with reference to social movements, examines the impact of their ideas on public discourse. It is also a major concern of the 'political opportunities' approach, which examines the structural conditions under which movements are likely to achieve some sort of impact. Taken together, these two approaches – which are now widely considered to be complementary – illuminate the cultural as well as structural dynamics that filter the impact of MACs.

Political Opportunities

The Political Opportunity Theory approach (POS) seeks to identify which political opportunities empower or restrict movements. It can therefore be used to shed light on the sources of the influence exerted by EU advocacy coalitions. The various strands of work on POS have reached substantial consensus on a set of key factors. For instance, McAdam (McAdam, McCarthy *et al.* 1996: 27) proposes a 'highly consensual list of dimensions of political opportunity' which consists of:

> the relative openness or closure of the institutionalised political system; the stability or instability of that broad set of elite alignments that typically undergird a policy; the presence or absence of elite allies; the state's capacity and propensity for repression.

These key concepts have been used by several authors to analyse the relations between movement and institutions.[2] And some of them can also be usefully employed to examine the prospects for movements in Brussels, although the multi-level governance system requires their consideration at different levels: openness, alliance formation and elite alignments should be examined at the international and supranational level, and in specific policy communities. At the international level and at EU level, the structure of regimes in different areas and geopolitical considerations shape political opportunity structures in distinctive ways (Risse-Kappen 1995; Risse, Ropp *et al.* 1999).

At each level, inquiry must focus on which events, alliances and structural factors strengthen or weaken the impact of movement coalitions. Movements often arise in conjunction with social controversies involving a nexus of interactions between the media, activists and policy-making institutions. Public debates on social issues tend to focus on a limited number of issues at any particular time. Some of these issues remain at the centre of public attention for several years and develop into articulated political and social controversies. Themes like the environment, regional devolution and racism have attracted sustained attention and controversy, giving rise to social movements which in turn have magnified them. In normatively charged issue areas such as these, specific events like an environmental crisis or a large influx of asylum seekers may generate the perception of a sectoral policy crisis – namely the widespread idea that a policy sector has gone adrift and that a profound shift in approach is necessary. Crises compel interested actors to propose new policy ideas and new structures, and to force a debate. They may break up previous elite alliances, and induce policy-making circles to open themselves up to new actors, such as movement representatives, and thus modify their political opportunity structure.

The impact of movements thus comprises a cultural component in which new policy ideas are aired, and a structural one in which activists may be able to affect decision-making, by either threatening or implementing disruption, or by being included in decision-making structures, or both. Here, movements will be conceived as the embodiments of broad ideas for social change; ideas which orient the action of networks of activists and sympathisers within and without institutions and take specific forms in different social and political contexts.[3] Movements produce plans for policy change, for the reorientation of cultural values, and sometimes for changes in lifestyles. After an initial disruptive phase, they often remain popular with the general public.

When, political, social and religious institutions are faced with the emergence of a new movement, they take up a position which varies in homogeneity and intensity and which may engender political realignments. To the extent that the demands of a movement are acceptable to specific institutions, activists will tend to be accepted as participants in decision-making and movements' goals will be pursued even if modified by institutions. In this study, the extent of activists' institutional acceptance will be examined by consideration of their own reports and the reports of institutional actors as to their involvement in consultation, in negotiations, their formal recognition and inclusion. As for movements' achievements, the goals stated by activists in personal interviews and in documents will be considered. These categories were initially proposed by Gamson in his influential *The Strategy of Social Protest*, which examined a set of protesting groups through a quantitative methodology (Gamson 1975). Here, focusing on three case studies, the book will utilise key actor interviews and rely on triangulation of the opinions and statements of several policy network participants in a set of different roles, citing statements which are representative of the responses obtained in interviews.

Movements are not the only source of innovation, however. New policy ideas are produced and reflected by several other actors. Consideration must therefore be made of the conflicts that arise when policy agendas are defined, and of the alliances made between movements and institutions. This analysis should be done within specific institutions, but also at the level of public discourse, articulating the impact between this level and decision-makers.

The contribution of 'frame-bridging' approaches

Mindful of the specific nature of EU-level politics, the analysis should begin by acknowledging the distinctive power position of elite state actors – heads of states and top policy makers – and the fact that their strategic considerations are decisively influenced by media discourse and public opinion. The elite state actors of the EU occupy a different and stronger power position than that of other actors, and their major concern, from which all their other goals derive, can be generally assumed to be re-election. To achieve this goal, they cater to all the components of advocacy coalitions, instrumentally seeking from them whatever is most likely to increase their chances of re-election: for instance, information from interest groups, the absence of disruption from social movements, influence on public opinion from trade unions or other mass organisations. One must therefore relate the impact of interest organisations of all kinds (including social movements) to their perceived usability by elected representatives, who are ultimately responsive to voters' opinions, which they try to guess and to influence. On the basis of empirical research, Burstein (1999) has stressed the particular importance of public opinion for interest groups. I concur with him by emphasising the importance of public opinion and, as the case studies will show, how it achieves diverse impacts on Brussels through a set of different channels operating in different areas. But I believe that there are intervening variables which moderate the impact of public opinion. I refer in particular to the impact of bureaucratic politics and the way public opinion affects the electoral considerations of various types of political actors.

Burstein (1999) considers the relationship between interest organisations and public policy. He argues that organised interests, of which social movements are a subcategory, are likely to be successful only if they express opinions that are already endorsed in society. This is because the key motivator for decision-makers is victory in electoral competitions. Thus interest organisations must either change public opinion or convince under-informed decision-makers that public opinion is in fact favourable to their concerns. In addition, a key element of public opinion is issue salience. Interest groups must heighten issue salience, and then profit from so doing only if the prevailing heightened opinion supports their positions. While recognising that there are mechanisms which limit the extent to which public preferences guide elected officials, Burstein argues that in general they are not sufficient to favour organised interest against the will of the general public. If a pressure group or a social movement is not achieving an impact in the policy realm, it is generally simply because the general public does not support that group or movement, and it is unable to change this opinion.

Accordingly, particular attention should be paid to groups' communication strategies: that is, how they choose to frame and attempt to re-frame issues. Attention should also be paid to attempts by groups to persuade decision-makers that they are popular. For their part, decision-makers are also active in this process of framing and re-framing, which they use to respond to any challenge against them, including those raised by the various components of advocacy coalitions. Framing mechanisms are also used for identity building purposes and they structure competition among different bureaucratic units, such as different DGs in the Commission (Morth 2000). It is therefore also necessary to examine decision makers' responses and their communication strategies in relation to each other and to organised interests, both private and public.

Useful insights into this emerging centrality of public discourse in the EU are again afforded by the social movement literature. The diffusion of movement ideas has been examined by the framing approach tradition, some key concepts of which can be usefully employed to shed light on the relationship between EU institutions and movements.

The concept of frame and frame alignment proposed by Snow and his colleagues (Snow et al. 1986), and the notion of consensus put forward by Klandermans (Klandermans 1988), facilitate description of the nature of the alliance that develops among advocacy groups in specific policy areas and comes to constitute an MAC. Snow points out that a movement needs a 'master frame' that condenses the grievances of its members into a single concept. By means of a 'master frame' certain aspects of reality are identified and given prominence while others are omitted. Certain connections between elements are highlighted and others are ignored. For a social movement to achieve wider support, its master frame must resonate with the priorities of sectors of the general public. Movements attempt to enhance this resonance by means of 'frame alignment' strategies whereby their frames become aligned with dominant cultural frames.

Working within this perspective, Klandermans distinguishes between consensus mobilisation and consensus formation:

> Consensus mobilisation is a deliberate attempt by a social actor to create consensus among a subset of the population . . . Consensus formation is the unplanned convergence of meaning in social networks and subcultures.

The two processes are interrelated in that actors attempting to mobilise consensus take the existing consensus as their initial reference. In unplanned consensus formation, dominant social institutions and the media play a fundamental role related to their social visibility and their influence on society and institutions. In order to mobilise consensus, movement organisations must refer to the existing discourse. One strategy is to attempt to subvert this discourse with an alternative one. This approach conceives social movement groups as strategically focused organisations. It also implies that they have and pursue clear, independent goals.

However, a different and perhaps more viable strategy is to borrow the discourse of powerful institutions and attempt (strategically or because of a cognitive merging of taken-for-granted frames) to modify it in order to legitimate activism or other forms of support for a social movement. This modification can take different forms. The linkages among the discourses of different organisations are of special interest. Snow and Benford (Snow 1986: 467), and the tradition of social movements research that developed from their work, call these linkages – which are a particular type of frame alignment mechanism – frame bridgings and define them in the following terms: 'By frame bridging we refer to the linkage of two or more ideologically congruent but structurally unconnected frames regarding a particular issue or problem.'

The concepts of frame bridging and of consensus formation and mobilisation are important tools with which to determine how positions emerge, change and are modified for strategic and identity reasons by social movements and their allies. These concepts appear in slightly modified version in several texts on policy analysis. For instance Cobb and Marc posit processes of issue expansion in the agenda building process (Cobb and Marc 1997). However, the concept of frame bridging well encapsulates the relation between two existing and potentially viable policy approaches which are supported by frequently competing actors. These frame bridgings can express instances of consensus mobilisation when they are intentionally pursued as a strategy, but they can also reflect consensus formation when they are of the unconscious, taken-for-granted kind.

Processes of consensus formation occur in institutions as emerging frames and are then re-interpreted in terms of the main institutional ethos. For the neo-institutionalist (Krasner 1988: 51), these re-interpretations are instances of institutionalisation where a newly emerging institution such as a social movement acquires links with specific institutional environments. They become deeply embedded in the identity of institutional actors and structurally connected with other institutions. Krasner's measure of institutionalisation is the breadth and depth of connection (1988: 76–77).

For analytical purposes, it is helpful to separate linkages that occur at the level of public discourse from linkages that occur within institutional realms. In-depth interviews can illuminate key concepts that define the ideational framing of advocacy coalitions. By interviewing several policy networks participants, it will be possible to extract and report typical definitions of MAC framings. Framings in public discourse emerge from media analysis. The two types of linkage have been studied by different bodies of literature but they are in fact interconnected. The linkages at the level of public discourse examined by the framing tradition (Snow *et al.* 1986; Gamson 1992; Ruzza and Schmidtke 1993; Zuo and Benford 1995), and the linkages that connect public discourse and policy areas (Rein and Schon 1977, 1994; Radaelli 1995; Ruzza 2000a), are separable only for analytical purposes, given that even very insulated institutions are immersed in broader inter-institutional culture. Differentiating between these different kinds of linkages are the mechanisms and the agencies that promote them. Thus the media are of central importance at the inter-institutional level. Institutional actors with multiple memberships and institutional gatekeepers (Bleich 1998) are important in mediating the relationship between public discourse and institutions and, additionally, internal networks are important in activating internal linkages.

Since the concept of 'frame bridges' refers to mechanisms of negotiation and formation of policy ideas, it is important to connect these mechanisms to actual influence, which is a crucial concern of all negotiations. Policies have what one can call 'a software' – the ideational part – and a hardware, the structures in which they operate (Alink, Boin *et al.* 2001). In our context, 'influence' is how certain organisations impose their objectives on other organisations – that is, how organised interests change public decision-making processes. Influence is a process that includes a variety of factors – both 'soft' and 'hard' – of which the framing of claims by interests and the response by decision-makers are only one aspect. The framing of claims and counterclaims shapes a policy area and orients the perception of the appropriateness of existing structures; it is therefore an important aspect of influence. For instance, whether the environment is sufficiently protected and whether additional protection is best achieved through legislative intervention or through self-regulation are controversial issues that set the social movement sector and other sectors against each other, but also allow for various possible compromises.

Because a frame bridge is often a compromise between competing institutional discourses, we may argue that the price of influence is often 'dilution'. However, no amount of dilution can ensure success, as other structural factors and processes come into play, and different approaches to 'diluting' may compete with each other. On the one hand, when frame bridges emerge spontaneously in society or in specific institutions as instances of consensus formation, we cannot properly speak of 'influence', which presupposes intention. On the other hand, bridging processes within specific institutions articulate general linkages in terms of the priorities of different institutional settings and often have strategic 'importers' of general frames, who may do this for normative reasons, bureaucratic politics, etc.

To summarise, two social movement theories will be utilised to examine advocacy coalitions in relation to policy-making: the POS and framing approaches. In discussing the case studies, particularly close attention will be paid to how claims have been framed by different actors involved in the decision-making process, and to the structural conditions that have determined their impact. This impact needs to be considered at different levels of governance. Equally important are the events and the political environments that have enabled or hindered movements.

However, difficulties arise in applying this framework to EU-level politics. The social movement literature places a certain amount of emphasis on aspects like repression, which is of no particular importance to institutionalised movements in Brussels.[4] Another difficulty is that important sectors of EU institutions largely share the agendas of certain movements; indeed, there is sometimes an overlap between policy-making role and movement membership.[5]

When analysing the case studies, I shall pay particular attention to the stable and effective interconnections that have developed between certain bureaucratic units and sectors of movements, a theme that is somewhat neglected in the social movement literature, but also in the advocacy coalitions and policy analysis literature (Sabatier and Jenkins-Smith 1993; Sabatier 1998). It is for this reason that, instead of focusing on movements, I find it more useful to combine movements' groups, movements' sympathisers in institutional settings, organisations that share most movements' goals, etc., under the heading of 'movement-related advocacy coalitions', thereby referring to the advocacy coalitions framework which emphasises the multiplicity of roles and the inter-institutional alliances that characterise activism at EU level. Focusing specifically on movements, rather than more generally on activism, would obscure the fact that organised movements are only a minor component of the complex world of advocates with multiple affiliations and strong activist concerns but often not directly connected to a social movement organisation.

Three levels of governance

MACs, as collaborating sets of individuals, networks and organisations which share a normative commitment to movement-inspired social change, are centred around the key ideas of a social movement but are not coextensive with their organisations. The new movements of the 1980s have become institutionalised, leaving in their wake a set of movement organisations, but also public- interest lobbies which have adopted many of the goals of one or more social movements, as well as committed but unaffiliated individuals operating in a variety of roles and institutions. In organisational terms, we can conceive MACs as inter-organisational fields – ideal spaces where communication takes place in more or less tightly knit networks of actors who donate their time, energy and resources for the pursuit of moralised policy goals.

Geographically these networks are polycentric. Their advocacy efforts in Brussels reflect and are connected with wider networks branching out in member states at all vertical levels of governance, and they reflect horizontal coordination among actors based in various institutions and movements. Functionally, at the centre of these activist networks are highly committed individuals, and on their peripheries allies and sympathisers. While it would be tempting to identify the centre with EU-level social movement organisations, this it is not necessarily the case. Coalitions incorporate people based both in Brussels and other EU institutional centres, and people based in member states. Hence, while the centre of EU movement advocacy coalitions is in Brussels, their borders are fuzzy and extend to member states. Several variables intervene to articulate the connection between MACs and member states, including the direct representation of national civil societies at EU level and the indirect representation of different political cultures through the action of elected representatives.

Key political elites in their turn attempt to advance not only the contingent priorities of their polities but also the founding principles and the legitimating myths that define modern states and are frequently the object of movement claims: Weiler, Haltern *et al.* describe this level of governance and its priorities as follows. At the international top level, governments establish 'Fundamental system rules; Issues with immediate political and electoral resonance; International "High-Politics"' (Weiler, Haltern *et al.* 1995). Here, states negotiate in an International Relations (IR) framework, generally through heads of state at European Councils and the like (Weiler, Haltern *et al.* 1995: 28). Their primary mode of interaction is diplomatic negotiation. They act in a scarcely institutionalised environment and respond to issues of immediate political and electoral concern. The competences electively attributed to this level have direct consequences for the public associations sector: in setting policy agendas, top governmental actors may permit the innovative approaches that movement coalitions advocate; in formulating declarations of principle that may be the prelude to policy innovations, they may legitimise the work of activists.

A second level involves the entire framework of EU institutions in Brussels. Weiler, Haltern *et al.* (1995) refer to this level as 'Supranational'. It consists of a highly institutionalised environment where the Union is a prominent player and influential institutional actors are concerned with the Union's overall legitimacy. Power resides with the negotiating institutions; which, to the extent that these institutions are hierarchical and bureaucratic, means that power lies with an elite of high-level civil servants and politicians. At this level, Weiler, Haltern *et al.* stress the role of 'the primary legislative agenda of the Community; enabling-legislation; principal harmonisation measures' as typical issues of governance. In terms of actors, playing a prominent role at this level are EU institutional elites and certain state actors. This level directs the researcher's attention to the impact of the presence or absence of common policies in delimited areas of campaigning. EU elites have traditionally expressed a keen interest in the activities of the third sector, and a specific examination of the positions taken up over the years is important in assessing the sector's growing importance. Increasingly, institutional documents connect the existence and role of the voluntary sector with issues of legitimacy and the meaning of democracy in the Union.

A third level of infranational decision-making takes place in the dense networks of administrators, interest groups, private and public associations, and experts which both in Brussels and in member states take the Union framework as a given.[6] The operations of this level cannot be explained without reference to the other two levels. It is the background within which they act and pursue a variety of goals that may coincide with those of advocacy coalitions. Low-level policy actors are generally not concerned with the larger issues of the Union's role and functions. Weiler, Haltern *et al.* (1995) identify a number of distinctive neo-corporatist and non-corporatist elements at this level. There is a dominant technocratic and managerial ethos which sets a premium on stability and growth and is suspicious of re-distributive policies, pushes for representational monopolies and emphasises a pragmatic concern for ends over means which is likely to encourage a lack of transparency and low procedural guarantees. At this level, the network of policy advisers, campaigners and advocates surrounding a specific policy field plays a fundamental role, which favours non-redistributive policies. The principal actors identified by Weiler, Haltern *et al.* – second-level organs of governance and certain corporate and social–industrial NGOs – may directly include, or be closely allied to, third-sector organisations.

Altogether, the three levels give differing articulations to the mechanisms that mediate the representation of advocates in Brussels. Understanding the outcomes of specific advocacy coalitions requires consideration not only of these three levels in and of themselves but also of the interactions between them. A unique interaction between the three levels characterises different periods and marks the political opportunities of movements' coalitions at any particular time and their framing strategies. The features of these three levels and their interactions now require clarification.

The domestic level

As already said, in EU agenda-shaping, the top level reflects short-term political calculations by heads of state and their symbolic adherence to state founding principles, such as categories of human rights and social justice. This latter concern is increasingly advanced by international NGOs and transnational activist networks. Thus, understanding the behaviour of heads of states in such areas as anti-racism requires one to consider the activities of these networks.

Transnational networks have been studied by a large body of literature which has focused on the international impact of social movements (Willetts 1982; Risse-Kappen 1995; Smith, Chatfield and Pagnucco 1997; Keck and Sikkink 1998; Risse, Ropp *et al.* 1999). This literature stresses the impact of activist networks which mobilise themselves to promote 'global ideas', the role of which has been depicted by scholars in various ways. Soysal (1994: 43) gives as examples the ideas of development (Ferguson 1990), progress (Meyer 1980), freedom (Patterson 1991) and adds the 'world-level organising concept' of human rights. Each of these concepts has at various times been entrenched in a social movement network. Similarly important concepts examined in the case studies that follow are the ideas of environmental protection, which is the subject of article 37 of the Charter of Fundamental Rights, and non-discrimination on the basis of race and ethnic origin, which are listed in article 21 (Parliament 2000).

As previously mentioned, the institutionalisation of movements depends on the extent to which emerging global ideas about key aspects of social organisation, the extension of rights and the politicisation of new aspects of life become institutionally entrenched in dominant social, political and religious institutions (Ruzza 1997). It also depends on the political legitimacy that transnational NGOs are able to acquire, which is in turn related to their ability to appear politically responsible defenders of universally supported ideas and therefore able to allay the fears that their presence constitutes a threat to the sovereignty of nation-states (Hudson 2001).

When successful, these ideas turn into taken-for-granted assumptions whose precise nature and actualisation may remain controversial and subject to advocacy pressure, but are no longer simply a matter of individual normative choice. My hypothesis is that, since these global ideas are not equally powerful, a movement that attaches itself by means of frame-bridging (see Klandermans 1988) to one of these powerful ideas will be advantaged (H1). Powerful ideas are ideas salient, long-lasting and popular in public opinion (the relation between global ideas and public opinion will be examined at a later stage).

The stress on global ideas points to the debate on the development of a transnational or supranational civil society and to the need to shift some of the analytical emphasis away from research on the nation-state to issues such as the impact of transnational activist networks and their relation to global ideas circulating in international and supranational organisations (Smith, Chatfield and Pagnucco 1997; Keck and Sikkink 1998; Boli and Thomas 1999; O'Brian, Goetz *et al.* 2000). EU case studies are of particular importance in this regard.

The literature on transnational activist networks is often inspired by an historical neo-institutionalist approach. Neo-institutionalists in particular, who stress path dependent approaches, point to the role of ideas in legitimating policies and opening new policy paths, and on the time dependent mutual adaptations of ideas and interests in particular social groups.[7] Summarising this field, and with particular reference to the IR literature,[8] Checkel (1999a) notes:

> Scholars are asking how global norms affect and constitute particular domestic agents, be they states, individuals or groups (NGOs, say). At issue, then, is how norms 'out there' in the international system get 'down here' to the national arena and have constitutive effects.

The specific mechanisms that transfer ideas to the global level and diffuse them in specific settings are still unclear, and criticism of the neo-institutionalist paradigm has focused on its inability to articulate mechanisms of diffusion (for a discussion see: Risse-Kappen 1994; Finnemore and Sikkink 1998; Checkel 1999a). I shall seek to specify these mechanisms in my case studies. It has also been argued that ideas are not necessarily driven by networks of professionals, as the literature on epistemic communities would have it, but may be disseminated by popular opinion even before professionals have been persuaded; they may also be driven by the media acting as a 'magnifying glass' (see Hall in Steinmo, Thelen *et al.* 1992: 96, 105). I shall argue that social movements as the popularisers of ideas can also propagate ideas in institutional realms through the voluntarism of activists in institutional settings, the pressure on polities applied by mobilised sectors of public opinion, the importation of external models facilitated by their increasingly transnational operations, etc.

Focusing on media and social movements is a useful corrective to the dominant thesis of the policy analysis literature, which even when stressing the role of ideas – as in the social learning and advocacy coalitions literature (Schlager 1995; Sabatier 1998) – tends to focus on the impact of epistemic communities (Haas 1989) and on other infra-institutional sources of ideal innovation (Majone 1989), and only secondarily on the generating and mediating role of media and social movements.

However, regardless of the source of ideal innovation, those scholars who stress cultural factors in policy, and the role of institutions in encouraging policy innovation, are making an important point. Stimuli to institutional innovation are not necessarily resisted by institutional settings. Hall points out that 'while we are used to thinking of institutions as factors of inertia, tending to produce regularities in politics, some kinds of institutional configurations may be systematically biased in favour of change' (1986: 107). The complexity and unpredictability of institutional dynamics invites explanation at the institutional–organisational level.

Applying these dynamics in fields where movements play a major role, such as environmental and social policy, a hypothesis of this study is that because some movements' ideas now refer to areas of generalised legitimacy, professional political actors, religious leaders, and business people will subscribe to them and even take their importance for granted, while re-defining them in terms consonant with their organisational/institutional cultures (H1a).

To anticipate examples from the case studies, with reference to the anti-racist movement, one notes for instance that there have been numerous declarations of principle by heads of state condemning racism and xenophobia which have legitimated initiatives at other levels. In association with international organisations, they have supported initiatives such as the 'European Year Against Racism' (EYAR) and similar schemes which have preluded new legislation in the field. At this level, coincidental political alignments and strategic calculations often develop on the basis of reactions to emerging social and political controversies sparked by unanticipated events such as environmental disasters, spates of racist incidents or violent regionalist conflicts.

One needs to enquire as to the factors that may increase or reduce the readiness of conventional political actors to support pro-movement initiatives. Their motives are best understood in terms of electoral calculations, public opinion dynamics and party political traditions. When considering the impact of this level, therefore, one must consider the ideological and contingent factors that may induce heads of states and other influential actors in member states to accept movement-supported policies. The specific reasons will be investigated in the case studies. However, it can generally be hypothesised that support for movement policies will arise when principles contributing to the self-definition of states are in question (H1b). Secondly this support will arise when a state acquires economic advantages by espousing movement-supported policies (H1c). Thirdly it will arise when damaging competition is avoided by regulating issues at EU level (H1d). In all these cases, as posited by the POS approach, movement coalitions will profit from selected elite allies.

The supranational level: organised civil society and the EU

The supranational level, whose fundamental processes can be identified in the priorities of EU policy-shaping elites, incorporates the joint contributions of a variety of institutional actors to the elaboration of formal procedures and a high level of process rules (Weiler, Haltern *et al.* 1995). In recent years in Europe, the entire system of functional representation has been affected by the protracted social controversy on the legitimacy of the EU and the proper avenues for representation of OCS, while specific types of public-interest groups have been affected by sectoral events. For this reason, in debating the role of public-interest groups, the Union has produced an extensive set of materials of a different legislative nature which constitute an empirical key to analysis of this level of governance.

These materials permit an examination of the dominant frames of the different policy areas. Through a frame analysis of policy documents of the environmental, anti-racist and regionalist sectors (which is discussed in appendix A) it will be possible to identify the key ideas circulating in the supranational policy arena among the key players – EU institutions, NGOs and other actors such as regions – and evaluate their connection to the dominant framings of movement advocacy coalitions. It will also be possible in subsequent chapters to identify efforts at frame-bridging – that is, attempts to connect movement themes and EU policy discourse. Here, it is useful to introduce in general terms the EU institutional discourse on civil society and its practices.

There has been much discussion over the years on the role of social NGOs and of OCS, and it has involved EU institutions, prominent EU actors at workshops and conferences and a variety of OCSs. The discussion has left a large paper trail of Commission discussion papers, opinions of other institutions and responses by NGOs. These documents constitute a coherent body of thought, and the most important of them are well known to all the actors involved in relations between NGOs and EU institutions.[9] They point up the importance of legitimacy considerations for this level of governance, particularly in relation to the public associational sector.

In addition to supporting OCS in general, EU institutions often promote specific movement themes. By espousing these themes, institutions strive to gain some of the popularity that movements have achieved, which is in some cases substantial and has remained so for several years. In so doing, the EU institutions may react to what has been called 'the crisis of politics', a perception that the political system as a whole, and particularly the mechanisms of political representation, are ineffective. Therefore, the broad issue of legitimacy should figure prominently in any analysis of movements' interactions with institutions.

An example is provided by the trajectory of the anti-racist movement. Just as in the 1990s there were numerous environmental initiatives, recent years have seen a plethora of declarations of principle and anti-racist initiatives by Commissioners, often connected to the issue of the role of the European level of governance as not merely facilitating the integration of markets but as supported by its additional legitimacy as a defender of human rights. It is thus necessary to stress the connection between the overarching institutional ethos of this tier – diffusing support for EU integration – and support for movements like the anti-racist movement. Similarly, one can hypothesise that EU elites' support for stricter environmental standards and regionalist autonomy stems from this endeavour to augment the legitimacy of the European process (H2). These hypotheses are supported by the literature that sees European institutions as 'purposeful opportunists' (Cram 1993; Wincott 1995). Thus, the crisis of legitimacy of the EU system of governance can be viewed as a political opportunity for movements. Different policy areas and different MACs can be expected to be seen by EU publics as differently salient and differently appropriate to be regulated at EU level. Thus, the perceived EU legitimacy and overall relevance of different policy areas can be expected to constitute differential political opportunities for different advocacy coalitions.

EU institutions and NGOs

To specify these hypotheses at EU level, it is now necessary to present a general examination of the relations of EU institutions to OCS, which illustrates the extent of concern with the legitimacy issue and the initiatives undertaken to improve it. Public-interest groups interact with all EU institutions. At present, the most important institutions for NGOs – including movement-inspired NGOs – are the Commission, the Parliament, the ESC and the CoR. All these institutions have debated and produced documents on OCS. I will first briefly review the history of the interaction, then examine the content of relevant documents and point to some of the factors that shape the developing relations between OCS and institutions.

The increasing centrality of themes related to public-interest representation reflects the fact that in recent years the Commission has undergone a set of changes with a direct impact on the role of associations; some are connected to the Kinnock reforms intended to introduce a more managerial, efficient, transparent and accountable approach.[10] The extent and the future consequences of these changes are still unknown. In this situation the presence of a complex, uneven and sometimes legally controversial set of relations with NGOs is potentially embarrassing and, as previously noted, it is at the same time an opportunity to inject some elements of much needed legitimacy into the policy process.

In EU discourse, the debate on OCS has centred on the concept of civic dialogue, which emerged as a counterpart of the more institutionalised social dialogue.[11] In institutional circles it was initially stressed by DG Social Affairs in 1996, which had a long-standing tradition of consultations with the NGO sector, and which found an ally in the EP Committee of Social and Employment affairs (Smismans 2002: 4). In the context of institutional support for civil dialogue a notable initiative is the biennial European Social Policy Forum which has typically involved very large number of European NGOs and over 1,000 participants.

Parliament and ESC

Other institutions are important as well. Parliamentarians often engage with like-minded institutions, sometimes brokering their relations with the Commission and more generally being part of broad advocacy coalitions which help NGOs with information and occasionally resources. Like other institutions, the EP has actively contributed to an examination of the proper role of lobbies. For instance, an attempt has been made to re-consider EP practices in relation to the accreditation practices of other parliaments (DG Research 1996).

The ESC's role of functionally representing interests specifically includes the category 'various groups', which comprises numerous single-issue movements and public-interest associations generally. It was, for instance, instrumental in setting up a 'First Convention of Civil Society', which was organised at European level on 15 and 16 October 1999, and regularly contributes opinions to the EU debate on OCS (see, for instance, ESC 1999a, 1999b, 2000a, 2000b, 2000c, 2001a, 2001b). The ESC is, however, a relatively weak institution whose role several observers recommend should be substantially re-defined.

NGOs

NGOs have consistently advocated a stronger role in policy-making, generally stressing the potential or actual importance of their contribution and their ability to offer solutions to difficult problems. For instance, Crook of ECAS has noted that NGOs are important in implementing policies that for political reasons governments find difficult to support. They are frequently leaders in developing new policy knowledge, new infrastructures for policy delivery and in experimenting with policy solutions subsequently adopted or 'mainstreamed' by public authorities (Crook 2000). NGOs have consistently and actively participated in the Commission's attempts to streamline consultation, and they have typically attempted to achieve their better inclusion in consultation activity, seeking to substitute ad hoc occasional and unregulated consultation with more stable forms of inclusion. This could take the form of legally recognised consultation which would give the Commission the right to fund NGOs and would be similar to the more formalised process of including the social partners in 'social dialogue'(see Commission 1996a, 1998b). In other words, a principle of 'civic dialogue' would have to be incorporated into the EU legal framework, as proposed by the Social Platform – a Platform of European Social NGOs formed in the context of the preparation of the first Social Policy Forum which constitutes the reference point for institutional consultation on matters involving the NGO sector (Social Platform 2000; Smismans 2002).

Interaction of OCS institutions

There are numerous occasions for exchanges of opinions between the movement sector and EU institutions since EU actors are frequently expected to become involved in public discussions, conferences and seminars and even to contribute in writing (Stevens and Stevens 2001: 143). This takes place both within specific policy sectors and at a broader inter-institutional level, where conferences and workshops are frequently organised with the inclusion of social movement and NGO representatives.[12]

NGOs have advocated an even closer relationship between the Commission and the voluntary sector, for instance by suggesting periodic stages or short secondments of Commission officials to NGOs, the purpose being to engender a mutual awareness of priorities, operating procedures and problems. In financial terms, NGOs would welcome longer-term funding, since this would help them allocate resources more efficiently. However, this proposal has been treated with suspicion owing to what is often referred to as their 'deficit of legitimacy'. One approach to overcoming the legitimacy problem is to encourage partnerships with local authorities, thereby increasing the impact of multi-level governance on OCS.

To summarise, the consultation of NGOs is a principle well entrenched in the EU's operations. However, it is considered insufficient by many NGOs and it is mainly limited to the Commission and the EP (and the relatively unimportant ESC). The Commission affirms the importance of consulting NGOs in countless documents, but there are only a few top-level fora where social interests are consulted – notably in our cases the fora for environment and social policy.

The affirmation of the importance of the third sector in institutional documents is not, however, inconsequential as it points to emerging aspirations and to focal areas of concern and dissatisfaction among the actors involved.

EU institutional discourse and OCS

A brief review of EU official views of OCS is useful as it allows a comparison of current practices with aspirations.

The Commission has reflected on its relationship with NGOs in a number of documents, the most important of those being 'The Commission and Non-Governmental Organisations: Building a Stronger Partnership' (Commission 2000a) and the White Paper on Governance and the related preparatory documents (Commission 2001b; Commission, Preston *et al.* 2001; Commission and Thogersen 2001). Commission documents on NGOs have naturally been proposed to the NGO sector for consultation. Several formal and informal reactions have accordingly been registered, including position papers by NGO coordinating bodies (Crook 2000; Social Platform 2000).

The Commission has traditionally favoured European networks of public interest associations both in accessibility and in funding. It has often encouraged, if not directly created and sponsored, umbrella groups based in Brussels (which effectively discriminates against NGOs from member states). Some NGOs see this approach as practically equivalent to a system of accreditation without the formal guarantees of such a system, and they advocate a broader consultation process. The Commission has given priority to Brussels-based umbrella organisations for the practical reasons of administrative simplicity and representativeness already mentioned. In doing so it has also been supported by some EU-level NGOs which welcome the recognition of a specific EU-level area of competence (Social Platform 2000). However, in recent years, the continuing stress on subsidiarity has required the re-thinking of this approach. Moreover, there is growing awareness of the potential of Internet-based forms of consultation.[13]

Reflecting academic analysis, in EU documents the exercise of political authority is seen as acquiring new characteristics of decentralised steering of social and political institutions performed jointly by networked centres of power which criss-cross territorial levels and include multifarious types of organisations (Kohler-Koch 2000). This diffused structure is the element emphasised with the use of the concept of governance – a concept of wide and positive utilisation in EU documents but of still recent diffusion.

As important actors in the debate on governance, EU institutions, and the Commission in particular, have manifested their expectations from the NGO sector. The Commission welcomes the role of NGOs in a number of contexts and assesses their performance with reference to a set of criteria. It welcomes the democratising impact of NGOs in the developing world and for this reason it funds development NGOs and stresses their contribution to policy-making, particularly their information-gathering activities, their feed-back on policy implementation and their reach throughout different levels of governance. It values their contribution to project management, particularly their abilities in monitoring and evaluating projects financed by the EU. It emphasises their contribution to European integration through their contribution to the creation of a European public sphere (Commission 2000a).

In several documents, the Commission and other EU institutions express a lack of satisfaction with current NGO performance when assessed through these criteria. However, there is a range of opinions within EU institutions on what the appropriate scope and power of OCS should be in policy-making, and to what extent institutions should take a proactive role in balancing the dominance of vested interests. Thus the Commission occasionally seems to advocate an interventionist role on the part of public authorities in fostering embryonic forms of civil society.[14] On the other hand, and particularly in recent times when state interventionist approaches are seen as unjustified forms of social engineering, many institutional actors dissent from this approach.

Doubts on the present functioning and proper role of OCS are also present in the NGO community. NGOs are not fully satisfied with their relations with EU institutions. In particular, as shown by the observation of operating mechanisms of policy areas where NGOs have a prominent role, the policy process is seen as too unpredictable and fragmented to give NGOs the possibility of performing their role appropriately. In particular, the ad hoc forms of inclusion of NGOs and the haphazard quality of consultation are singled out for criticism. The Commission is aware of these criticisms, as evidenced by the report of the WPG working group on civil society (Commission, Preston et al. 2001), which notices that on the basis of the team's consultation it emerged that:

> All the representatives of civil society stressed the need for the Commission to adopt a more systematic and coherent approach to consultation. They felt that existing formalised or structured consultation procedures should be made more transparent.

However, if there is general agreement in the NGO community to increase the frequency and relevance of consultation of OCS, it is less settled how this should be done. Opinions range from advocating an article in the Treaty giving a legal basis to dialogue with NGOs, activating an accreditation system, to open consultation to smaller NGOs which, it is argued, would better represent emerging sensibilities and ideas in society (Commission, Preston et al. 2001).

These conflicting and cross-cutting expectations in the institutional and NGO fields can be elucidated by reconsidering with reference to empirical case studies the standards of good practice whose indication recurs in official documents.

In their relationship with OCS the Commission, but also more generally other EU institutions, may value representativeness and accountability, together with openness, information and a connection with local communities and subnational levels of governance, but the exact meaning of these qualities is related to what OCS finds in the EU environment and the pressure and constraints that this environment puts on OCS. The connected qualities of representativeness and accountability need to be reviewed, as they are particularly recurrent in the EU list of desirable qualities.

Representativeness and accountability are in several ways directly connected. Through the organisations in question, the first quality indicates the necessity of a real flow of information from civil society to political institutions, the second an inverse flow back to civil society. The possibility of these flows rests upon a receptive and collaborative policy environment. Representativeness presupposes an environment that does not select organisations on criteria other than their relevance in society. Accountability presupposes an environment that provides information that can be relayed back to political principles. Whether these qualities are typical of the EU system needs to be evaluated. This can be done with reference to the case studies. Nonetheless a few general points can be made with reference to the aspiration emerging in institutional documents.

OCS, representativeness and accountability

Representativeness is emphasised by several EU institutions, not only the Commission (Commission 2000a). For instance, the ESC stresses that a 'basic precondition and legitimising basis for participation is adequate representativeness of those speaking for organised civil society' and that 'when consulting civil society organisations, the European institutions should check how representative these bodies are' (ESC 2001a).[15] However, there is also a certain margin of ambiguity in the institutional discourse. If the dominant view emphasises representativeness, there is also an awareness that good policy advice is in principle a different issue from representativeness. For instance the Commission recognises that 'representativeness, though an important criterion, should not be the only determining factor for membership of an advisory committee, or to take part in dialogue with the Commission. Other factors, such as their track record and ability to contribute substantial policy inputs to the discussion are equally important.'

In other words, good policy ideas are not necessarily representative ones. There is also an acknowledgement of the difficulties that OCS encounters in developing good ideas without appropriate resources. However, in the NGO community it is not agreed what constitutes evidence of representativity and whether only representative organisations should be consulted (ESC 2000b). NGOs and Social Movement Organisations (SMOs) point out that increasingly civil society expresses fluidity in the type of formations that represent its values and opinions. New organisations often emerge quickly with strong popular support and dissolve or change into different organisations in a short time. Therefore an insistence on calculating memberships would exclude an important part of civil society.

The same ambiguity that emerged with representativeness also emerged with accountability. A first important issue is 'accountability to whom?'. Here the commission distinguishes different forms of accountability that may well be, and often are, at odds: political and social accountability. For instance, one of the teams involved in the preparation of the WPG argues that 'in addition to the traditional forms of accountability, public administrations are accountable towards society as a whole' (Commission, Preston *et al.* 2001). As the EU-level public administrator, the Commission seems to imply an acceptance of a responsibility to society, which is different and presumably broader than accountability to elected representatives and institutions. However, in the same document, accountability is ultimately subordinated to the electoral process, which implies a conception of relations with OCS in which they are seen as mainly channels of information in the policy-making process.[16]

The Commission in frequently emphasising accountability but also 'The need to respect diversity and heterogeneity of the NGO community', and 'The need to take account of the autonomy and independence of NGOs' assumes that the two concepts can be combined (Commission 2000a). But in many ways the two categories are different and not easily reconciled.

Implications of the relationship between OCS and the EU

To sum up this section, the role of the OCS is to some extent embarrassing because it may be seen as clientelistic, lacking the legitimacy of majoritarian institutions, and as evidence of lack of planning and consistent operating rules. But it is an opportunity precisely because it allows the claim to be put forward that an unachievable concept of democracy based on representative mechanisms can be replaced at the EU level by a Madisonian concept of democracy in terms of preventing the tyranny of the majority through the inclusion in the policy process of a set of independent and conflicting voices (Majone 1996: 286). The Commission may also be trying to compensate EU problems of input legitimacy with a measure of output legitimacy – the legitimacy that springs from performing necessary tasks and doing so satisfactorily (Scharpf 1999). And crucial to this end is the information-providing role of NGOs. For these reasons, there is much ambivalence within the Commission and the EP on the best way to frame relations with OCS.

This indecision is also rooted in the political socialisation of parliamentarians and senior Commission officials. As for the latter, their political values are naturally related to what model of Europe they favour and therefore what role they are prepared to attribute to OCS. In general they tend to be supranationalists and in any event to believe that Europe should be more than a common market, therefore implicitly recognising a role for EU OCS (Hooghe 1997).

More specifically, one source of ambiguity concerns the selection of NGOs to be included in consultation. One view is that the Commission should move toward some kind of accreditation system, similar to the one operating in several international organisations whereby inclusion is conditional upon recognition by other NGOs and or evidence of size of representation. This approach is, however, rejected by several NGOs, which see it as potentially institutionalising a system that would marginalise smaller NGOs in favour of large and established organisations. This approach could defeat the purpose of including NGOs as sources of alternative policy solutions, of lesser-utilised expertise and of unpopular but correct approaches. For smaller NGOs, the principle of inclusion should be that all relevant voices on a specific policy area are heard, regardless of claims of representativeness. However, this approach will be difficult to accept by a Commission which frequently faces accusations of lack of representativeness itself. A second source of uncertainty is the awareness that, at present, the Commission has too few administrative resources to improve and standardise the consultation process. For a perception of increased efficiency to come about, the Commission would have to be more selective in its choice of which organisations to consult and which budget lines to continue, particularly in view of the legal uncertainty of several areas of funding which first came to light in 1998 (Bates 1998). Yet, there is much reluctance to restrict the Commission's involvement in a set of small grants related to policy areas of uncertain legal bases. Numerous officials believe in the substantive importance of these areas, and are aware of the strategic advantages of the Commission's involvement in the public interest associations sector.

The policy-communities' level: advocacy coalitions in the policy process

Turning to the third arena defined on the basis of Weiler's scheme, the second-level organs of governance (Commission Directorates, Committees, etc.), and relevant corporate and social–industrial NGOs (Weiler, Haltern *et al.* 1995) require examination. This level deals with the administrative process, the role of networks, and low level of process rules. New issues constantly emerge in the political and media arenas which require policy solutions. However, a complex set of institutional filters intervene between the cultural acknowledgement of a problem and its translation into a set of new policies. At the level of policy communities there operates a number of variables that mediate this translation. One consists of the specific values and interests of bureaucracies and in the case of EU institutions, the distinctive mix of political and sectoral interests that characterises the EU system of governance.

As in all bureaucracies, EU civil servants are sensitive to budget-maximising and bureau- shaping considerations (Dunleavy 1991), which adherence to the practices of particular MACs may well promote (H3). In addition, historically different bureaucratic units express different ideological preferences (Michelmann 1978). There are, however, common traits in the EU policy environment that make it particularly conducive to the emergence of advocacy coalitions. One is an entrenched tendency to solve conflicts through their technicalisation and secondly through their diffusion in a system of extensive deliberation which relies on the interaction of a large number of actors. It should be noted that there are institutional reasons for maximising interaction. The frequency of interaction is part of an intentional design intended to promote consensus in a system that cannot easily use legislative solutions in cases of conflict. In such cases, the strategy has traditionally been that of technicalising and bureaucratising conflict (see Peters in Sbragia 1992), and resolving technical problems through negotiations. The consequence is a global inter-organisational field in which there are frequent contacts and, at times, role exchanges. For instance, EU personnel not infrequently become lobbyists after retirement – often early retirement. A case in point is the environmental field, where environmentalists take positions as *stagiaires* in the DG Environment, or other environment-related positions, and at times remain as permanent personnel in EU institutions. As we shall see, similar dynamics occur in the broad family of pro-inclusion movements, and to a lesser extent among regionalists.

Essentially, we can conceptualise the work of policy communities as conducted in an inter-institutional space where a plurality of actors negotiate the rules of the game. Within this space, a fundamental distinction is drawn between private and public groups. Public groups are funded by the Commission. In the

words of the Commission, a substantial amount of resources are used to give the
sector relative parity with its status in member-states. The Commission notes:

> At present over €1000 million yearly is allocated to NGO projects directly by the
> Commission, the major part for development co-operation and human rights and
> democracy programmes in the external relations sector with other important
> allocations in the Social (approximately 70 million), Education (50 million), and
> Environment sectors within the EU. Several hundred NGOs in Europe and world-
> wide are receiving funds from the EU. The Commission has therefore contributed
> substantially to matching the support of the members of the European public given
> to NGOs and thus highlighting the continued importance of high levels of public
> support for the role of NGOs. (Commission 2000a)

Despite this declaration of good intentions, the Commission recognises the
financial and administrative differences among policy sectors in the treatment
of NGOs, the different traditions that set different standards and typologies of
inclusion in the policy process, the lack of reciprocal information between EU
institutions and the rapidly changing nature of the NGOs' sector. Not only
access to information, but also the way in which dialogue and consultation are
organised and the availability of core funding differ across policy sectors (Commission 2000a). All these factors contribute to a relative lack of transparency in
relations, and a relative ignorance of funding practices, which are not logically
organised. As the Commission notes:

> At present the Commission is faced with a high number of budget lines with their
> respective legal bases which are not coherently organised either in terms of their
> position in the EU budget and nor in the complementarity of their objectives.
> (Commission 2000a)

In both the NGO sector and EU institutions, there is an element of disorienta-
tion which the existing set of guiding documents produced both by institutions
and by the NGOs sector is not sufficient to alleviate (Sluiter and Wattier 1999;
ECAS 2002).[17] Nonetheless, in several policy sectors the general climate is
favourable to a contribution by MACs to agenda-setting. For instance, one
can cite in this regard the bi-annual meetings between the Commission services
and the member organisations of the Platform of European social NGOs. Also,
there is a twenty-five-year tradition of meetings by a Liaison Committee of
Development NGOs to discuss policy issues. Similarly, twice a year, the larger
pan-European environmental NGOs ('Group of Eight') meet with the Director-
General to discuss the work programme of the Environment DG and the general
relationship between the NGOs and the DG. This body also reviews recent
events and the policy agenda (Commission 2000a).

   This relatively positive climate is also encouraged by the fact that there are
important niches of activism within the ranks of institutions – particularly the
Commission and Parliament. The impact of activism at policy-community level
can be substantial. For instance, it has been noted that the rapid progression
of gender equality measures can be explained with relation to the work of a

committed number of activists working within the institutions (Hoskyns 1996; Hubert 1998; Stevens and Stevens 2001: 140). The importance of institutional activists has also been documented in the case of environmental policy (Judge 1992; Cini 1997; Ruzza 2000b) and of anti-racist anti-discrimination policy (Favell 1998; Geddes 1999; Ruzza 2000a). This literature points to an important political opportunity for MACs supported by committed institutional actors.

Institutional activists

Clearly, movement coalitions target a different mix of institutional spheres, and, as Santoro and McGuire (Santoro and McGuire 1997) argue, the type of movement–institution relationship matters for the advocacy outcomes of specific movement advocacy coalitions. Movements can be integrated to a greater or lesser extent in different institutional spheres, which determines their chances of success. On the basis of a comparison between two US movements – feminist and civil rights movements – in relation to political institutions, Santoro and McGuire (1997: 517) argue that:

> First institutional activists should play more dominant roles in policy outcomes for social movements that enjoy substantial access to the established political structure ... Second institutional activists should be particularly important when movements face strong insider opposition to their policy goals. Institutional activists are in an advantageous position to prevent government resources from being co-opted by such oppositional groups ... Third, government insiders should be particularly important in policy outcomes when the policy in question is highly complex or technical in nature.

These hypotheses (H3a) will be considered in the examination of movement coalition outcomes that follows in this book. Some evidence that institutional activists play an important role in a variety of movements is provided by descriptive and historical studies of social movements – particularly the new movements of the 1980s. However, the extent of institutional activism is still not fully appreciated. This feature will be documented on the basis of personal interviews with movement-sympathetic civil servants and activists using direct citations from interviews . In the course of this, both the outcomes of the policy process, which are determined by the complex interaction of levels of governance, and the processual elements of policy-making and the structures for the formal and informal incorporation of MACs into the Brussels policy machinery, will be stressed.

Conclusions

In this chapter, a research strategy to explain the influence of the movement-inspired advocacy coalitions that address EU institutions has been stressed. By distinguishing three levels of political decision-making – intergovernmental, EU elites, and policy communities – involving different actors, arenas and processes, it is argued that movement coalitions play distinct roles at each of these levels. As regards the intergovernmental level, a scarcely institutionalised arena has been observed in which electoral calculations play a significant role, and where subscribing to the policy ideas of social movements may yield advantages for political actors. When examining specific movements it will therefore be necessary to investigate the key events in their emergence and affirmation and to identify the strategies of top-level political actors at the times of movements' emergence. Discussion of these strategies will also require a mapping of the range of opinions on the themes raised by these movements.

At EU elites' level, the role played by the legitimacy of the EU system of governance in the calculations of EU elites has been stressed, as have the benefits that may accrue from subscribing to successful movements. When presenting the case studies, it will therefore be necessary to inquire into the legitimacy benefits that sponsoring specific advocacy coalitions can bring.

At the policy-community level, two mechanisms that can generate support for social movements have been stressed. One is a process whereby organisational selection is made of personnel with a normative commitment to a movement's ideas by institutional activists. There are also self-selection processes of activist-minded civil servants who opt to work in MAC-relevant environments. The second mechanism involves considerations of budget maximisation and bureau shaping which are similarly able to generate support for movements. The three levels interact when new political opportunities arise and policy ideas, political opportunities and politics converge. These processes are likely to come about in different ways in different policy areas, which affects the chances of movement groups at EU level. In any policy field, policy innovation is rare, and movement coalitions are a source of new policy ideas that are generally marginalised by mainstream electoral politics. They are effective 'on those relatively infrequent occasions when three usually separate process streams – problems, politics and policy ideas – converge'. Processes of frame-bridging in which extreme and unacceptable ideas of movements are tempered and merged with dominant institutional foci can aid this convergence.

Considered together, the literature and the reflections presented here point to a set of hypotheses and identify areas requiring empirical investigation. First, it has been stressed that EU movement coalitions maintain a social movement character, particularly in relation to their international and member state connections. In the light of the literature on social movements, one would expect to find that the presence or absence of elite allies is crucial for predicting movements' policy effectiveness, and that the relative openness or closure of the institutionalised political system will have predictive capacity with regard to policy outcomes. Institutional openness in the EU depends on the different legal bases and traditions of different policy sectors. Furthermore, from a different perspective in social movement research, one would expect that the amount of resources at a movement's disposal will play a role in its advocacy effectiveness. Given the institutionalised nature of the EU environment and of movement coalitions, it can be assumed that repression or threats of disruption by movements will be of little empirical relevance.

Secondly, as suggested by the recent literature on EU OCS, special attention should be paid to the issue of the legitimacy of the European construction in all its diverse meanings at different levels of governance. The hypothesis presented here is that this will prove a powerful predictor of the amount of support for movements forthcoming from institutional actors (H2a). Thirdly, with regard to the policy analysis literature and its suggestion that non-distributive policy areas are regulated more easily, because change is possible without alterations to the balance of power among actors, this claim will be examined in relation to the activities of the movement coalitions examined by the case studies (H2b). With regard to the literature on ideas in policy, the role of sympathetic intellectuals, scientists and experts in advancing movement causes will be examined with the expectation that their contribution will be found to be substantial and possibly institutionally path dependent.

At the third level, that of policy communities, the impact of institutional activists on movements' outcomes has been stressed. As with Santoro and McGuire (1997: 514), it is posited that institutional activists play a crucial role in institutional settings, particularly when there is internal institutional opposition and when issues are highly technical. The factors that have been identified as contributing to the influence of movement coalitions are of two kinds: institutional mechanisms and public discourse dynamics affecting society. The institutional factors are processes of mutual selection by movements and institutions on the basis of compatible ideologies, and the likelihood that institutional activists occupy work roles that enable them to impact upon movements' objectives. Influence, as the outcome of pressure applied by institutional activists, is specified as their ability to influence agenda-setting and issue-formation, to affect institutional procedures, policy change and discursive positions. Public discourse, as the inter-institutional environment that affects all institutional action, is also important. It is argued that since some movements' ideas now refer to areas of generalised legitimacy, professional political actors and business people will subscribe to them and even take their importance for granted, while re-defining them in terms consonant with their organisational/institutional cultures. The extent of this re-definition will be determined by the cultural and social power of institutional activists.

Traversing these three levels, it is argued, are global ideas embodied in international organisations and states which movements can use as resources. Movements are, however, not equally powerful, since a movement able to attach itself to one of these ideas will be advantaged. It is also argued that not all institutions process ideologies similarly. Path dependencies, recruitment strategies and gate-keeping structures influence the manner in which different institutions process movement ideologies. This study will focus on the ideal and moral aspects of movements as easily exported to a variety of institutional domains and to observe the differences in how movements are incorporated in institutional environments when they are mediated by relational and non-relational channels. The hypothesis presented here is that goal displacement, distortion and pre-emption will be less likely when there are relational channels available for movements' advocacy in institutional contexts and when a wide range of institutions give movements' ideas strength and resonance in everyday practices.

Summary

In this chapter, a set of hypotheses have been presented with references to the literature on social movements and their institutionalisation, and on policy analysis. The importance of both institutional dynamics and public opinion in determining the viability of social movements and the advocacy coalitions that promote their views have been stressed. In relation to institutional environments, the role of institutional selection in re-defining the character of movements has been stressed. It is argued that as movements change their nature, becoming more professionalised and institutionally useful for legitimacy purposes, they become part of larger movement advocacy coalitions and can be selectively incorporated by policy-making institutions.

It is argued that when a movement coalition can be connected to internationally validated ideas, such as human rights and freedom, institutional activists will be able to support it from within institutional settings. But influence will be effectively exercised when these activists occupy powerful institutional roles and are able to coordinate tactics with movements. Such influence will be assessed in terms of agenda-setting, institutional procedures, policy change and dominant institutional discursive frames.

Notes

1 Using an inclusive classic approach, social movements can be seen as 'a set of opinions and beliefs in a population representing preferences for changing some elements of the social structure, or reward distribution, or both, of a society' (McCarthy and Zald 1982).
2 For a review of the literature on the institutionalisation of social movements see Seippel (2001).
3 There are several definitions of 'social movement' in the literature. They have been conceptualised in similar terms by McCarthy and Zald (1982).
4 The social movement literature also concerns itself with debates that are not particularly relevant to the EU environment because it has traditionally focused on emerging movements. For this reason, some of the concerns of this literature will not be addressed. While its recurrent debates on the relation between activism and public policy are of relevance here, two of the classic issues addressed by the social movement literature cannot be analysed with Brussels-level observational data. See Giugni (1999). One is the debate on social movements' impact in relation to their moderate versus disruptive strategies.

It is unlikely that disruption will occur in Brussels: many social movements represented in EU institutions emerged decades ago and are now fairly institutionalised. The issue of disruption can only be examined peripherally by asking actors whether disruption occurring elsewhere has an impact on EU-level dynamics. This will require broadening the field beyond Brussels-level dynamics, but empirically it is not a central issue. The second is the debate on whether movements control their environment through their strategic choices or whether they are mainly shaped by external influences. Again, in Brussels movements are a minor component of a vast system of interest representation, so that the question is of secondary importance.

5 The fact that movement activists are also frequently institutional activists is difficult to conceptualise in a theoretical framework which asserts that institutional dynamics constitute opportunities for movements, because it is premised on a strong distinction between the two. POS, an influential methodological framework in social movement research, can conceptualise institutions as allies but not so easily as hosts for movements. This is because it would then be difficult to identify movements' outcomes as separate variables and relate them to institutional dynamics, which is a long-standing concern of the social movement literature. This is generally not a problem, as movements' scholars concentrate on the protest activities of movements, but it is a problem when very institutionalised entities are considered.

6 One also needs to consider intergovernmental relations – that is, relations between administrative units acting in a partially autonomous manner from their governments. To the extent that these relations affect specific policy communities they should be framed at the third level of analysis. To the extent that they are ultimately kept out of the EU system of governance they are reflected at the first level of analysis.

7 Well known, for instance, is the work of John Hall on the diffusion of monetarist ideas and the contributions of historical institutionalists to ideal innovation in different contexts (Hall 1986; Powell and DiMaggio 1991; Steinmo, Thelen *et al.* 1992; Immergut 1998). Neo-institutionalism points to the role of gatekeepers in filtering ideas in institutional domains (Bleich 1998) and to the role of previous institutionalised ideas in determining which new ones are incorporated and how (Ruzza 1996, 2000a). Following John Meyer's lead, the role of 'global ideas' in influencing specific contexts has been empirically studied by institutionalists (Meyer and Scott 1983; Soysal 1994; Klotz 1995; Checkel 1997, 1999a, 1999b; Ramirez, Soysal, *et al.* 1997; Risse, Ropp *et al.* 1999).

8 For a review of the IR literature on the role of global ideas and more generally 'knowledge approaches' see Hasenclever, Mayer and Rittberger (1997) Hasenclever, Mayer *et al.* (1997).

9 Important documents are, for instance: Commission (1992, 1993, 1995, 1996a, 1997a, 1998b, 2000a, 2001b); Diamantopolus (2000); ESC (2000a); Platform (2000).

10 Neil Kinnock, a member of the Commission since 1995 and former leader of the UK Labour Party, was given the task of internally reforming the Commission. His aim, as declared at a hearing in the EP, was to modernise and reform the management culture of the Commission by injecting a stronger emphasis on responsibility, value for money, accountability and transparency, particularly by increasing the transparency and professionalism of communication within the Commission and between the Commission and EP and the public.

11 This was given a constitutional basis with the adoption of the Social Agreement added to the Maastricht Treaty. Conversely, the role of NGOs is merely recognised in Declaration 38 annexed to the Amsterdam Treaty which underlines their important contribution to social solidarity.

12 For instance, in November 1998, the Commission organised an event to present a 'Vademecum on grant management' to representatives of Brussels-based NGOs – an audience of about 200 representatives, inclusive of campaigners for the environment, social affairs,

development aid and human rights sectors. As the Commission notes, 'representatives of these four NGO "families" are in regular contact with the Grant Management Network on the implementation of the Vademecum, and the steering group sees the current informal cooperation as useful and wish it to continue' (Commission 2000a).

13 Several interviewees from NGOs have also emphasised the role of the Internet, which has facilitated the work of NGOs first by making information previously restricted to policy-making bodies widely accessible, and secondly by lowering the cost of participation in the policy process. For this reason, smaller NGOs find that a stable presence in Brussels is less important and cost-effective because they are now able to acquire relevant information on funding and contribute position papers directly from member states. This would be facilitated if the Commission could create channels for consultations in member states, but without additional funding for the consultation process this is unlikely to happen (Crook 2000). However, at least some initial work in classification of the sector has been done. The Commission has utilised the Internet to start and then stimulate the growth of a public register of groups. In January 1997, a first version was published which comprised more than 600 non-profit organisations working at EU level and covering approximately 100 branches of activity. An electronic version was launched in 1999 which included over 800 organisations. Since 2000 the service has been automated and expanded, and in 2001 the service known as CONECCS included over 1000 organisations (see http://europa.eu.int/comm/civil_society/coneccs/index.htm). The information is provided on a voluntary basis. The Commission also intends that the directory should provide a means to promote awareness and therefore increase consultation of the less well known types of organisations.

14 For instance, a key document reads: 'It should not be assumed that less-advantaged stakeholders are already in existence as relatively easily identifiable entities, and organised to a greater or lesser extent. It may be the case that, as an issue arises, important stakeholders are not at all organised, and may not be at all well-informed about the potential impact of them. Redressing material and cognitive imbalances may therefore, first and foremost, involve public actors in assisting the emergence of stakeholders as organised entities in order that they may make a meaningful contribution to the policy process' Commission (2000b).

15 The ESC also stresses that 'representativeness must be qualitative as well as quantitative . . . meaning that representatives are able to participate effectively and constructively in the opinion-forming and decision-making process through the provision of appropriate organisational structures and expertise' (ESC 2001a).

16 The document reads: 'It is nevertheless apparent that the decision-making process in the EU is first and foremost legitimised by the legislator, i.e. the elected representatives of the European people . . . However, consultation, if carried out properly, can provide valuable expertise laying the ground for – technically – sound decisions. In particular, consultation helps reconcile the views and concerns of different actors throughout the policy-cycle (i.e. in policy-shaping, implementation and evaluation), thereby obtaining wide support and social acceptance for decisions.'

17 ECAS was created in 1990 to help the non-profit sector counteract the rapid expansion of business following initiatives for the completion of the single market and the anticipation that new NGOs areas of policy would be part of EU competence. ECAS has been instrumental in the development of the overall sector of public-interest representation in Brussels: For instance, it has assisted with the establishment of over twenty EU associations such as the European Consultation on Refugees and Exiles (ECRE). One of its main tasks is to help NGOs acquire the skills necessary to obtain EU funding. It produces a funding guide, now in its seventh edition, and trains NGO personnel.

3

Environmentalism

In recent decades, environmental policy has been one of the newest and fastest-growing policy areas in the West (Weale 1992). Since emerging in the 1970s as a result of pressure applied by public opinion and environmental movements, it has grown into a comprehensive set of concerns about new problem areas, spreading across a variety of other policy areas. European institutions are crucial for environmental regulation, both because of the integrated character of the European economies and of the cross-border nature of many environmental threats. For this reason, institutions such as the European Commission and the EP have aroused a great deal of interest among industrial lobbies and public pressure groups.

The EU has been highly active with regard to environmental matters; even more active than one might expect on the basis of pressure from member states. As Majone (1993) points out, environmental regulation has significantly increased in a period of general de-regulation. Without stressing the role of new ideas in the policy process – specifically a new awareness of the environment promoted by a committed MAC – it would be difficult to explain the emergence of environmental regulation. But how ideas relate to actual policies is not self-evident. Particularly in the case of a horizontal and highly technical policy area like environmental policy, which is connected to concerns about health and safety, a complex set of institutional and cultural dynamics separates the emergence of environmental themes in the political and media arenas and its impact on policy-making. In this chapter, the diffusion of environmental policy into the legislative bodies of the EU will be examined and related to the work of the environmental advocacy coalitions in Brussels. This will involve an examination of the changes that have come about, and the accommodations reached by business people, policy-makers and environmentalists, these being the main parties with specific interests at stake. This will also involve consideration of the specific contribution made by the notion of 'sustainable development' to creating the cultural and structural conditions necessary for these accommodations.

On the basis of over fifty key-actor interviews with participants in the environmental policy community,[1] the idea of sustainable development will be connected with the impact of the environmental movement. The way in which this impact is mediated by the distinctive dynamics of the EU decision-making centres, and by the logic of the institutional environment of business, will be highlighted.

The political role of sustainability

'Environmentalism' entered wider societal awareness on the coat-tails of the environmental movement, whose objective is now well encapsulated by the key term *sustainable development*. The term conveys the utopian vision of a society that, while continuing to progress economically, does so in a way that prevents further damage to the environment. From the political point of view, establishing the concept of *sustainability* has been the ultimate achievement of the so-called 'Ecological Modernisation' coalition. The middle-to-late 1980s saw Western governments fully recognise the legitimate status of the environmental problem, and take on the challenge from a more global perspective, whereas the 1970s and early 1980s had mainly witnessed the scattered enactment (and poor implementation) of local and sectoralised policies.[2]

In part because of its very ambiguity,[3] the concept of 'sustainable development' has freed industry from its earlier uncompromisingly negative role, enabling it to recast itself as a potential partner to governments in the development of technologies to solve environmental problems. The influence of industry should not be underestimated, as the EU's Fifth and Sixth Programmes recognised, for they incorporate some of the key concepts on compatibility between market principles and environmental protection (through 'working closer with the market' and in partnership with business as advocated by the Sixth EU Programme, and through 'market instruments' of regulation like the Eco-Label and the Environmental Management and Audit Scheme (EMAS), as advocated by the Fifth Programme) (Commission 1992, 2001a).

The concept of sustainable development, and similar concepts, were frequently cited by the actors interviewed in Brussels. Some of them posited sustainability as an ideal to be approximated in the real world; others were cynical about the idea but acknowledged that it could be a source of legitimacy, and an indicator of goodwill when employed in consultation procedures; yet others believed that it should be refined by scientific and or social research. However, all of the interviewees used the term and were aware of its importance in the policy discourse on environmentally related issues.

But why has the notion of environmental sustainability been so successful that it has become a sort of institutionalised myth? The hypothesis presented here is that since environmentalism is now an approved societal concern, a wide range of actors subscribe to it, and even take its importance for granted, whilst re-defining it in terms consonant with their organisational cultures. In addition to the cultural factors affecting EU environmental policy through the influence exerted by actors from member states, there are institutional ones, notably those that will be analysed in the EU policy-making environment.

EU actors in networks of environmental policy play a crucial role in linking their organisation with a fragmented world of political institutions and vested interests. Their knowledge, values and operating practices are constantly questioned and exchanged in their multifarious inter-organisational relations, and over time they become institutionalised. Lobbying, both private and public, is fairly formalised and integrated. There are lobbyists who act individually for single clients, but there are sectoral associations which represent large and small constituencies. For instance, UNICE, the general association of European industry, and the European Confederation of Chemical Industries (CEFIC), are two lobbying organisations of different types. As these organisations interact with EU institutions, they constitute a new inter-organisational field in need of legitimacy *vis-à-vis* other policy communities, and, it is argued, they use the concept of sustainability to acquire it. First, however, the way in which concepts like sustainable development can emerge and become dominant in a policy domain must be explained.

The literature on discourse in policy domains has pointed to the social construction of problems and solutions in the policy arena. Rein and Schon (1977: 239) maintain that 'the complementary processes of naming and framing mediate the transition from disaggregated worries and scattered perceptions of situations toward the cognitive experience of meaning' that helps define a policy problem and envisage solutions. Frames select elements in a policy domain for attention; they have both explanatory and normative functions, and hence orient action. This normative and explanatory dimension is evident in the concept of sustainable development, which constitutes a 'frame-bridging', that is, a merging of two frames: the 'development' frame, which is widely shared in society and particularly in the business environment, and the 'sustainability' frame, which has emerged only relatively recently, acquiring power and credibility by dint of its association with the first frame. Sustainable development both implies a moral aspiration to a more harmonious relationship with the environment and provides a lens through which a range of policy areas can be scrutinised. A similar point is made by Michael Freeden, who sees ideologies in general, and the green ideology of environmental sustainability in particular, as able to assume different forms within the broad limitations of a family of resemblances. Freeden argues that ideologies are more or less cohesive aggregations of concepts comprising beliefs that are central and others that are peripheral. He sees the green ideology as having a particular capacity to relate to a wide variety of ideas: 'The indeterminacy of the green core concepts suggests that their mutual proximity can take a number of paths, which wave in and out of a wide range of political traditions' (Freeden 1995: 6).

As previously mentioned, the insights of the 'framing' literature are insufficient if they are not anchored in institutional factors which articulate the political opportunities of specific actors, and specifically MACs. By stressing organisational and political dynamics, insights will be qualified in terms of the role of environmental values and grounded in specific institutional processes. Affinities between interests and world views can then be unpacked. In other words, we need to ask why, and under what conditions, innovative elements in environmental policy discourse are accepted by all the participants in a policy community and come to constitute the underlying assumptions, or even simply the 'legitimated myths', of policy-making. This question is particularly relevant to environmental policy, since this is an area that requires the cooperation of a broad set of actors.

Explaining why the frame of 'sustainable development' has been so widely accepted requires a distinction to be drawn between the impact of general features of EU policy style and the specific dynamics of the main sectors regulated by environmental policy.

Reasons for the incorporation of sustainability in the EU framework

There are several reasons why environmentalism has found a welcome reception in some key EU institutions. First, at a global level, the EU has advanced through thematic shifts in areas of least resistance. In the 1970s and 1980s, the environment arose as a new and under-regulated area, one in which supra-national intervention made sense and attracted the support of public opinion. The level of support has remained high as public opinion data show, even if it has declined somewhat in recent years (Figure 3.1).

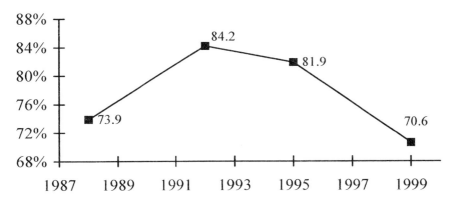

Figure 3.1 Importance of environment protection in Western Europe, 1987–99 – people responding: 'An immediate and urgent problem' (%)

Source: EB 29 (q242), EB 37.0 (q74), EB 43.1Bis (q15), EB 51.1 (q3)

Second, as already noted, EU policy-making relies heavily on discourse because of its de-centralised decision-making procedures. Several observers have pointed out the complexity and diversity of EU decision-making on environmental policy. EU personnel must perform a delicate role of mediation and consensus formation which requires many multilateral and non-bureaucratic contacts of a collegial nature across Commission DGs and more generally across institutions. This collegial style is uniquely suited to the discursive resolution of conflict, to the importing of new ideas into the policy arena and to their use as tools by deliberating parties. The collegial aspiration of the Commission (Edwards and Spence 1994: 36) is often stressed by officials. Collegiality as an inspiring principle derives from Commission decision-making procedures as a way of counteracting the divisive impact of national allegiance (Mazey and Richardson 1994: 172), and it is facilitated by professed allegiance to a common set of values. Majone points out that 'Because uncertainty is so pervasive in policy-making, the values of administrators and experts count a great deal' (1989: 26). But, if values are important, they play an even more crucial role in an organisational structure like the EU's comitology system (Christiansen and Kirchner 2000). In this system, extensive deliberation is institutionalised and, when possible, the profession of common values like sustainability injects cohesion into the policy process.

In general, relations among actors in the environmental field are characterised, not by conflict but a general tendency to negotiate and cooperate. This tendency arises from necessity, for often there are no clear-cut chains of command upon which to rely. The institutional framework is still relatively new and constantly changing, and is therefore difficult to predict. In such a situation, as previously noted, constant negotiation becomes a necessity. The EU is a system in which there are institutional reasons for maximising interaction, and this is particularly the case for horizontal policies.

The tendency to cooperate is facilitated by a professed common concern for the shared value of 'environmental sustainability', which provides negotiating partners with at least the semblance of a common ground, a goal that can be approached in different ways but allows participants to define their interaction as cooperative. Only if a unifying cultural frame like that of environmental sustainability is intentionally adopted can collegial relations be possible. Collegiality in the name of sustainability thus acts as an interaction rule which holds out the promise that people belonging to different communities may nevertheless be able to arrive at collaboration-based solutions if they can agree on a set of ideal values that they might be tempted to pursue, albeit in different ways. While collegiality fosters the production and diffusion of ideas, other processes are also important in channelling these ideas into the system.

Thirdly, the EU architecture is particularly open to external influence. It is, therefore, here more than elsewhere, an institutional setting that can be biased in favour of change rather than against it.[4] In general, European institutions have several different ways of gathering information about ideas and processing that information in the policy-making process. Their staffing by a multinational bureaucracy already provides an important source of information. And ideas and information are also supplied by epistemic communities and MACs (Mazey and Richardson 1994: 177–180). This is a major factor in the environmental field, but others can play a decisive role as well. Clearly, the political parties represented in the EP are of crucial importance in linking ideas and policies together, a case in point being the Greens and their focus on environmental regulation.

The consequence of this openness is a global inter-organisational field in which frequent contacts – and, at times, role exchanges – take place. For instance, in the environmental fields, environmentalists take up positions as *stagiaires* (temporary assistants) in environmental jobs and may stay on thereafter as permanent personnel in EU institutions. Some NGOs scientific advisers have also been experts at the ESC. Even some industry insiders have been defecting to NGOs, and as already noted, some EU personnel become lobbyists after early retirement.[5] These 'boundary-spanning' personnel play a key role in imposing normative and cognitive cohesion onto the macro-organisational field. This is a field that spans levels of government, and to a certain extent unifies environmental policy-making throughout Europe, shaping policy cultures and legitimating action. It is significant to the extent that it involves the public sphere, where elected officials are accountable. It is at this public level that environmental sustainability is a key concept and is connected to the relevance of environmental issues in public opinion.

Public opinion

The results of a 1999 survey show evidence of a long-standing and substantial concern with environmental issues. From this survey it emerges that one in two Europeans is concerned about the deterioration of the environment. In all, 83 per cent of Europeans said that they considered the protection of the environment as a priority for the EU and 55 per cent believed that decisions should be made at EU level.[6] As the Commission notes, these results show considerable uniformity throughout the EU and indicate that there is in all countries a desire to take action. The survey indicates that 56 per cent of Europeans believe that 'it is necessary to fundamentally change our way of life and development if we want to halt the deterioration of the environment'. Over half of Europeans are worried about the environment and as a source of information they trust environmental protection organisations more than they trust government sources (although this trust has been eroded in recent years). The preferred approach to environmental problems is a regulative one. Economic instruments are much less popular than stricter legislation and punitive state intervention against polluters. Trust in government is also deteriorating: compared with a previous (1995) survey, Europeans in 1999 judged public bodies to be acting less effectively at all levels of government: local, regional, national, EU and world-wide.

At the level of EU elites, the public opinion relevance of environmental concerns has a direct result in the legitimating strategies of EU institutions.

Environmentalism as a policy principle

As a policy principle environmentalism has been debated through the concept of sustainable development. The concept of sustainable development is repeatedly cited by such key Commission documents as *Toward Sustainability* (1992), by conferences and workshops – for example, the Commission-sponsored workshop on 'Global Environmental Change and Sustainable Development' (Wuppertal Institute, June 1994) – by study groups and by advisory fora such as those created by the Commission after the Fifth Environment Action Programme. However, as we shall see, the concept does not find direct resonance at the level of detailed policy deliberation. This point is well illustrated by the following extract from an interview with a head of unit:

> You will not find today, I would argue, anybody who argues that he is against the environment. There is nobody who argues that he is against sustainability. It is just poor little detail which is disturbing. The big principles, yes, everybody is in favour of those. I would say, you see, the environmental sector is different from many other sectors in my experience. Whenever a problem is being discussed publicly, and in a way that is detailed enough, there is a potential for environmental policy solutions that take 'sustainability' seriously. And the more the discussion takes place in closed shops, offices, and so on, away from public awareness and opinion, the less these things are taken into consideration. So I would think, where public opinion is involved, the words 'sustainability', the context, and so on, will be pronounced, and will be used ... But many of the solutions which are made in the environmental sector are initiated outside this public sector. So there is this discrepancy between public speaking and private deciding on public issues. (Commission Official, Head of Unit, DG Environment 1997)

This interviewee emphasises the importance of legitimacy in the environmental sector. In private, 'sustainability' loses much of its importance and, as some interviewees pointed out, much of the ambiguity of the concept becomes apparent in specific policy deliberation. However, the fact that sustainability is widely believed to be nothing more than a sop for public consumption does not lessen its importance. Because legislative initiatives are taken in its name, those actors committed to it will to an important extent be able to hold all participants accountable, using the principles to which they publicly subscribe for the purpose.

Limitations are set on the concept of environmental sustainability by its advocates' comparative lack of power. Environmental networks are largely composed of industrial lobbyists and civil servants, with environmentalists constituting only a relatively small minority, whose lack of resources increases its marginalisation. As the same head of unit pointed out, when environmentalists survey the field from the point of view of conferences and public consultations, they gain an exaggerated idea of their success. EU environmental organisations are included in top-level discussions with EU elites together with leading environmental political actors from member states. For instance, EU environmental organisations meet the President of the Commission once a year (http://www.eeb.org/activities/general.htm): in 2000, they discussed the 'Sustainable Development Strategy' prepared by the Commission and examined issues related to access to documents. They are also an active component of the sector of public interest organisations with which several MACs are connected. For instance, they were part of a Contact Group of Civil Society organisations with European organisations active in social, human rights and development issues set up in December 2001 to establish dialogue with the Convention and to prepare proposals for the substantial revision of the EU Treaties. However, owing to a lack of resources, this high-level inclusion does not necessarily translate into influence on specific policy events.

Business, on the other hand, is extremely active in lobbying at all levels, and the number of business lobbyists has increased markedly in recent years (Fouloy 1994; Greenwood 1997). In the environmental networks, their outlook shapes the field in distinctive ways, although they are faced by a pro-environmental ethos, particularly in the Commission and EP.

The fourth reason for the institutional affirmation of environmentalist policies is the influence of environmental regulators. Northern European countries have selectively recruited regulators with environmentally sympathetic ideologies. When European environmental policy first emerged, there were few policy-makers competent in the field, and they tended to be from Northern countries, where environmentalism was stronger and legislation more advanced. A process of selective recruitment into the EU bureaucracy ensured that the EU ethos acquired a markedly environmental character.[7] In several cases, these officials achieved rapid career advancement that placed them in prominent roles, and their commitment to environmentalism maximised their selective retention in environmental policy-making. For instance, a head of unit from a Northern country said that he had been appointed to his post when he was still in his thirties, and that he had remained in a key position for a very long time, stimulating environmental thinking in a variety of fora. Processes of self-selection were also apparent in the form of environmentalist-minded civil servants who opted to remain in politically relevant positions despite the relatively low status of DG Environment (Stevens and Stevens 2001: 197). This has had the consequence of increasing the concentration of institutional activists.

The fifth and last general reason for the success of the sustainability frame is the 'crisis of politics' – a phenomenon frequently observed and analysed in recent years[8] and which has induced institutions to seek legitimacy from policies endorsed by advocacy groups or the media, and to show a concern for environmental sustainability. In doing so, they want to appear responsive to civil society and concerned with issues popular among European publics.

That said, one should not conceive EU institutions as cohesive and there are important pockets within EU institutions where support for sustainability is at best lukewarm. Ideological conflict frequently characterises views of environmental policy, counterposing on the one hand, for instance, DG Industry and DG Environment and on the other hand OCS and EU institutions. While a frame analysis reveals substantial agreement on the importance of sustainability and sustainable development between OCS and institutions, OCS actors stress this slightly more and despite the ideological agreement express a strongly critical stance towards the work of EU institutions, particularly with reference to a frequently emphasised *implementation* deficit. This is a critique and generally a debating style which utilises very technical and detailed information and the critique concerns the *effectiveness* of the policies adopted, revealing the high degree of pragmatism and professionalisation of this movement coalition.

There are also specific reasons, pertaining to the operations of the level of detailed policy making, that help explain the acceptance of environmental sustainability.

The environmental policy milieu

Multinational corporations, associations of industrialists and even smaller companies generally have the resources and technical expertise with which to argue their case on the environment and to sell their ideas, at least in part, to the relevant committees, and to an institutional structure permeable to their input. The policy community that has formed in the field of environmental policy is therefore a broad and ramified one.

However, the members of this policy community know that a purely resource-maximising approach would be unacceptable to the regulators in charge of protecting the environment. Conversely, merging environmental and wealth-creation frames by advocating sustainable development appears to be a legitimate strategy. For instance, certain chemical industries spend substantial sums on environmental advertisements and are among the most generous sponsors of environmental charities. Concerns about the environment are exhibited by all the highly regulated corporate actors, and also by state contractors, such as chemicals manufacturers, biotechnology firms and water treatment companies.

However, business does not simply act strategically. Rather, there is ambivalence as well as genuine interest in 'sustainability' as a policy principle. Those actors most closely involved in consultations with the Commission often develop a common culture with those who regulate them. While some business lobbyists see sustainable development as a difficult issue which cannot be ignored, many others view it as having a crucial bearing on the future growth of their industries. As a consultant for an agricultural consortium explained:

> I will say at the outset that for us it is the most important issue, sustainable development. So we are not aliens, we consider it our top priority . . . Our industry has an input in agriculture, and agriculture's role in achieving sustainability of the environment is crucial. So although we are indirectly involved, we have a crucial input. (Interview, Brussels 1996)

Obviously not all business actors subscribe to the concept of sustainable development. Some business people seek to promote an understanding of environmental issues that is more clearly pro-business, advocating for instance the concept of 'sustainable growth' where the emphasis is mainly on the concept of growth. Some of them are sceptical about the intelligibility and feasibility of the project, which is not to say that they do not recognise its political importance. For instance, an EU consultant for the car and transport industry described sustainable development as :

> a dramatic phrase . . . a sort of a catchword . . . [but] . . . not a realistic concept because, as I see it, we must not go back to living in caves ... if we really want sustainable development. But that is not really important. The fact is that it has provoked a lot of environmental thinking, and the fact that the Fifth Action Programme picked up the theme, I think has had a big impact and it's made us think 'what do they mean?'. (Interview, Brussels 1997)

Even when consultants do not directly endorse the pro-environmental policies debated by the Commission, there are some who nonetheless demonstrate that they have adopted both the language of the EU environmental networks and the general goals of environmental policies. Indicative of this is the following statement by a representative of the chemicals industry:

> they (DGII) speak about what they call the PER, polluting emissions register . . . we have the impression that they have taken the wrong direction. A register is not a good instrument. But the objective is right in the concept of 'sustainable development' and of partnership. (Interview, Brussels 1996)

This emphasis on 'sustainability' is becoming a common cognitive scheme for some industries. Studies of corporate cultures have often pointed to the binding role of organisational cultures, which provide corporate identity given that no two organisations share exactly the same culture. At the same time, corporate cultures are never entirely dissimilar because business organisations dynamically relate to societal culture by importing the cultural markers of a particular historical period. If environmentalism is to some extent an accepted value in society, it is difficult for those who operate in an environmental field to deny its importance.

Firms producing environmentally sustainable goods will obviously promote sustainability more than those whose main concern is to resist regulation. But, as previously pointed out, roles are sometimes reversed, and regulation is welcomed for a variety of reasons. Significant among these are first-mover advantages. That is, some businesses gain an advantage from environmental regulation because it excludes those businesses that either cannot match the technological level required for compliance or are not sufficiently sensitive to market demand for environmental products and therefore respond to environmental regulation with non-compliance strategies. Consequently, there is no clear correspondence between environmental attitudes and market position.

In addition, as Héritier (1996: 151) has pointed out, industry's first-mover strategy of welcoming regulation is supported by some highly regulated member states which seek to avoid the cost of adjustment to European legislation and to equalise the cost of environmental compliance of their industry. They try to favour their market for environmental products and protect themselves against their industry's lobbying efforts, which could otherwise point to laxer standards elsewhere. Thus environmental business lobbyists do not necessarily adopt a defensive stance on environmental regulation. The relationship between business and the regulators can at times be very strained in the environmental field, but it can also be a symbiotic one. Commenting on industrial strategies to influence environmental regulation, a Commission official pointed out: 'Industries do not always oppose regulation. Why should they? It might not be cheaper in the short run. But some of them plan in the long run' (Interview, Forward Studies Unit 1993).

Reactions are frequently positive, particularly since environmental regulations are frequently drawn up in consultation with industry, whose input is expressly welcomed. For instance, when commenting on the Fifth Environmental Programme a CEFIC official noted:

> The Fifth Environmental programme is a remarkable book which sets the agenda for the next five years. And I think we, every partner, has recognised the quality of this book. And effectively there is in many places of this document a call for working together, and working together, maybe, may lead to new instruments compared to the traditional government control approach. (Interview, Brussels 1997)

Lobbyists know that notice is taken of their pro-environmental attitudes; indeed, they are the first to point them out. The reaction of civil servants to industry lobbying is one of acceptance and encouragement, although at times there is irritation at the frequent attempts made to exert influence.

A further reason why business does not necessarily oppose regulation is the threat of negative publicity from environmentalists. In the absence of a bureaucratic or political organiser – such as when the Commission organises working groups including both industry and advocacy groups – contacts between industrial lobbies and environmentalists may be infrequent and sometimes strained. However, they may also prove constructive and useful for both sides. Business realises the potential threat of a direct appeal to public opinion and needs information. As both industries and NGOs become more global, political regulation loses some of its power, and direct relations between the two sides become necessary. As Offe (1990) has pointed out, the 'crisis of politics' has translated into a 'crisis of policy' in which political powers are no longer sufficiently legitimated to be able to impose policies, relying on the lack of popular scrutiny or the trust of the electorates. To be viable, policy change increasingly needs the support of public opinion. In addition, processes of globalisation have put many policies beyond the reach of national politics. Global advocacy groups in some fields have sufficient hold on the media and public opinion to be powerful shaping influences on policy, and therefore invite independent negotiations with industry. Events like the Brent Spar[9] fiasco have conveyed the clear message to industry that expert opinions or political influence are not enough. As for environmentalists, they are convinced that, in many instances, there are affordable environmental solutions to business problems which business ignores at its peril. A Commission official noted that 'lately, industries have been more attentive to the problems of image. They are now more open even in Committee work' (Interview, DG Environment 1997). He added that this openness extended to the relationship with 'green producers', citing groups 'like Ecovert in cosmetics' which are at times obviously misinformed about the technical specifications of mainstream products, and yet command an audience.

However, direct contacts between business and NGOs are still in their infancy. The 'greening of industry', to the extent that it is coming about, is not the direct outcome of the environmentalists' work. Rather, one should look at the cultural influence of political–administrative environments.

Political–administrative environments

When discussing the role of elected officials and environmental civil servants in Brussels' networks, it is important to stress that they have substantially more power than the other actors, public and private lobbies. Although as a category they are highly fragmented, they have specific interests in common that they are often able to advance. Smith makes the point clearly: 'Frequently it is not pressure groups that determine state policy, but state policy affects the activities of groups' (Smith 1993: 7). Civil servants are often in a position to decide who is to be included in environmental consultations and who is to be excluded. However, they have an interest in regulating the environment, and can do so effectively only with a degree of compliance from industry. Crucially, they need information from industry because they often do not have the resources to conduct studies themselves. Moreover, their careers may profit from environmental regulation. For instance, a civil servant noted:

> my friends should be called the 'envirocrats' because although they can claim they want to protect the environment, they are interested in their own survival and importance, and they emphasise the importance of their regulation. (Interview, Forward Studies Unit 1993)

But more generally, the belief of civil servants in environmental protection and in furthering the progress of advanced industrial society spurs them to seek effective regulation based as far as possible on consensus, because in EU institutions even limited opposition may block the policy-making process. In some countries only minor resistance is necessary to stall legislation in controversial areas. This is particularly true of new legislation, as environmental legislation was until recently, and in part still is:

> The directives drawn up by politicians are interpreted by non-elected officials in the framework of an organisational culture[10] that has traditionally been rather sensitive to environmentalism in the EU environment-regulating bureaucracy. For instance, a DG Environment official stressed the need for sustainable development to be considered right from the outset: It should be in everybody's head that anything they propose should be sustainable. It should be obvious. But the point is, that we are living in a world where we've only just discovered that we're hitting the limits of sustainability. (Interview, DG Environment 1997)

However, there are significant variations across different Directorates-General. In addition to DG Environment, which is largely but no longer exclusively environmentalist, there are now small environmental sections within all the other DGs. Some barely exist, and some are actively resisting more stringent environmental regulation in their sector.

At times, these environmentalist ideologies arise in forceful reaction to some external threat. Ideology can infuse bureaucratic work with motivation. It provides legitimacy internally through commitment from colleagues, but it can also be used externally to 'sell the product' of EU policy-making. As one civil servant noted:

> European consumers are very favourable towards the Community's environment policy. If you look at surveys, you see that the environment comes out among the highest in terms of public acceptability in terms of community responsibility. And that is important because assuming that there is a profound environmental awareness, we should try to use that enthusiasm for building up the European Union as such. So this is a very global point, but it's an important one.

Consequently, environmentalism as an ideal stance is particularly viable in EU institutions because it addresses the 'crisis of politics' issue by bringing together a set of timely concerns: the discourse on the 'construction of Europe', an industrial modernity respectful of environmental protection and, in appealing directly to public opinion, concerns about subsidiarity and a more direct connection of the European policy machine with citizens.

Environmental values have another powerful promoter in EU institutions: NGOs and environmental movements.

Public-interest lobbies and the environmental MAC

An environmental MAC formed by environmentalist social movements, together with sections of the media and certain epistemic communities, played a key role among the early popularisers of environmental concerns. The influences exerted by the components of this MAC were often not distinct, either in terms of ideas or in terms of actors, because there was an overlap of roles, particularly at the onset of environmental activism. As is often the case, social movement groups with differing degrees of institutionalisation unwittingly support one another, with the extreme ones attracting media attention and being instrumental in agenda-setting, and the institutionalised ones offering credible alternatives to the public and policy-makers (Gamson and Modigliani 1989). Unlike epistemic communities, their range of views is wide enough to accommodate different causal beliefs and knowledge bases (Haas 1992: 18), and yet the moral commitment of activists leads to the donation of time and energy to certain policy areas and occasionally to high-risk protest activities.

There are eight NGOs active in the environmental field operating in Brussels and eight smaller ones (for a summary of their competences, see Neveso, Schoeters *et al.* 2001).[11] Some have worked in close collaboration with EU institutions for a long time: the European Environmental Bureau (EEB) – an umbrella group representing 1,500 European environmental groups – has been active for twenty years; others are much less firmly established. But in relative terms they are hampered by a substantial lack of resources. Their success, however, is at the problem-definition and agenda-setting stage, where their presence is crucial in the moralised public arena of global policy debate.

Over the years, the environmental movement has undergone a process of institutionalisation, and by and large has accepted the language of science. As Butter and Taylor put it: 'the rising persuasiveness of environmental and global change data has contributed to shifting the essential thrust of modern environmentalism towards an increasingly thoroughly "scientized" Weltanschauung and mode of movement's strategy' (1994: 223). This trend tends to be intensified by the institutional selection of interlocutors in Brussels. The Commission's money and interest has the effect of partially marginalising the anti-technology, anti-market and anti-science voices in the environmental movement. Hence, environmentalism becomes more acceptable to business.

As Smith (1993: 48) points out, what is crucial in the relationship between pressure groups and the state is the form that it takes, even more than the amount of resources available to each participant in policy communities. If a state's actors have an interest in certain groups, they can promote their expansion. This is in part what happens to certain groups in Brussels. The EEB, in particular, receives a substantial portion of its resources from DG Environment and is in frequent consultation with civil servants and Euro-parliamentarians.

By way of summary, the environmental movement has undergone an extensive process of institutionalisation; yet its successes are more evident at the agenda-setting stage than in detailed policy-making.[12] Environmentalist themes have affected EU decision-making through environmentally sensitive bureaucrats and a global cultural change in environmental discourse. In this sense, the influence of the environmental movement should be re-assessed as being crucial at the stage of discourse formation in the policy domain, but limited by resources at most stages of the policy process.

Different types of environmentalists

It is always difficult to formulate typologies of social movements' groups. Positions are at times quickly reversed, there are transfers of activists and issues and a division of labour arises on issues so that positions cannot be compared among groups. Nonetheless, a useful distinction with regard to the organisations operating in Brussels is that between generalist organisations, sectoral organisations and 'false environmentalists'. I shall deal only with the large organisations. Sectoral organisations have a smaller scale of operation. 'False environmentalists' are those organisations which claim environmental credentials for purely instrumental reasons. An EEB official described their role as follows:

> a huge number of people who are presenting themselves as NGOs ... are purely consultants or business oriented. Everybody can pretend to be an NGO nowadays. We have decided to have our own police. And this selected network is our way to police. They are doing it for money. Being an NGO nowadays is the best way to get a contract from the Commission. The environment is a big market nowadays ... Several DGs have environment programmes ... So they represent themselves as environmental NGOs to get contracts. Sometimes they have a good expertise, but as consultants, not as NGOs. We are refusing to recognise NGO organisations having no membership.

The reference here is to the NGO coordinating committee which screens out false environmentalists without membership and with commercial priorities.

The three large generalist organisations adopt two main approaches: a more cooperative one best represented by the EEB, and a more confrontational one best represented by Greenpeace. I shall examine these two types of organisation in the light of their views on sustainability and their relations with institutions and industry. However, it should be stressed that they cooperate on many issues, and that the difference is one only of emphasis. On other issues they accept or even encourage a division of labour: for instance in 1996 an EEB activist described some typical areas of competence as follows:

> Packaging: Friends of the Earth ... Hazardous waste: Greenpeace. Structural Funds: WWF, and anything regarding nature, nature protection issues. EEB has been very busy on the vivisection campaign. We are now very much involved in anything concerned with eco-labelling, eco-audit, standardisation.

But on other issues there may be synergy or competition. One activist described the relations thus:

> whenever there are basic or very important things, we issue documents together, or we try to put pressure as a single group. It also is important for us to have these

co-ordinating meetings to prevent one organisation going against the other, so that we are well informed and really are a coalition.

However, competitive relations do to an extent exist. The same activist explained that all environmental groups (aside from Greenpeace, which used only its own funds) were 'applying for the same funds from the Commission' so that there was a sort of competition for public recognition and so on. Though this was seen as 'quite healthy'. Nevertheless, the difference in tactics is evident:

> In tactics there are differences, . . . from the media campaigns and so on, Greenpeace actions have a completely different approach. EEB would never do . . . these, wild actions, trying to block the ships, these very media orientated campaigns . . . it's a different approach and to draw public attention to it, it's very good. [but] EEB has far more a political approach.

These excerpts outline substantially different approaches to tactics (theatrical forms versus collegial involvement), ideology (confrontation versus cooperation) and funding sources (acceptance versus refusal of institutional funding). Nevertheless, in practice both groups engage in collegial fora, although on different bases.

Different types of fora

Among the various types of fora created by EU institutions, some are more frequently attended by environmentalists and have been for several years. This quotation from an interview conducted in 1995 with the EEB coordinator in Brussels gives an idea of the typical involvement of environmental groups:

> What you observe in recent years is that we as environmentalists are now invited to participate in expert committees . . . where there are representatives of the member states and each of the sectors, such as the environmentalists, the retailers, the consumers, the trade unionists and so on ... and we are part of committees like these in the field of EMAS, in the field of car emissions . . . Another kind of forum is the Ecolabel, where you only have representatives of the sectors getting together, and the Commission is there on the side [but] not chairing the meeting, ... in these two kinds of fora you have people meeting on a regular basis coming from different sectors and getting to know each other very well and in touch formally and informally, of course.

In addition to these two institutional arrangements there are fora where representatives of several sectors meet, like European Partners for the Environment (EPE), an initiative the EEB launched in the early 1990s where representatives coming from different sectors meet on a regular basis with a specific agenda. In these fora no binding decision is generally achieved but the presence of a variety of ideologically different actors nonetheless shapes the agenda and occasionally engenders re-alignments. A complex system of shifting alliances emerges from these fora. The same EEB activist described these shifts:

> All these things are very informal and very fragmented. And the reason they are fragmented is that we don't have permanent alliances. So the alliances will differ from one issue to another. Sometimes you are with one guy and sometimes you are against him. Networks last the time of the discussion [of an issue]. That does not mean that there is no influence. What happens is that, because people get to know each other better, because also they are defining their own political line considering what the other political line will be, to a certain extent it has an influence. It is bringing people more close together. If you look at the position of the sectors, the business sector and the NGOs for instance, the fact that we are dialoguing all the time, because we are, they feel they have to define themselves according to the message *we* are sending.

Clearly, these constant re-definitions of positions, this overall fluidity of the field, mainly concern those groups more willing to cooperate. Groups less willing to compromise must be considered as a category apart.

The cooperative environmentalists

Cooperative environmentalists are still attentive to their social movement provenance, but they now largely share the dominant views and practices of the macro-institutional environment. Like many civil servants and a number of industry representatives, they believe in the concept of sustainability and place special emphasis on this concept because it has broadened the sphere of environmental concerns. As one activist explains:

> In the beginning we [the EEB] had contacts mainly with DGII, now we have to work with all the different DGs. If you think of regional policy with all the structural fund money, whether that's tourism, whether it's energy, agriculture, single market, transport – all the different DGs should really draft their programmes on the basis of sustainability now . . . you have got this principle recognised in writing, so we can refer to it and make requests. Which helps us to come up with demands and requests.[13]

Groups like the EEB tend to adopt a cooperative attitude in their relations with the Commission. They receive money from the Commission, and from other sources as well, such as national governments, and fees from members, and they compete for the Commission's research projects. In some cases they intervene at all stages of the policy project and even formulate proposals for Commission initiatives, highlighting their importance for the policy process:

> Sometimes we even start launching projects where we think the Community should get active. So we sort of bring things into discussion, initiate it, or draw attention to it and ask to have it added to the Council agenda. Then, of course our work programme is very much oriented on the Commission work programme, as we want to lobby them, so of course there must be a coincidence between the two work programmes. Commission having the right initiatives, of course that's our first point where we try to get over our demands and our positions. So we have got now everyday work, very regular contact with the Commission people.

A similar tactic is adopted in relation to the EP:

> We have contacts with the Parliament . . . sometimes helping MEPs draft a paper, or we circulate information from our members asking them to comment on it, or to prepare amendments and so on. We have been lobbying in Strasbourg as well . . . and from there into the Council and so we manage to really have an influence there and a shift in the approach to revisions of the legislation.

This underlines the efforts made by these groups and their pride at being influential. Consultations are frequent – they occur almost daily – and they are appreciated.

However, like other groups, they complain that their resources and influence are too limited for them to be able to counteract the overpowering influence of industry effectively, especially in times of recession. They are careful about the impact of their inclusion in the policy process and on how they invest their resources. They express concern that their inclusion is just providing a measure of legitimacy to institutions which comes to be granted in exchange for only very limited policy returns, or that their inclusion in committees has the implication of providing only an arena for endless discussion which remains, however, inconsequential.

A rather different approach is taken by groups like Greenpeace. These are much more suspicious of incorporation in the institutional realm, in its culture and practices, and wary about cooperating, although they do not reject collaboration in principle. They are rather pessimistic in their evaluations of the policy process and its outcomes.

The oppositional environmentalists

Oppositional environmentalists are aware of the ambiguity of sustainability. One declared:

> But it [sustainability] is a word that has very very nice principles in it but needs a great deal of definition and is only going to be really useful when it is made very clear what it means and what it doesn't mean.

And on the same subject:

> I think [sustainability] is another one of these words. I think it is a total pile of crap because the reason that is has been so widely adopted and has been so popular is that everybody simply takes it to mean exactly what they want.

As regards the Commission, one interviewee thought that it was only in the business of technological fixing, and that it did not really take charge of environmental problems but only engaged in 'remedial work':

> You don't ever really get to discuss anything but 'band aid' work with the Commission, because they are not in a position to do anything except 'band aids'. When they try to, and there have been instances where they've tried to and have run into

> terrible trouble . . . DGII particularly tends to be reasonable the first time around, until industry gets on to them and then of course that is the end of it. But it certainly never comes out reasonable in the end and what is adopted is just always almost inevitably garbage.

This activist then complained about the rarity of 'real' consultations, claiming that when they take place they were 'staged' to achieve what the Commission wanted in the first place. She added that the Commission was far too reluctant to take on really controversial problems, and that the environmental unit was in any event much too weak. However, the environmentalist commitment of environmental officials was generally not questioned. Describing the commitment of institutional activists one environmentalist noted:

> I think it is a genuine attempt. I think the people in DGII, I would say the majority of people, obviously not all of them, but I think a large number of people in DGII are very serious about the environment. They are in DGII because they want to be there, they want to be there because it is a subject they care about. There are exceptions, the most notable of course, being ****, who doesn't even know what the environment is, which is unfortunate given his position. But I think that a lot of people there, particularly in the lower positions, I mean the people who are just sort of in charge of dossiers, are interested in the environment. And they feel, and rightly so, that the views of the NGOs are useful, because they get a great deal of industry input whether they want it or not. A huge amount of industry input. And frequently, certainly what we have found is that industry doesn't do its homework very well.

Oppositional environmentalists like Greenpeace are more sceptical about the effectiveness of business' approach to environmental policy, and they are less ready to cooperate:

> [sarcastic tone] I'm sure that in a thousand years we will just be able to inject ozone into the stratosphere and that will solve this problem. And I suspect that this is probably not an unusual stance for people in the business community. Certainly the ones that I speak to, that I deal with, tend very much to have this sort of Mr Fixit attitude of 'it's all right we'll take care of it if it gets too bad'.

Despite this negative attitude, however, the importance of consultations is not denied. The same interviewee went on to emphasise the importance of consultation, which suggests that the ideological dimension differs more from the macro-institutional field norms than does actual practice:

> But generally I find that it is much more useful to be in a room together because I know that, that for instance, when I talk to people from industry it is very useful to me, because I find out what their problems are, I can say to them, 'too bad we don't see this, this, this as a problem', and they say 'yes they are, because here we have this here we have that and here we have the other'. And they'll put forward seven different problems that are just absolutely impossible for them to resolve. And usually what will happen is that at least three of them, lets say, will be things where it's perfectly easy to solve their problems. It's just that they haven't heard about a particular technology or a way of doing something, or a methodology. *And they're very*

pleased to get the information from us. And in other cases it turns out that they have got an argument that simply has to be taken into account.

But it is not just for useful exchanges of information that contacts are sought. They can also be used strategically.

> But its that kind of dialogue that can only take place if you have your parties in a room together. And for the National experts I think it is particularly important to be in a room with the NGOs. Partly because the industry tends to sound like total fools and I think its important for them to hear that. Secondly because frequently the industry itself is not united, and one part of the industry is being played off against another and that's something that they need to hear. And it's important for them to hear what environmental NGOs are saying, because sometimes they are not sure of their own arguments and it gives them things to either think about or to realise they had better look into or ignore.

The desire of the NGOs for a stable system of consultations is opposed by an influential part of industry. Many in the Commission would welcome such a system, but are possibly unable to impose it. And not infrequently when consultations do take place they turn into ritualistic affairs where the information that officials release in private is simply withheld in public. For instance, an environmentalist described a meeting as follows:

> The people who were there from DGII, with whom I'd spoken on the same issues many many times before, all of whom had admitted at various times, over the phone or in private meetings that there were problems with certain aspects of the way [a certain type of policy work] was being carried out now in the Commission and there would be further problems in the future . . . refused to say anything of the sort in this public meeting, and simply said everything was fine, and thank you so much for coming, hope you enjoyed the coffee, would be delighted to see you again, goodbye. A total waste of time.

And on the same subject:

> My experience has been that the information which I get from the Commission, which is real information and useful information, is always off the record. What I get from them on the record tends to be either very partial, much too late or not at all.

This prompts the question as to why consultations continue to be held in such circumstances. It is difficult to give an unequivocal answer, for a number of factors may be at work. One is that Commission officials may be sympathetic both personally and politically to environmentalists, but still feel that appearing to take sides is too risky. They want to be inclusive, but they do not want to be seen as partisan. The second reason is that excluding environmentalists can be risky. An environmentalist interviewed in December 1995 noted that a few years before, under a particularly unhelpful Commissioner:

> The only thing you could do under **** was, you could call up and say, I've heard this is going on, if I'm not allowed to put in a submission, or to talk to you about

this, or to get information about it, I'm going to go to the press and make a huge stink, and embarrass you terribly. So you might as well be willing to discuss it, because you'll have to discuss it with journalists otherwise; and that worked reasonably well. But that was the only thing that worked.

The climate has changed in recent years, however, and relatively more relaxed and fruitful relations are in place. Why has this happened? There are several reasons for the movement's shift to a less radical stance; they are mentioned in the following two excerpts from interviews conducted in 1995 and 1996.

Reasons for a changing movement

One set of reasons is cognitive: activists value professionalism and expertise and find that an overly radical approach may sometimes be unhelpful and simplistic. There are strategic reasons as well. An EEB activist with a history of activism dating back to the 1960s described the changes in the nature of environmental campaigning as follows:

> We are still extremely flexible and we don't have rigid structures like institutes or institutions, but what is certainly very important when you look at the evolution of NGOs, we are not any longer protest groups but in order to be able to influence anything we need the expertise. In the 1960s it was very important to draw attention to things politicians would have liked to hide, so we drew public attention to that. And now we have our own proposals, we have our experts and they are extremely well informed, otherwise we wouldn't be able to influence anything. That means . . . that includes knowing very well the issue, knowing all the scientific data, what is possible, what is not possible . . . So you really need all the facts in order to be able to influence something. Just this moral or ethical argument and big protests . . . that time is over, you can't move anything anymore. So that certainly is an evolution.

Another EEB activist argued along the same lines, pointing to the strategic reasons why dialogue is useful:

> The question is that everybody [industry and the movement] has to define themselves legitimately vis-à-vis its membership but also vis-à-vis public opinion. And the two elements have always to be considered together. So that is why I think that you have no more the same *very radical* positions you had in the past. People start to know what the constraints are and we do accept and internalise the economical constraints we have, although we think that some alternatives have to be considered and explored much more than they are, and the same for the business sector . . . So the field is less polarised. Even Greenpeace is now open to dialogue with the business sector.

In short, the environmental movement has undergone an extensive process of institutionalisation; yet its successes are more evident at the agenda-setting stage than in detailed policy-making. Environmentalist themes have affected EU decision-making through environmentally sensitive bureaucrats and a global cultural change in environmental discourse. In this sense, the influence of the environmental movement should be re-assessed as crucial at the stage of discourse formation in the policy domain, but more limited at other stages of the policy process.

If at this stage we address the more general question of the overall impact of the environmental movement, we must necessarily consider issues of implementation, even if only briefly. While there is a substantial literature on environmental policy in different member states, brief discussion of the specific impact of Brussels movements will shed useful light on their relative importance.

Discussion

For all the actors involved, and particularly for business, environmental regulation is both an opportunity and a threat. Environmental regulation may provide industry with an opportunity to expand its market share through product standardisation, and with a competitive advantage over competitors unable to meet the time schedule, costs, or technology required for regulatory compliance, given that it may undermine profit margins by increasing production costs. It may provide bureaucrats and lobbyists with an opportunity for budget maximisation. For all these actors, environmental policy must be regulated by means of various information-gathering strategies and the deployment of influence. For these reasons they must produce a viable answer to the environmentalist challenge – for example by re-defining its nature and its priorities – and they must do so in a complex and fast-changing institutional framework.

Concentrating on environmental regulation, I considered the relation between the cultural frame of environmental sustainability in the policy discourse and EU institutional dynamics. Policy ideas – specifically a limited set of views on what constitutes environmentally 'sustainable development' – give cohesion and legitimacy to the environmental policy community, and they are used by different actors for organisational and institutional purposes. 'Sustainability' constitutes a symbolic space in which business can become a valued participant in a community that also includes such diverse actors as politicians, civil servants and social movement activists. Several factors should be considered when examining the relation between ideational factors and institutional dynamics. They are not in opposition but jointly give rise to outcomes in environmental policy.

At a global level, the field of environmental policy is characterised by a moralised idea, that of sustainability, which is supported by public opinion and proclaimed by advocacy groups. The intervention of these groups in deliberating public fora has a powerful impact, mainly at the agenda-setting stage. There is a donation of time and energy by a number of activists which modifies the policy process, and which shares some of the features of other policy areas where social movements have a marked presence (for instance those involving gender relations, poverty relief, asylum issues, etc.).

Because the impact of environmental movements is limited by their lack of resources, and because their ability to cause disruption is limited by their de-centralised decision-making structures, in several instances their inclusion in the policy process does not simply result from a concern with public legitimacy but is also due to an ideological similarity between advocacy groups and dominant actors in the policy process. Their inclusion is therefore guided by rules of collegiality which are in principle distinct from interest intermediation. However, as has been shown here, concern with the overall legitimacy of the 'European project' also plays an important role.

This chapter has also demonstrated how institutional factors have shaped the evolution of environmental policy in the EU. First, the institutional memory of the EU policy process has determined sequential aspects of policy-making which can be appreciated simply by looking at the gradual progression of EU environmental regulation. Originally absent from the Treaties, and then introduced as a health and safety issue, environmental regulation is now entrenched in the Union's architecture because of a succession of policy events. It is recognised as being of central importance by the Maastricht Treaty, and there are environmental units in all DGs. Environmental themes recur in all action programmes. A progressive shift of focus from restoration of environmental damage to the Precautionary Principle to the Polluter Pays Principle has resulted in a general emphasis on sustainable development. The nature of environmental regulation as a new field, its policy initiatives and ideas, are the outcome of a closely linked series of steps. Sequential mechanisms are crucial for explanation of what is presently prioritised and what is neglected. For instance, it is no coincidence that only minor progress has been achieved in the relationship between agriculture and the environment. As a historically powerful policy community, agriculture has successfully repelled environmental regulation (Ruzza and Adshead 1995). Indeed, one might argue that it is in fields such as agriculture that real environmental influence should be, but is not, exerted. At present in the policy process, the importance of sequential mechanisms emerges more clearly in the agenda-setting mechanisms that powerfully orient proceedings because they are largely controlled by a pro-environmental body in the Commission.

If the history of environmental regulation orients the range of regulatory practices and possibilities, it can be classified as organisational institutionalism. This offers a better analytical tool with which to explain dynamics in the environmental policy community. Institutional factors relating to the budget-maximising desires of environmental regulators illustrate rational choice institutional dynamics and help explain the expansion of the field, as the interviewee critical of the 'envirocrats' pointed out. But a resource-dependency interpretation of environmental activism in EU institutions is not sufficient if it neglects the importance of policy-makers' ideal interests. The profound impact of environmentalism on society has found echoes among civil servants, and to a certain extent business, and it resonates in the language that the policy community has adopted.

Neo-institutional theory provides an 'embedded' view of the organisation process in prevalent cultural codes. This chapter has concentrated on the cultural value of 'sustainable development', showing that the embedding process is of constructionist nature, and different actors formulate it on the basis of the global configuration of their interests, cognitive practices and cultural values. The various institutional environments – bureaucracies, business and social movements – are storehouses of cultural examples which define the scope of environmental sustainability.

Moreover, organisational dynamics have contributed to the spread of environmental ideas and their legitimation. The following hypothesis from organisational neo-institutional theory is central to the examination carried out in this chapter: the greater the extent to which the organisations in a field transact with agencies of the state, the greater the extent of isomorphism in the field as a whole (DiMaggio and Powell 1991). A concern with environmentalism is paramount for an EU bureaucracy that regulates environmentally sensitive areas, and which is in a position to dispense resources on the basis of alleged conformity to environmentalism. Actors whose resources are controlled by the EU bureaucracy will be motivated to express a similar concern and will in time increasingly resemble each another. Isomorphism results from normative, mimetic or coercive processes, and is facilitated by the search for common cognitive schemes encapsulated in the adoption of keywords with the symbolic status of markers indicating membership of the policy community.

The extent to which participants are instrumental in this adoption and aware of their search for legitimacy varies. Some actors take the legitimating character of organisational action for granted. In other words, things are customarily done in a certain way, and to the individual actor, who does not necessarily share any evaluative structure intended to legitimate specific organisational modes of operation, the situation appears unchangeable and unthematised. Organisational viability imposes mimetic practices that are institutionalised in the field. One such practice is the profession of allegiance to sustainability which eventually turns into an 'institutionalised myth' (Meyer and Rowan 1991: 55). As the institutionalists have pointed out, a gap tends to emerge between what is done for legitimacy purposes, which is more visible at the level of public pronouncements, and what is done at the level of actual organisational practices.

For many participants in this policy field, environmentalism has a normative status rooted in cultural values. This is particularly evident among pressure groups and many Commission officials. There is also a coercive element resulting from the dynamics that have placed environmentalist civil servants in powerful positions. However, the institutionalisation of cognitive schemes like sustainability carries unexpected consequences. While a new social conflict emerges between those who know how to reach the centre of the regulatory system and those who do not, a new discursive way of reaching the centre emerges, as actors with limited resources like NGOs find that they can appeal to public opinion to shape the policy process. In making this appeal, they are helped by the institutionalisation of sustainability and its acceptance by political institutions.

This chapter has suggested that resistance to the regulative impetus is curbed by conflict among the actors subject to environmental regulation. Internal tensions in business, movements, and regulators promote wide-ranging alliances, both within and across fields. Business may promote stringent regulation that requires a unique type of technological know-how. Regulators are split along political lines and may openly side with activists. The result is a general isomorphic process at the level of the inter-organisational field. All these factors together are shaping Brussels' EU institutions, moulding them in a unique fashion and creating something quite different from all the previous models of the Western nation-state.

The development of this macro-organisational field has crucial consequences. Particularly affected are the rules governing the participation of citizens in collective decisions. As several observers have pointed out, European unification is only the most visible development in a process which is draining the nation-state of much of its classical functions, notably the establishment of economic policies, in this case environmentally relevant ones. Traditional forms of interest representation are undermined if decision-making processes occur in a field so complex that the consequences cannot be fully comprehended, either by citizens or by the policy-makers who work on them. This is certainly the case of environmental policy, which is established by means of a complex multi-arena game.

Conclusions

The impact of movements on agenda-setting is of great importance because it trickles down to member states. In all EU countries a sizeable amount of legislation originates at the EU level. On the one hand, it is clear from the foregoing discussion that EU-level environmentalism would be impossible without the strong movements active in the Northern European countries. These movements provided the first cohort of institutional activists in Brussels, and they still channel public opinion support to the Brussels institutions, in many ways and notably through the EP. Thus, in a sense, the impact of EU environmentalism is predicated on its entrenchment elsewhere. However, full appreciation of the impact exerted by the European environmental movement requires us to ask what kind of environmental legislation would be in place without the EU institutions. Given the history of environmental regulation in some member states, we would have to conclude that the impact of EU movements is stronger precisely where environmental movements are weaker: namely Southern Europe (see Ruzza 2000b).

Southern member states which did not autonomously develop an environ-mental policy until EU institutions directly or indirectly coerced them to do so are a test case for the indirect impact of EU movements – even if they are also a test case for how exogenous environmental legislation can be distorted and neglected. Thus, reference to the European South reveals the long-term and long-range impact of environmental movements in Brussels.

There are two different ways in which this impact is exerted. One is through the relations among movement activists. Southern European environmentalists belong to the organisations represented in Brussels. They travel to Brussels, gen-erally for short periods, to express the voice of their national organisations in Brussels' umbrella groups, and they return with information and movement cultures. The second way is more important, and also more difficult to docu-ment. To the extent that institutional activists shape EU environmental policy, and to the extent that it trickles down to member states, Brussels' impact can be observed in the changes made to the environmental policies of member states. While in Northern countries the EU level has frequently been instrumental in conveying the views of movements, it is arguable whether the entrenchment of environmentalism would be any weaker in the absence of EU policies. A possi-bly more interesting issue is its impact in the relatively passive region of south-ern Europe. As several studies have shown (see Hanf and Jansen 1998, for a review), the South European region is fairly homogeneous in terms of relatively unconcerned attitudes to the environment and environmental policy. Yet, the environmental movement through its impact at EU level has had a profound influence even there.

Summary

European environmental policy-making emerges from competition in a cul-tural arena where business people, bureaucrats and environmental activists interact. Across different sectors, the concept of 'sustainable development' oper-ates as a catchphrase to guide regulatory discourse. It gives identity and profes-sionalism to the environmental regulation issue network. At the same time, the ambiguity of the concept allows for conflicting framings of the state of the envi-ronment, of regulatory priorities and of interpretations of scientific evidence, and creates the basis for a debate. It is argued in this chapter that EU environ-mental policy is influenced by (1) the EU bureaucracy's interest in expanding its influence and power *vis-à-vis* national bureaucracies and polities, and its acqui-sition of legitimacy by supporting pro-environmental action; (2) the EU's selec-tive recruitment of regulators with environmentally sympathetic ideologies; and (3) a pro-environmental attitude which contributes to the societal legitimation of business. A distinction was then drawn between interest group intermedia-tion and collegial policy-making. The latter is driven by a normative consensus on values of sustainability and a response to a generalised need for media and popular support. It favours the issues embraced by advocacy groups, particularly at the agenda-setting stage.

Notes

1 In addition to personal interviews, the methodology of this study involved analysis of archival materials and media sources in order to bring out the cultural and strategic factors operating in the decision-making processes. Interviews were conducted in Brussels between 1992 and 2000 in the context of three EU-funded environmental research projects. These were studies of (1) institutional decision-making in the environmental field with particular attention paid to the role of social movements, business and civil servants; this involved examination of e-packaging policy and trans-European networks, and the framing of environmental issues in EU documents; (2) Media framings of environmental issues in Europe and (3) tourism policy and environmental sustainability.

2 See Weale (1992).

3 See, for instance, Redclift (1992).

4 For the concept of institutions biased in favour of change, see Peter Hall in Steinmo, Thelen *et al.* (1992).

5 For instance, in 2000 Ben Plumley, international programs director at Glaxo Wellcome, joined UN Aids, the joint programme run by the United Nations, World Health Organisation (WHO) and World Bank. David Earnshaw, formerly a senior political lobbyist with SmithKline Beecham, joined Oxfam in 2001, to campaign on the price of Aids drugs.

6 Commission (1999).

7 See Héritier (1996).

8 See, for instance, the many works on this issue by Jurgen Habermas and Klaus Offe.

9 In 1995 Shell tried to dispose of an oil rig in the North Sea against the advice of environmentalists, but with the support of the British government. In response, Greenpeace occupied the platform. A spontaneous European-wide boycott followed that cost Shell dearly, was widely reported in negative terms, and as a consequence forced it to abandon its original disposal plans (Rootes 1997). A newspaper article noted 'Shell's about turn over Brent Spar shocked the business world . . . As a result they are trying to come to terms with demands for better corporate governance, improved environmental performance, and a recognition of other stakeholder groups besides shareholders' (Roger Cowe and Jon Entine 'Fair Enough?', *Guardian*, 14 December 1996: 30).

10 For an examination of the role of ideology within DGs see Michelmann (1978).

11 The larger ones are: EEB, Greenpeace, European Federation for Transport and the Environment, Friends of the Earth, Birds Life International, Climate Network Europe, WWF, Friends of Nature International.

12 Some long-term observers of environmental policy in Brussels argue that in the early years of environmental regulation business was inexperienced, and thanks to their knowledge NGOs had a more powerful role. One head of unit (DG Environment) maintains that much early regulation proposed by DG Environment was approved simply because business was not fully aware of its consequences. Whilst it is problematic to verify these statements, they are clearly no longer applicable.

13 These words and those of other activists are not those of native English speakers. Rather than risk misunderstanding, I have left their words essentially unchanged even if they are somewhat ungrammatical.

4

Anti-racism

Territorial belonging

In recent years, geopolitical factors such as increased immigration rates in several EU countries have given renewed importance to issues of 'territorial belonging'. Movements and parties have emerged which define belonging in essentialist terms, so that issues of 'race' have now acquired new salience. A right-wing populism rooted in perceptions and fantasies of the ethnic community has sparked a resurgence of the extreme right in several EU countries, resulting in attacks against immigrants and increased coverage of themes concerning racial identity by the media. The counter-movements – the anti-racist movements – that oppose these developments have also acquired prominence. They reject claims that ethnically non-West Europeans – and, more generally, ethnic minorities – constitute a threat. The cultural exchanges between the two types of movement reflect debates ongoing in public discourse and, in turn, influence them. As the expression of anti-immigrant sentiments and coded racist sentiments have grown more frequent, rejection of those sentiments has also become visible. A coalition of anti-racists has now developed in all EU countries and has put down strong roots at the EU level. This coalition originated with smaller immigrant associations and has turned into a counter-movement against racist attacks. This has combined with principled opposition to social exclusion within churches and the institutional left. It is a movement that, besides protesting against the mistreatment of racial minorities and immigrants, also promotes an ideal of tolerance and multiculturalism, raising an independent voice in public discussion on the nature of integrated Europe.

However, the wider population continues to conceive immigration as a threat, and 'Islamophobia' is also mounting, particularly after the revival of Islamic fundamentalism in recent years. In this context, education policy, welfare provisions and employment rights emerge as the key issues around which a struggle for resources takes place, and collective belonging is politicised. In the EU context, this debate takes on a novel articulation as it grows increasingly interwoven with the debate on the direction that European integration should take, an issue which has engendered some of the conditions for the renewed salience of territorial and ethnic identities. This chapter will examine the anti-racist movement's relations, influence on policy-making and prospects at EU level, taking account of the impact of the broader European political and cultural context.

It will concentrate in particular on the events leading up to approval of article 13, the first instance of European legislation which provides a legal basis for anti-racism, and the initiatives that appeared in its aftermath. Immediately before and after approval of article 13, the EU institutional apparatus proved extremely efficient in formulating and approving a range of institutional struc-tures, support measures and legislation to combat racism. This is intriguing, for it came about in a context where public opinion was rather hostile to immi-grants, and to issues associated with migration like racism (Commission 1998c). As public opinion data show, Europeans tend to be reluctant to accept people of other races even more than people of other religions and nationali-ties (Figure 4.1). In fact, since the events of 11 September a marked and wide-spread 'Islamophobia' has also appeared throughout Europe (Allen and Nielsen 2002). To account for these phenomena, one must consider the politi-cal opportunities, the framings of the battle against discrimination and the interests of EU actors.

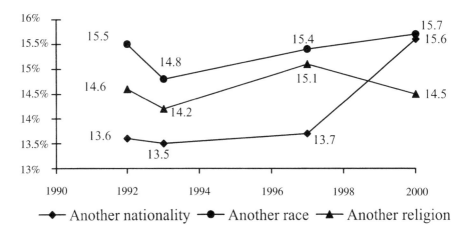

Figure 4.1 People disturbed by the presence of people of another nationality, race and religion in Europe, 1990–2000 (%)

Source: EB 37.0 (q.73), EB 39.0 (q.36), EB 48.0 (q.44), EB 53 (q.46–48)

Anti-racist movements in Europe

The anti-racist movements at EU level reflect, albeit in a modified form, the features, framings and internal divisions of European movements. The latter should therefore also be considered. Europe has a long history of anti-racist mobilisations which have taken action in a variety of ways, mounting protests or working within institutional domains. I shall broadly refer to them as 'anti-racist movements' – although I am aware that they apply very different forms of pressure, some disruptive, others not – with a view to stressing the empirical continuity of people and purposes in the two types of mobilisation. The nature of the anti-racist movement is difficult to define, because anti-racist protests have occurred in a variety of contexts, and in a time frame not marked out by large-scale geopolitical episodes like the Cruise missile crises or the Chernobyl accident in 1986. The UK is an exception in Europe, for it is the country that has had a robust and diversified anti-racist movement for the longest period of time. Typical of the mobilisations in the UK are those witnessed during the1970s and 1980s, when tensions in certain inner-city settings exploded into what at the time were called 'race riots'. Also typical of the UK are anti-racist movements lodged in public-sector institutions, particularly educational establishments (Bonnett 1993b, 2000). But anti-racist movements also emerged early on, although not as prominently, in France, where groups like SOS Racisme have for many years been supported by the Socialist Party.

One may therefore usefully take the British and French literature as a starting point for description of some features of a movement that, with the advent of large migratory influxes since the early 1990s, has come to characterise several European societies. As Bonnett (2000) and Ben-Tovim (1997) observe – and the point can be extended to other similar movements – the UK anti-racist movements have been in a state of crisis for years, a crisis due to multifarious causes connected to both internal and external factors. Examination of these factors is useful in that it sets the context of anti-racist action at the EU level.

Internally, there has been a lack of solidarity among its different components, which are too fragmented in terms of their occupational, religious and ethnic features to agree on a definition of objectives and methods. In fact, as Modood and Werbner (Modood 1997; Modood and Werbner 1997) argue, there has been a revival of ethnic assertiveness whose consequence is a rejection of the anti-racist's unifying category of 'black' as homogenising and insensitive to cultural and religious diversity. This has divided the movement, with some members advocating a curb on the narcissistic tendencies of a fragmented ethnic assertiveness (Gilroy 1990), and others arguing, for example, over whether separate schooling for Muslims would fragment the movement or whether on the contrary it would provide it with social sites of aggregation. Similarly, at the ideological level, some have argued that anti-racism should be a set of dimensions of the multifarious and changing identity of various ethnic groups connected to their religious and cultural identities. Others have given priority to a cohesive political identity whereby the anti-racist struggle takes place in association with, or is even superordinate to, class and gender conflict. A further division has often emerged between minorities and 'white' anti-racist activists, with some arguing that anti-racists should let minorities speak for themselves while others advocate a broader and more inclusive movement: that is, a movement of people from different backgrounds who deal with racism in their everyday professional and social lives, such as educationalists and other professionals. There are also those who see education of the public at large as the main goal of anti-racism, although they are criticised for concerning themselves only with the white majority (Gilroy 1987). This split is connected with controversy over the origin of racism, with some focusing on individual dispositions and others on institutional procedures (Ben-Tovim 1997: 219). In institutional settings, particularly in UK schools and local authorities, but also among social workers, probation officers and social security officials, disputes have arisen over what should be the focus of attention: racism or multiculturalism (Ben-Tovim 1997).

Externally, the popular press has attacked the ideology of anti-racism, which it associates with the traditional left and with what it regards as a culture of intolerance within the movement. These issues have also been addressed by movement analysts and advocates (Gilroy 1990).

However, in the UK as well as other European countries, anti-racist movements to some extent set aside their internal divisions and interpretative self-doubts in the early 1990s, when their response to racial attacks re-united them, strengthening their counter-movement character and re-invigorating older counter-movement organisations like the Anti-Nazi League in the UK (originally formed in 1977). This counter-movement character has been conducive to the formation of broad alliances but, as we shall see, not of cohesive framings. Anti-Nazi anti-racism has also emerged in limited contexts, a case in point being football, where coordinated national campaigns like the 'Show Racism The Red Card' initiative have been successful (Merkel and Tokarski 1996). There are, moreover, broad-ranging anti-racist groups like 'SOS Racisme' in France. All mobilisation episodes have attracted support from a variety of groups not directly involved in their organisation, and of which many are committed to other causes. As a consequence, the identity of the anti-racist movement is somewhat difficult to define. Yet there are a large number of anti-racist organisations in Europe, some national, many local, which constitute the background for the anti-racist movement active in EU institutions.

As a whole, it is a movement that varies significantly in terms of tactics, scale of operations, and areas of specific concern. It ranges from the militant British Anti-Nazi League to specific-issue groups like the Austrian ones opposed to discrimination against Roma and Travellers, to more institutional groups like the European Council of Refugees and Exiles (ECRE). What unifies this broad movement is a principled aversion to social exclusion.

This has, however, attracted limited scholarly attention. Although racial intolerance has been broadly covered by the European media, the specific academic literature is rather small, and it has dealt more frequently with racist movements than with anti-racist ones. While there is an abundance of early work on race and immigration issues in the UK – which also includes studies on anti-racism (see, for instance, Gilroy 1990; Bonnett 1993) – the work done in other EU countries is limited (see for instance Massinger 1955; Silverman 1991; Wrench and Solomos 1993). The area of anti-racism is especially bereft of comparative studies and EU-level studies. Lloyd (in Wrench and Solomos 1993) analyses the reasons for these gaps, and points to the vastly different ways in which race relations are regulated in different countries, to academic traditions that frame race and migration issues very differently and to linguistic and cultural difficulties which obstruct comparative work.

These differences include the difficulty of locating racism socially: that is, of identifying the institutions in which racism must be tackled, its causes and the appropriate methods to combat it. As Wrench (in Wrench and Solomos 1993: 12–13) points out, it is often denied that racial and ethnic inequality is pervasive in European society, and there is confusion about the link between EU and national policy-making in combating racism, as well as about the role of anti-discrimination legislation. This, however, does not imply that anti-racism is not generally accepted as a worthwhile endeavour. In fact, as activists report, anti-racism is more highly valued in societies that have been only marginally affected by racial conflict. For these societies, both racism and anti-racism are relatively new phenomena, and social reflection on the nature and implications of racism is still in its infancy. By contrast, in countries where there is a tradition of anti-racist mobilisation, it has become clear that, apart from its reactive character, the movement is fundamentally divided on ideological grounds between assimilative and multiculturalist strategies – between an emphasis on cultural differences and a demand for recognition by society and its institutions, on the one hand, and an emphasis on fundamental human similarity and a demand that differential treatment should stop, on the other (Modood 1997; Modood and Werbner 1997). Despite this profound division, however, anti-racism as a general political value is now beyond dispute.

Like other social movement frames, such as 'environmental sustainability', 'anti-racism' is now an approved societal concern that stimulates discursive institutional compliance. Combating racism has traditionally been a defining characteristic of the left and has in recent years attracted the attention of the media and mainstream politics as a reaction to the substantial advances achieved by the extreme right in several EU countries.

Movement and political party activists engaged in the fight against racism are aware of this broad anti-racist ethos, and they attempt to turn what they perceive as a universally approved declaration of principles into specific cultural and policy initiatives. Their efforts, however, may merely result in limited and controversial institutional initiatives because their work is resisted, re-defined and ignored by a substantial right-wing political coalition.

The framings and politics of anti-racism in member states

Two framings of anti-racism are dominant within European movements: assimilationist and multiculturalist. As Lloyd (1994) points out, the former views anti-racism as a civil-rights issue bound up with the French revolutionary and republican tradition that stresses the equality of citizens before the state, and tackles it with the French model of integration based on unrestricted access to nationality and citizenship. This tradition encourages the overcoming of differences under a common conception of citizenry. Conversely, in the UK, the affirmation of a politics of identity has resulted in an emphasis on minority cultures. The drawback of the former tradition is that it may erase all differences by focusing on the lowest common denominator of the dominant culture, while the drawback of the latter is that it may produce a proliferation of particularist identities which hinders unified mobilisation. Lloyd (1994: 237) argues that anti-racist organisations have been unable to overcome this contradiction between universalism and particularism.

Unlike other movement concerns – 'environmental sustainability', for instance – 'anti-racism' is a less cohesive cluster of ideas and organisations, because it does not possess an all-encompassing and widely recognised discursive frame. Although it is backed by a very broad family of movements advocating the social inclusion of discriminated-against minorities, it has only limited internal ideological cohesion and is generally recognised as a set of individual components rather than an overarching movement. Each branch of the family may incorporate anti-racism among their main grievances and re-interpret it as one of their competencies, but it is often not the grievance that they most forcefully assert. Gender and class issues, poverty, migration, human rights, labour disputes and so on, are all seen as affected by racism, and all the sectors of the movements concerned devote time and energy to it. While this is an advantage for the anti-racist movement because it makes it globally important, it is also a disadvantage because the specific constituency of victims of racism is often too weak to claim its own discursive space. The issue is tagged on to the other movements, which makes it more difficult for anti-racists to retain their own relevance. This polarisation of views is however decreasing as advantages and disadvantages of the two approaches are being identified and more mixed models are emerging.

Public opinion

The impact of the dilution of this movement in a set of connected causes is accentuated by its relative low salience in the general public. A large proportion of EU respondents admit to being quite or very racist – 33 per cent in 1997 with much higher proportions in countries such as Belgium (55 per cent) and France (48 per cent).[1] In a survey conducted in 2001, one in five EU respondents supported the view that all legal and illegal immigrants and their children should be sent back to their country of origin, even if the children were born in Europe.[2] This clearly negative view of the relevance of anti-racism in a situation of declining fertility and widespread need of labour has been connected to an attempt by EU decision-makers to Europeanise this area of policy, in order to remove the possibility of political blackmail ensuing from its prominence in the domestic electoral arena, even if it concerns one of the areas most important for states' sovereignty: control of their territory.

These results need to be qualified in terms of the meaning and placement of racism in the views of respondents. To the extent that racism is connected to issues such as violations of human rights it touches upon a fundamental area of concern of Europeans. For instance, in a 1999 survey 'Non-respect of human rights' concerned 39.5 per cent of Europeans.[3]

The politics of anti-racism

Anti-racism is an example of policy made in response to crises. Before approval of article 13 of the Amsterdam Treaty, most observers would have identified it as an area in which there was an obvious reluctance of member states to engage in anything more than ritualistic efforts to halt racism through EU-level action. There had been an abundance of statements in support of anti-racism, many of them issued by a group of highly committed anti-racist activists in the EP. But there was a fundamental reluctance to develop a policy area with significant implications for the status of third-country residents within the EU framework, given that it touched directly on one of the most closely protected areas of state policy – immigration, with its direct implications for territorial sovereignty.

However, approval of article 13 and the subsequent spate of activity surprised many analysts. Approval of the article has been explained with reference to a shift of position by the Council, which has been traditionally reluctant to accept integrationist approaches in social policy, and particularly so in this area, with its close relation to migration and the mobility of workers, these being two issues with a close bearing on a fundamental prerogative of states, namely control over their territory. The Council's change of position was due to events such as the increasing prominence of extremist parties, which worried the mainstream electorate of several member states, and the exploitation by racist groups of the absence of uniform legislation (Bell 2002: 64). The institutionalisation of anti-racism as a concept was closely connected with the internationally sanctioned concept of human rights and the need for states to appear able to coordinate efforts. As immigration increased during the 1990s, realisation of the burgeoning threat of racism began to permeate the Council and was no longer restricted to a minority of activists, along with growing awareness that attacks on immigrants were growing increasingly common. Racism was discussed at the 1990 Dublin Council, the 1991

Maastricht Council, the 1992 Edinburgh Council, the 1993 Copenhagen Council, the 1994 Corfu and Essen Council and the 2002 Seville Council. A decisive factor in approval of article 13 was also the contingent prominence in Europe of centre-left governments, and the absence of committed anti-integrationist governments following the British switch to a Labour government in 1997. In any event, after 1997 and the European Year Against Racism, activism in the field of anti-discrimination became more broadly legitimate and inspired institution-building activities ranging from increased support for anti-racist NGOs to the creation in 1997 of the European Monitoring Centre against Racism and Xenophobia (EUMC) as an independent body to combat racism, xenophobia and anti-semitism.

Anti-racist activism developed apace after approval of article 13. The Commission had debated and prepared a set of measures even before approval of the Amsterdam Treaty, so that it was ready to produce concrete proposals well before it was even possible to do so (Ruzza 2000a). At the end of 1999, a racial equality directive was presented which outlawed racial and other types of discrimination in specific sectors – employment, education, social protection, social advantages and access to goods and services – and formulated an Action Programme against discrimination.

The progress of this package of measures was accelerated when a new political opportunity arose for the anti-racist MAC: in February 2000, Jorg Haider, the representative of a right-wing party (the Freedom Party) was invited to join the Austrian government. This invitation provoked public protests from other EU leaders and prompted the Portuguese presidency to accelerate anti-racist legislative proposals, with the result that the directive was approved in June of the same year. The publicly announced priority of combating racism and the need for rapid action committed the Council to action and empowered anti-racist activists within and without the EU institutions, allowing a strengthening of the proposal at the hand of the EP (Bell 2002: 74).

It is clear, then, that these considerations are crucial for understanding the expanding political opportunities for the anti-racist MAC. However, they should be supplemented with considerations concerning the legitimacy of the European project. These issues came to the fore as popular support for European integration declined after the Maastricht approval debates of the early 1990s. These concerned not only the strategies of the EU elites but also, and increasingly, the realisation by heads of states that their reliance on a benevolent if distracted attitude towards European integration could no longer be taken for granted, and that attempts to utilise symbols to ensure support for European integration were failing (Shore 1993). Finally, as will be discussed in more detail below, the impact of a committed EU-level advocacy coalition including activists from several institutions as well as representatives of NGOs must be stressed (Ruzza 2000a).

Anti-racism as a policy principle

In EU institutions, anti-racism is an institutionally approved social value which has left little space for any major inroads by the right-wing coalitions distinguishing the politics of some member states.[4] The question as posited by some institutional elites is whether present institutional efforts to combat racism can be considered substantial, adequate or grossly insufficient. Some MEPs viewed the issue as somewhat marginal until the escalation of attacks against immigrants attracted widespread media attention in the mid-1990s. A period of heightened interest, but also of what might be described as ritual declarations of concern, ensued. This attitude is noted by anti-racist activists who are generally supportive of the efforts made by EU bodies, although their attitudes vary from scepticism to belief in the personal commitment of specific institutional actors. When noting the reiteration in EU bodies of anti-racist concerns, one activist said:

> Regulation of racism is a matter of fashion. Everybody says they are concerned about racism. You had the Council of Europe's campaign, 'All different all equal', then the following year there was the 'European Year Against Racism'. Now you hear much more about it on TV and the radio. In the newspapers it has become a fashion. You have to be anti-racist. It is something in the wind.

EU institutions have performed a generalised facilitating role in the establishment of anti-racist movements in Brussels. However, despite widespread awareness of, and a frequently stated concern for, the evils of racism, legislative change has been slow in coming.

The issue of anti-racism made its formal substantial appearance on the agenda with the EP-produced Evrigenis Report of 1986. Nonetheless, writing in 1991, Glyn Ford (1992: 87), the former leader of the European Parliamentary Labour Party, noted:

> Of the 40 recommendations of the Evrigenis report only a few have been fully implemented so far and none has led to significant changes in anti-racism legislation, nor to action at the Community level to confront and tackle the root causes of racism and xenophobia.

The situation began to improve when a commission of independent experts headed by Jean Kahn was set up on a Franco-German initiative and produced a report in 1996 which *inter alia* recommended the creation of a European monitoring centre.

In recent years racism has been an increasing focus of concern. As Chopin and Niessen (1998: 18) pointed out in 1998:

> There is evidence of willingness among the Union's institutions to proceed towards effective action. The EP produced the Evrigenis report in 1986 and the Ford report in 1991, and has continued to press for measures, including a directive. The Commission has done everything possible within the constraints of the old treaties: giving some financial support to anti-racist projects, co-operating with the social

partners in producing a code of good employment practice against discrimination, sponsoring studies of anti-discrimination laws in member states, and most recently working successfully for the establishment of a Monitoring Centre on Racism, Xenophobia, and to make 1997 the European Year Against Racism, Xenophobia and Anti-Semitism. The Economic and Social Committee has long urged legislative and other measures. The Committee of the Regions has also called for action.

However, despite the variety of initiatives (in addition to Ford 1992, for a more recent summary of initiatives and selected texts see Commission 1997b), progress has been slow, hindered by both institutional dynamics and the fragmented organisational structure of this policy area among several DGs. Although connections are generally good at a personal level, institutional fragmentation is a source of inefficiency that has prompted some Commission officers to advocate closer inter-DG cooperation.[5]

Politically, it is a weak policy area. As Ford points out (1992: 88), it is not sufficient for the Commission to submit documents or initiatives to the Council of Ministers, because the qualified majority rule in this policy area means that initiatives are easily blocked, or the Commission is forced to dilute them substantially until it becomes questionable whether they can any longer be considered a step forward. Thus institutional actors committed to anti-racism within EU bodies are faced with the difficult task of deciding where they can most effectively direct their action. Nevertheless, as mentioned, the task has become much easier in recent years since the approval of article 13.

As previously noted, social movements are important for the Commission and the EP because of the perceived need to establish the democratic legitimacy of the 'European Project'. This point emerges clearly from interviews with Commission officials, who often refer to 'the European value added of their operations'[6] in tackling racism, and also from interviews with Commission institutional activists, who feel themselves valued as a means for an otherwise isolated bureaucracy to reach out to citizens. In the words of a European Youth Forum (EYF) activist, 'The main idea is that as many young people as possible should know that Europe is good for you'. A Communication from the Commission (by DG XXIII) emphasises the importance of voluntary organisations, and the sector is extensively reviewed with a view to increasing its resources and influence.[7] Awareness of its significance has permeated all sectors of the bureaucracy and has impacted on the politicians in the Commission, which as the frame analysis documents, readily acknowledge the importance of civil society. This is an emphasis that finds frequent expressions of support from OCS organisations.

As the field of anti-discrimination policy is still relatively new and several policy approaches are actively debated without a stable consensus, policy documents of both the EU and OCS sectors emphasise the importance of *implementation*. This term refers to the application of EU-level decisions to the public policy of member states. Also stressed are *improving knowledge* and the *exchange of information* aimed at reaching accepted criteria of good practice and including civil society in broad networks. There is, however, a fundamental difference between EU institutions and OCS. Institutions focus on combating discrimination and do so with particular attention to the economic dimension, which includes combating the markers of discrimination in the labour market, such as unemployment. Conversely, OCS pays markedly less attention to economic issues whilst sharing the rest of the policy agenda. Thus, the negative impact of racism on the job market and its connection to unemployment is particularly underlined in EU documents. However, differences of emphasis in documents does not imply difficulties in personal relations between EU actors, many of whom are institutional activists and members of anti-racist organisations. As a policy community all actors agree on the importance of forming networks. This call for cohesion may in part reflect the awareness that anti-racism is a diffused concern that needs to be organised in a set of more stable and interconnected actors to become effective. In part it also reflects the awareness that new collaboration is needed to take full advantage of the opportunities opened by the approval of article 13. There is therefore some ground for optimism but also a realisation of the difficulties in achieving unity.

A different movement family in Brussels

Although in Europe concerns with social exclusion and the environment may both be promoted by left-libertarian movements, in Brussels they belong to two distinct families of movements, with scant contact between them. However, the anti-racist movement has close personal and institutional contacts with a variety of other movements concerned with social exclusion. Diverse organisations with different tasks and philosophies lobby EU institutions for legislation and funds. And then there are the few large and loosely organised networks that encompass a variety of social exclusion causes: the Social Platform, Solidar, the Youth Forum, the European Federation for Intercultural Learning, the European Human Rights Foundation (EHRF), and religious organisations. Solidar, for instance, coordinates activities at EU level on social welfare and aid, and last year waged a campaign against racism. The Social Platform coordinates around twenty-five umbrella organisations, each of which in its turn coordinates organisations numbering from a few to several hundreds and whose focus ranges across disability rights, ageing and racism. All these organisations have good contacts with EU institutions, and at the same time support the protest activities of some of their activist member organisations and the service and welfare activities of others.

Although anti-racism is embedded in other movements, it is a distinct social movement with its own identity and a variety of *loosely collaborating organisations* directly connected, even if based in other networks. Some organisations have stressed their anti-racist concerns only in recent years (particularly in 1997, the European Year Against Racism), while there are others for which anti-racism has always been the main or pre-eminent concern. The most prominent of the latter are the European Migrant Forum (EMF), the Anti-Poverty Lobby, and to a lesser extent the EYF and the EWL. Together they give voice in the EU institutions to the concerns of a broad European movement comprising several hundred organisations and unaffiliated individuals. This MAC Brussels representation, as in the case of the environmental MAC, excludes the more radical, small and institutionally peripheral groups but includes a wide variety of concerns, philosophical positions, and strategic orientations.

Given so many connections and potential synergies one would expect these movements to be influential and successful. But this has not generally been the case. Success has come belatedly, and to understand why one must consider a variety of issues which I will discuss after reviewing the role of bureaucratic and political environments, and the social movement organisations. Unlike in other movements, such as environmentalism, in this case the business sector plays only a marginal role and does not warrant separate consideration.

Political and administrative environments

This institutional commitment to anti-racism exhibits features similar to those of environmentalism. There are intensive institutional and personal contacts among the actors engaged in anti-racism, who all together constitute what was earlier described as a 'macro-organisational field' where, as noted, normative, mimetic and coercive behaviours take place. As an activist pointed out:

> The institutions with a mandate on racism collaborate closely. In particular, the relevant sections of the Commission, particularly DGV, and the EP, particularly the Committee on civil liberties, collaborate closely. The head of the relevant unit and some staff go to most of the meetings of this committee, and there are frequent personal contacts.[8] Relations with movement representatives and NGOs are also frequent, and were so particularly during the 'Year Against Racism'.

There are broader generational and ideological factors at work behind the close connection between EU institutions and NGOs. One activist said:

Activists very often have links that go back to the 1960s and the 1970s with the people in government. I was able to tell a Commissioner that he was a founder member of one of our organisations. Especially now that there is a social democratic majority in the EU, many ministers were supporters of NGOs.

The Commission

The Commission has long been concerned with racism, but the bureaucratic strength of the field of anti-racism is limited when compared to the environmental movement. The main bureaucratic referent for anti-racism is a unit of DGV which concerns itself with the free movement of workers in the EC – and thus engages essentially in legal work (revision of free movement legislation, action on complaints of infringement against member states, etc.). The unit also deals with the social integration of immigrants, employment programmes for recognised refugees and action against racism. The latter, therefore, is only one of its areas of concern. Activists describe the former head of unit, who retired in 2000, as very committed – a 'super-convert' – and they value her political good sense, her ability to be realistic and effective in her demands, and to achieve results.

The unit was created in 1958 and deals with matters such as the free movement of labour already covered by the Treaty of Rome. The integration of immigrants and refugees came later, and anti-racist policy was added in 1986. There are twenty people employed in the unit. The number of personnel working on racism varies: in late 1999 only one person was working full-time on racism and three people on a half-time basis. The previous year, however, some extra staff had been taken on to cope with the extra work created by the establishment and administration of the European Year Against Racism. The work on the integration of immigrants involved contacting and subsidising NGOs working with migrants or NGOs drawn from migrants, and promoting social integration.

The main policy initiative of recent years has been the decision to organise the European Year Against Racism. Given that hitherto the Council had argued that there was no legal basis in the Treaties for action against racism, the establishment of the 'Year' must be considered a breakthrough. Building on the success of the initiative, in 1998 the Commission adopted an action plan on racism (Commission 1998a); and the establishment of the Agency in Vienna has been a policy success as well. Article 13 against discrimination in the Treaty of Amsterdam was drawn up by the unit and was considered to be a significant achievement. Similarly, the initiatives launched after approval of article 13 testify to the unit's proactive role.

This is not to imply, however, that all its efforts have been successful. The former head of unit said that she had hoped for more money for the European Year Against Racism, arguing that 4.8 million ECU was a trifling sum for the EU. She would have liked article 13 to allow for majority voting (at present, the Council must be unanimous, and this is a handicap), and she would also have liked it to have direct effect (at present, the Commission must make proposals and Council is also involved). Moreover, the article falls within the Free Movement normative and does not define a specific political right. Expressing some disappointment, she reiterated opinions voiced by other institutional activists not only within the Commission but in the EP as well, where an MEP said of the measure: 'Many of us hoped it would go a great deal further than that.' The former head of unit, however, pointed out that the entire issue is to a significant extent out of the Commission's control. She noted that Chancellor Kohl himself had removed some words at the last minute, and that when issues are debated between heads of states, issues go well beyond the sphere of influence of a head of unit.

Unfortunately, as the former head of unit further noted, there is a high level of mobility in DGV and it is encouraged by the hierarchy. Racism is a very special field; if a position is posted, only personally committed people tend to apply. They are generally not directly activist, although they might – like the head of unit – be members of Amnesty International or similar organisations. She argued that hiring like-minded experts and consultants in DGV is no longer possible in the present money-conscious climate. She had a couple of '*auxiliares*' from the NGOs but they could be employed only for the European Year Against Racism. Over the years, this head of unit had seen her job and her unit change. It had started as a unit which occupied itself with a purely legal set of concerns and then progressively turned itself into a unit that maintained a legal concern. But it also concerned itself with 'societal aspects of policy', and its budget had gradually increased over the years – a development encouraged at all levels of the hierarchy. At present, the unit's activist climate continues to support a steady flow of proposals connected with the Action Plan Against Racism of 1998 and, more generally, with the mainstreaming strategy which, since the Action Plan has sought to integrate anti-racism into all Community actions and policies, and at all levels when general actions and policies are drawn up (Commission 1998a). It is interesting to note that in the documentary analysis the emphasis on mainstreaming which appears strongly in other movements, notably the women's movement, occurs principally in the documents of EU institutions, rather than in those of civil society. This may suggest a process of spillover from the concepts and institutional activists of a movement to another movement.

The anti-racist work undertaken by units other than DGV is similar in its fairly activist orientation – particularly the work of DGXXII, but also that of DGXVI and DGVIII. As with DGV, the ideological orientation is sustained by an endeavour to promote Europe, not only to provide legitimacy for EU bodies but for broader reasons as well. Some activists reported that there is an entrenched belief in the Commission that the European model has been an effective social model for many years. It has provided security against wars and promoted affluence, and there is a desire to promote it as a philosophy not just within the EU but outside as well. Hence, voluntary organisations such as youth organisations and their activists' concerns are funded in places as far afield as Georgia or the Maghreb. Since the Commission requires input on societal trends, voluntary organisations can provide spaces for reciprocal knowledge ranging from activists and volunteers brought to Brussels for consultations and represented in Brussels to EYF-staged 'Youth in Parliament' events (where 500 young people are brought to Brussels for a two-to-three day debate on their living conditions, with the participation of representatives from EU bodies).

The division between an assimilationist and a multiculturalist approach characteristic of European anti-racism is replicated in Brussels. There is uncertainty over whether to address racism with the assimilative Jacobin French tradition or to adopt the more multicultural Dutch approach.[9] In Brussels, this contradiction hinders the anti-racist community's progress towards identifying shared goals – for instance, agreement on how best to spend money, where to concentrate efforts, which groups to support. However, some activists maintain that the dominant institutional ethos is an assimilationist one, and indeed an assimilationist ethos seemingly emerged from interviews with civil servants. For instance, one of them stressed that all steps should be taken actively to encourage the access of immigrants to 'majority' culture, but awareness of immigrants' cultural diversity was never expressly mentioned. Much emphasis is placed on, and funds are spent on, promoting the integration of minorities, but policy provisions to promote minority cultures and to safeguard religious rights are more limited.[10]

The two approaches are not easily combined, but conflict between them is more of a problem for the unity of the movement as a whole than it is for institutional activists. From their small units in Brussels, the latter can simply espouse a policy of channelling as much in the way of resources as they can to a wide variety of organisations, which may have contrasted aims.

Institutional activists in the Commission

As in other units, the purpose of those concerned with anti-racism also shapes their ideological alignment (Michelmann 1978). However, it is difficult to determine the extent of institutional activism because Commission officials are torn between conflicting demands in their self-presentation. On the one hand, institutional activists need to safeguard their legitimacy as professional impartial bureaucrats. On the other hand, they have to show commitment to the ideology of their unit, the taken-for-granted rules operating in that particular environment. Consequently, stressing that racial discrimination is intolerable and must be combated is part of the job. Personal participation in extra-institutional activities is revealed with more caution, however. Yet, in general, the EU civil service in movement-related areas is in principle open to sympathetic observers, even if it is cautious about subjecting itself to external scrutiny.

Institutional activism is somewhat less clear than it is in institutionally strong movements, such as environmentalism. The head of the relevant DGV unit declared that she did not think there were any activists or ex-activists in the unit, only a group of highly committed people. But another civil servant noted that to work well in such a demanding and politicised DG, it was necessary to have a personal commitment beyond the call of a civil servant's duties. Institutional activism in the Commission merges the overarching value of European construction with commitment to the specific ideology of the unit. Thus the same civil servant continued:

> And if you want to do something which is creative thinking, something that has been done all those years by the NGOs, what can we at the European level add to that which is appealing to the NGOs but which is also appealing to the general public? Because if you think about it, our biggest challenge is to reach the general public. Because we reach the converted, people who are even more convinced than we are, but we have to reach your neighbour.

In its strategy of addressing the concerns of the 'average European public' – which has required an endeavour to appear reasonable, to choose credible interlocutors and even to accommodate the preferences of specific governments – the Commission has not infrequently been seen as erring on the side of caution.

Relations with movements

On conclusion of the European Year Against Racism, DGV and the relevant NGOs decided to continue with their close collaboration, and the Commission encouraged them to coordinate their efforts at EU level and to be represented by a coordinating structure – the MPG – given that it would otherwise not be feasible to consult the some thousands of EU NGOs in the sector directly. A successful conference jointly organised by the Commission and the NGOs ensued in 1997 and other similar initiatives took place in the following years in conjunction with, and after, the First Action Plan Against Racism of 1998. This included, for instance, the conference held in Strasbourg in October 2000 entitled 'All different – all equal: from theory to practice'.

Speeches by an ex-incumbent of the most important post for setting the Commission's social policy agenda – Commissioner Flynn – testify to a personal and institutional commitment to anti-racism; a commitment that an MEP reports to be generally appreciated in Parliament. The attention to OCS typical of the EU policy-making style has been clearly enunciated by Commissioner Flynn, and is seen as encompassing the field of anti-racism:

> I see a role for a strong representation of European level. A representation that will complement those which exist for other major social issues such as equal opportunities, poverty and disability . . . A representation that will enable you to participate in the development of European policy against racism.

The main problem for the Commission is that, as in other movements, organisations speak with too many voices. A head of unit recommended as follows:

> There should be a secretariat or a small platform, whatever they want to do, with an agenda. The purpose of having a platform is that they should have *one* programme, decide what they want to accomplish. So that will be our partner for all the activities in the area of racism . . . There are thousands of these groups and they should really come together . . . So this is one reason why the Migrants' Forum was set up.

NGOs are consulted for a variety of reasons: to gather information, to co-organise events, and occasionally to discuss their financial needs and project proposals (there are over 600 of these for each call for proposals, so that an initial selection is made without consultation).[11] Trust in movement organisations varies significantly. Those with better accounting procedures, punctual delivery of reports and a record of accurate research are clearly favoured. On the other hand, the 'well-meaning amateurs' are seen as an all-too-frequent source of problems.

The Commission is also trying to involve trade unions and employers, given that the workplace is considered a locus of much racial discrimination. The

Unions adopted a joint declaration signed by trade unions and employers in 1995, and there is optimism that their role is significant and will grow in the future at EU level.

The European Parliament

The EP has also been very active in anti-racism. Its nature is such that MEPs are free to involve themselves in anti-racist work, or otherwise, according to their personal interests and party affiliation. The EP is traditionally high-minded in terms of principles, possibly because it has little power to implement resolutions, but it also has a high absenteeism rate and not infrequently a back-log of tasks at national and EU levels that imposes a strict selection of interests. Consequently, there has emerged over the years a core of institutional activist MEPs with a specific interest in anti-racism; an interest which, for some, is long-standing and has involved participation in the committee that reported on racism in 1986 and in 1991, as well as a continuing commitment. These MEPs often work on anti-racist issues, at both the national and the EU level, where much anti-racist policy work is concentrated in the Civil Liberties Committee (LIBE)[12] and the anti-racist working group.

They also have excellent and close relations with the anti-racist organisa-tions in Brussels, although there are more specific ideological affinities as well. Thus EYF tends to work mainly with the Socialist group, and particularly with the same few members. And in general all groups have worked more closely with the left because, as an activist pointed out, welfare and the inter-ventionist role of the state in society are leftist concepts. MEPs often take the initiative in contacting the representatives of movements when they have to be *Rapporteurs* on issues for which they need information. They establish contacts directly, or through their assistants or, often, through the Commis-sion list of contacts.

The anti-racist MAC

The same ambiguity on the scope and focus of the battle against racial discrim-ination that emerges within EU institutions also emerges within activist net-works. Some activists with a belief in 'mainstreaming' do not see the need for a unifying key concept; others believe that anti-racism has not been correctly framed at EU level. The secretary general of a medium-sized group argued that many of the early problems encountered by anti-racist work in Brussels stemmed from the fact that the issue was incorrectly framed, in that it was seen as connected to migration instead of being resourced by EU institutions and independently conceptualised by activists. However, following the Commis-sion's efforts in conjunction with the European Year Against Racism, a specific anti-racist network emerged. A constitutive conference of a 'European Network Against Racism' (ENAR) was held in October 1998, and the first board meeting took place in December. This network was substantially financed by the Commission, which saw it as an independent counterpart to the more institutional EMC (Bell 2002: 86). This network is widely seen as still in its infancy.

In addition to institutions and networks specifically committed to anti-racism, the issue is often on the agendas of other networks and federations of NGOs, which subordinate it to their major institutional aims. As one activist noted:

> Many organisations approach racism as one concern among a set of related concerns and might focus on it for a campaign, but then move on to other topics keeping a more limited reference to it. For instance, the Youth Forum's main campaign against racism was called 'All different all equal', but when it came to an end other themes emerged.

This contextualisation of anti-racism, which emerges in the programmes of women's groups, trade unions, socialist parties and churches, embeds anti-racism in the left-liberal family of movements, and in the mainstream of the European institutional left, through its generalised concern with social exclusion. In this sense, anti-racism is a universal concern for a variety of MACs in Brussels, and not just for social movements.

The social movements

Movement activists are frequently personally and officially engaged, supporting protest activities in their own countries, as well as pursuing initiatives in Brussels. In performing the latter role, their function varies from the purely legislative lobbying typical of Starting Line (SL) before it was dissolved, having achieved its main goal of providing a legal basis for anti-racism, to the mainly consultative function of EU institutions characteristic of the EMF, which is entitled to lodge collective complaints, to a combination of the two roles for particular constituencies like women and youth (the women's lobby EWL and youth forum EYF). Members of these networks state that protest and lobbying are complementary activities.

Although activists with a general interest in racism outnumber those concerned with environmental issues, the number of people with a specific interest in race issues is probably similar – about fifteen to twenty-five permanently in Brussels and a larger group working occasionally on anti-racism. The precise figure is difficult to estimate, not only because some organisations may focus entirely on racism for several months and then move on to other connected issues, but also because concern with racism is frequently expressed under other headings. For instance, the majority of recent immigrants into Europe are non-white. Work on immigrants is closely linked to work on issues of racial discrimination, even when it is not expressly stated.

Several organisations, for instance the EMF and SL, started to be active in the late 1980s and early 1990s, and have been substantially helped by the Commission and EP in establishing roots in the EU. Their budgets vary greatly because their funds, or a large proportion of them, derive from one-year projects.[13] They are sufficient, however, for these organisations to maintain some permanently employed staff and to refund the expenses of national activists travelling to Brussels for short periods. The EMF has about six staff members and three elected members permanently in Brussels, and an executive committee of seven which is convened several times a year. The SL and the other groups before dissolving had fewer full-time personnel – often just one or two full-time workers and several frequently changing volunteers. There are, moreover, a number of general-purpose organisations that may have one full-time anti-racist activist in Brussels. For instance, the EWL has one; the EYF, which has seventeen full time workers (seven campaigners and ten staff), does not have a specific person but several activists who have worked on anti-racist issues. Solidar has one person working on anti-racist issues in 1998, and a few working on other projects.

The strategies and cultures of anti-racism

The anti-racist sector displays a division of labour and affinities for different activism styles. The EMF sees itself as performing a coordination function for anti-racist European social movements, and views protest and lobbying as complementary. One activist noted:

> Protest is the job of our base organisations. The Migrant forum is an institution established by other institutions, but it is made up of local groups. This means that if I act within the EMF or the supporting groups, it is the same thing. So if any organisations need demonstrations or protests they can ask here to the EMF. For instance, last year [1997] the EMF organised a big conference in the Netherlands with the participation of EU institutions and the Dutch support group. Outside the conference the supporting group engaged in protests and demonstrations.

The EYF similarly organises petitions in parallel with its lobbying action. For instance, in 1997 it mounted a campaign to collect signatures on a petition to 'end exclusion'. Conversely, SL sees its role as solely involving the lobbying of EU institutions, but admits that its members are activists on a personal level and as such engage in protest events. They consider groups like EMF to be somewhat too close to EU institutions, or even as 'creations of the EU', but are in principle not opposed to collaborating with them.

A somewhat more cautious relationship exists between churches and other groups. Potential conflicts of interest and philosophical differences may arise between groups envisaging a stronger role for state intervention to curb racism and those who rely on private organisations. This undermines the value of churches as institutional allies. EMF is in favour of collaborating with churches and reports frequent and good relations, whereas other groups such as SL are more wary, noting that churches are reluctant to accept any regulation of their sector.

These differences, however, do not preclude collaboration on specific issues, particularly when the national levels are involved. A triangulation takes place between EU institutional activists, EU movement activists and the national levels. For instance, an activist commented on these relations in two cases, in 1997 and 1998, one successful and one unsuccessful – a German campaign to grant citizenship to the children of immigrants, and a French campaign to grant citizenship to selected illegal immigrants.

The unsuccessful German campaign concerned the issuing of children's visas. The German anti-racist coalition called for visas to be issued to the children of immigrants born in Germany. All the German organisations, the Turks, the Kurdish groups and so on, were closely involved and received strong support from television stations, newspapers and radio stations. However, despite intensive mobilisation, the initiative failed.

As an example of a successful campaign, the activist described a set of initiatives organised in 1998 in France to help illegal immigrants (*sans papiers*) and which succeeded in having them granted resident status. In both cases, she reported that the preparation work for mobilisation was done in Brussels. French activists, for example, travelled to Brussels, while EMF representatives and French cadres jointly attended meetings at the EP to coordinate support in France and EMF activists subsequently went to lobby politicians in France. After extensive preparations, the EMF organised a conference, two weeks after which resident status was granted to migrants. The interviewee placed special value on this success because it provided a valid example of transnational coordination. In the German case, she reported that the EP was as committed as it had been in the French case, but she ascribed the failure to a lack of political opportunity. The conservative German government, and especially the minister for internal affairs, was radically opposed on ideological grounds to changes to immigration laws.

Reports on these experiences highlight the mix of national and EU institutional activism, the alliance between various EU groups and cross-national groups, but also the fundamental impact of national-level politics when legislation takes place at national level. In the environmental case, EU institutions would instead have been able to formulate immediately applicable directives and regulations.

Obstacles against mobilisation

Although the anti-racist movement has organised significant protest events in several EU countries, it has not taken off in such prominent and concerted fashion as the environmental or peace movements. Its successful mobilisation of the early and mid-1990s is now dwindling, and this is reflected in Brussels. One EYF activist noted 'a sense of fatigue towards the organisations, but also towards the topic'.

Effective mobilisation is hindered by the difference between the conscience constituency – white Europeans working as institutional activists and lobbyists – and the representatives of immigrants. This feature is illustrated by the experience of an activist who took part in the Council of Europe initiative entitled the 'European Youth Campaign against Racism, Xenophobia, Antisemitism and Intolerance' between 1994 and 1996 and which, although it occurred within a non EU institution, is indicative of the difficulties that arise when attempts are made to connect the different components of the movement together. This activist coordinated the European Youth Train initiative[14] and represented minority youth organisations on the Campaign's European Steering Group. She noted that:

> events of the campaign conformed to the stereotype of a 'young, middle-class, global elite'. The aim of reaching out to grassroots organisations of marginalised minorities was generally unsuccessful . . . It was largely felt that there was insufficient representation from groups affected by the problems that the campaign aimed to tackle.[15]

An additional problem concerns the difficult issue of representation. Brussels activists would like to consult their members, but consultation is often difficult, time-consuming and inconclusive. They are consequently obliged to decide for themselves on issues of strategy, for instance, or on how to advise the Commission on the channelling of funding to national projects. This may lead to accusations that they are insensitive to local views, bureaucratised, or that they cater to vested interests.

Inter-organisational relations

EU institutions are the only effective referent for EU-level movements.[16] Attempts to involve business, as in the case of the environmental movement, have proved fairly unsuccessful. EMF personnel say that a lack of time has to date limited attempts to contact business, and the SL was of a similar opinion. The EYF engages in minor amounts of market consulting and intends to increase its efforts in this area in the future. Others have no particularly close connections with business. The EU institutions, on the other hand, have permanent and generally positive relations with movement organisations, and the latter have a positive attitude towards them. Individual Commission officials are often praised for their competence, their sense of strategy and their commitment. Access is readily available for many organisations.

This is not to imply, however, that inter-organisational relations are unproblematic or that the line between institutional activists and other activists is simple to cross. Not only do institutional activists have much better personal resources and institutional power, there may be some resentment among movement activists over the 'brain drain' that EU institutions engender, and the mutual interdependence may give rise to what one activist described as a 'love–hate relationship'. Organisational interconnections create problems of loyalty besides the brain drain. One EYF activist said:

This is political work and people have an interest in making political careers, being in the Parliament, being in the Commission. So it often happens that people from here [the EYF] jump on to the administrative level, become Eurocrats. People win concourses, they are asked to put themselves forward.

He also noted that two previous members of the secretariat had found jobs in the Commission. This finding cannot be generalised, however. Other organisations, Solidar for instance, see entry in the Commission as rare, and they report inter-organisational transfers as being more frequently in the opposite direction, with EP assistants becoming movement lobbyists. However, he described the sector as generally static:

The NGO community in Brussels is quite static. In the time I have been here [several years] there have been a handful of changes at the level of general secretaries and below. And most organisations are three to five people. I probably know most of them. It is quite static really. Most directors of networks have been there for some time.[17]

Nevertheless, since several projects are short-term, there is a relatively high turnover at low levels, although some groups try to promote members internally so that they can retain good personnel.

Discussion: success or failure?

Despite long delays in achieving a legal base, slow institution building and belated action programmes, the anti-racist advocacy coalition has been successful in promoting legislation in an area where public opinion is in the main against it. This fact invites explanation for it gainsays the existence of any direct relation between popularity and policy initiatives.

As mentioned with regard to the first level of the strategies adopted by state actors, the literature often sees a direct connection between public opinion and policy making. According to Burstein (1998), interest groups are able to exert an impact which at best is somewhat stronger than the body of opinion that they represent in society. This happens when they are able to misrepresent and magnify to policy-makers the strength of the opinions they claim to represent. However, in this case public opinion is known and is of a different orientation. Explanation of this situation requires us to move from interest groups to advocacy coalitions. This re-orientation helps account for the measure of success achieved by the anti-racist coalition despite unsupportive public opinion. When policy-makers address a broad advocacy coalition, they are no longer dealing only with lobbyists but have to consider the motives and efforts of wider networks; and this calls into question the conditions for their electoral performance and their normative commitment and mimetic practice as state actors. Appearing to condone racism would, for instance, mobilise churches, trade unions and other social actors against them.

These considerations also apply to the second level of EU elites. Is has been widely noted that the EP has frequently taken up principled positions. Critics have explained this with reference to the fact that the relatively powerless Parliament has never had to deal with the consequences of its statements. Appearing principled is thus portrayed as a viable strategy with which to acquire legitimacy. This may to some extent be the case, and in this sense the support for anti-racism parallels the EP's support for stringent environmental regulation as a normative choice. Similar considerations apply to the Commission. For anti-racism, as earlier argued with regard to environmental policy, Europe can be regarded as one of the strongest defenders of an undervalued policy area in a period when the issue is still not of central importance to much of Southern Europe, so that 'Europe' can put itself forward as performing a necessary and useful role. The fact that environmental issues are more popular than anti-racism does not undermine the principled character of anti-racist policy.

At the level of policy communities, determining success is not as straightforward for those involved in advocacy efforts. Viewed from close up, the field can appear as a confused succession of victories and defeats. Deciding the issue of success or failure is difficult for movement organisations and lobbies which collaborate closely with institutions, since it is hard to see a connection between action and results. One activist noted:

> It would be very difficult if we want to measure our success on the programmes. We do not. We find it very difficult to evaluate how effective our lobby capacity or policy work is . . . We have joint objectives. For us it is an achievement when we can say 'we raised the issue'. But it is a love–hate relation because they want to keep us short of funding and still they want us to do things.

While it is hard to judge success from outcomes, it is less difficult to do so in terms of how activists play their game. Another activist pointed out:

> I can watch the comments being put in from organisations, and from Parliamentarians. And I can tell you on that basis who is working and who isn't working. It is the quality of the interventions, the speed of response, the regularity of information, all those things. I think that you are being assessed all the time, and if you make a mistake people know.

Consequently, not only do other activists know, but institutional activists do so as well; and this, according to some activists, directly rebounds on their chances of receiving financial support.

The activists interviewed maintained that anti-racist organisations do not always deliver as much as they could, and that some of them make much more effective use of their money than others. The same point was made by an MEP, who also complained about the fragmentation of anti-racist organisations. This situation of relative organisational ineffectiveness was argued to be one of the main contributing factors to the lack of influence and the small size of anti-racist initiatives in EU institutions. This, some believed, will improve when ENAR, the specific anti-racist network, becomes fully operational in the near future, complementing the present immigration network, which now acts as the main channel for anti-racist initiatives:

> Another problem concerns delegation and turnover. Some activists noted that, although effective delegation may not conform with their movement's principles, it is nevertheless necessary. Yet they feel uneasy and are unable to undertake it effectively. Turnover is a problem for several organisations. An activist pointed out that the entire 'family' of left-liberal movement organisations comprises no more than 200 or 300 people permanently in Brussels, and that over time one meets most of them. On the other hand, people move across projects and organisations, causing problems of organisational learning deficit.

These problems of resources and work method do not cause concern among institutional activists, many of whom feel that they can do a great deal of successful work even in difficult conditions. In fact, small size can be a benefit, according to a Commission official, because it sustains team spirit and commitment.

Yet, when the anti-discrimination policy area is compared with other EU areas, such as environmental policy-making, it appears fragmented and weak, reflecting the overall weakness of the field in member states. Anti-discriminatory measures have appeared in piecemeal and ad hoc fashion everywhere, without coherent strategies, and state responses have often failed to recognise that migration is a permanent phenomenon for political reasons (Wrench in Wrench and Solomos 1993: 24). The EU institutions' evaluation of success must be framed within this general European situation. The successes marked by approval of article 13 and its aftermath are indicative that the anti-racist coalition is advancing, but it is still on a different scale from the centrality of other advocacy coalitions, such as the environmental coalition, at EU level and in member states.

Conclusions

Overall assessment of the anti-racist movement in Brussels points to a movement well supported by institutions, well-resourced, with competent and motivated activists from every part of Europe, but which is nevertheless weak and fragmented. As an MEP noted, with the exception of the extreme right, there is an ample consensus on anti-racism across the political spectrum. The recent spate of racist attacks on immigrants has provided the movement with political opportunities, and it has engendered sympathy in the European publics for the plight of racial minorities vulnerable to xenophobic intolerance. Yet the movement saw only a brief revival in the early 1990s and its policy achievements have been modest.

It is hard to attribute these difficulties to a lack of political opportunities in the strict sense of those that arise from dynamics operating within the political system. Anti-racism is a movement with numerous elite allies. It is not particularly repressed, it operates in an inclusive political environment, and there is a desire by the moderate right in the EU institutions to distance itself from the extreme right by condemning racism even when attempting to limit migratory flows. However, if one conceptualises opportunities more broadly and focuses on the cultural–political opportunities of this movement, some fundamental difficulties with anti-racism are apparent and which explain its predicament: a movement whose success is due less to the anti-racist organisations than to its institutional allies, institutional activists and normative and mimetic pressure on heads of states. Two orders of factors require separate consideration in this regard: the movement's ideological crisis and the general cultural context. The latter more directly explains success than does the former.

As regards the movement's ideological crisis, this stems from a fundamental indecision between assimilative and multicultural strategies. This is an uncertainty that has fundamental policy repercussions in that it occasionally restricts the activity of institutional activists unsure of which measures to prioritise, but even more importantly it restricts the ability of the movement to coordinate its efforts.

The second factor relates to the global cultural context and operates at several levels. As previously mentioned, the escalation of immigration and the increased visibility of racist attacks occurred in a period when it was culturally unacceptable to call for centralised solutions at a European level unless they were strictly necessary. Hence anti-racist policy is less easily considered within the framework of social policy, as it would have been in another period. It is still often defined in terms of individual liberty and in terms of an economic right – for instance, the right to mobility in labour markets.

Some governments are still not ready to accept common deliberation on their immigration policy, which is closely connected with racist behaviour, even if this connection has been seen as hindering the movement. However, in this respect the situation has changed considerably. For instance, the British Conservatives opposed the establishment of the European Year Against Racism on the grounds that it was a threat to sovereignty; New Labour has taken a very different approach. Yet substantial difficulties still persist for this MAC. The current crisis of legitimacy afflicting the European construction process makes insistence at the political–cultural level on increasing Brussels' visibility with substantial inroads in new policy areas, particularly controversial ones like anti-racism, of doubtful utility. The only option is to de-politicise anti-racism, which is indeed what EU policy-makers have attempted to do. But this tactic has run into problems because it has clashed with the traditional militant left-wing nature of anti-racism. Evidence of these problems is provided by the wrangling among the representatives selected as interlocutors by the Commission.

The crisis of anti-racist movements has been particularly closely studied in Britain, which has the oldest and strongest anti-racist movement. Some of the difficulties besetting the British anti-racist movement also explain the problems at the European level. As Bonnett (1993: 57) points out, the recent revival of anti-racism has glossed over some of its traditional problems by focusing on the urgency of reacting to right-wing attacks. This, however, is ultimately an unsatisfactory strategy because it relies on unforeseeable violent events and does not address the substantial ideological divides within the anti-racist movement that prevent coordinated action. Of course, coordinated action and synergy are goals that have proved unachievable for many movements, which are successful only when they find valuable political opportunity in externally provided grievances, and in the context of anti-racism they might even be undesirable because they would reduce the richness of anti-racist approaches (Solomos 1993: 216–17). But a common political opportunity of the kind available to the environmental movement is unlikely to result from racist attacks, even when they are particularly repellent. Such attacks tend to be confined to specific locations, and at most to entire European member states, but they are unlikely to be significantly reflected in EU level politics without the viable co-ordination of groups and initiatives.

While in many EU countries the anti-racist movement has recently concentrated narrowly on opposing right-wing extremism, this has not happened at the Brussels' level. Precisely because of this broad European focus, in Brussels there has been a deficit of transfer of the detailed policy elaboration, high-quality activist expertise and movement-generated resources available to other movements. Moreover, different priorities and unresolved ideological controversies remain in the background, preventing the onset of real synergy among groups.

Yet, despite all these problems, the changes made to the Amsterdam Treaty may engender positive developments for the movement. They could, for instance, result in legislation that stimulates the emergence of a new brand of institutional activist: people in business and public institutions who review race relations and promote a constant stream of new initiatives to curb racism; they could stimulate more research by universities and government think-tanks on racism that would entrench anti-racism in a broader range of institutions. A similar development could soon take place in Brussels. The current debate on 'civil dialogue', which centres on the formation of a European Social Policy Forum, is moving in this direction. NGOs are pressing for formal consultative status and EU institutions are considering whether to organise and formalise the relationship between the EU and NGOs as a counterweight to the present dominance of the economic dimension in Brussels. This initiative could expand and empower all social exclusion institutional activists, including anti-racists, whose cultural importance is not likely to decline.

Throughout Europe, the legal and hidden immigration rate continues to be significant, and the issue of the rights of Muslim minorities is still high on the political agenda. Accordingly, the attendant issue of race relations is unlikely to fade in significance. The anti-racist movement will continue to be a substantial presence in the political arena, and even if it is fragmented and sometimes unfocused, it will continue to represent a powerful moral concern, one likely increasingly to permeate European civil society.

Summary

This chapter has considered the agenda-setting strategies of the anti-racist advocacy coalition operating at the EU level. It has examined how decision-making takes place in the area of anti-racism regulation in EU institutions. It has analysed the role of different concepts of anti-racism and their implications for the policy process. The data used were drawn from observation, personal interviews and analysis of archival materials.

The chapter has suggested that policy-making emerges from a fragmented coalition of NGOs, politicians and civil servants operating in connected but distinct regulative environments. Various conceptions of anti-racism operate across the different sectors involved in the policy process. Those that focus on implementation and also on acquiring knowledge of racial discrimination act as the dominant condensing paradigms that guide most agenda-setting attempts and regulatory discourse, although several definitions of the nature, causes and ideal solutions of racism coexist with them. Altogether these conceptions give identity and professionalism to the relevant policy network, but in a fragmented and contested fashion.

Notes

1 Commission (1998c).
2 Thalhammer, Zucha *et al.* (2001), cited in Bell (2002).
3 Eurobarometer 51.1, cited in Commission (1999).
4 As the head of the Civil Liberties Committee, Michael Elliott, pointed out, there is virtually universal rejection of extreme right positions in the EP.
5 For instance, at the EP-sponsored conference 'Tackling Racism in Football Across Europe' at Manchester United Football Club (30 January 1998), a DGV official noted that there was a need for different Directorates of the Commission to cooperate more actively.
6 When civil servants consider policies, they are obliged to take account of what has been termed 'the European value added'; that is they must consider whether policies make a positive contribution to furthering the process of European integration.
7 Communication from The Commission on Promoting The Role of Voluntary Organisations and Foundations in Europe – DG XXIII, 1995 (en/23/95/00891100.W00(EN)). DG VIII has also issued a document entitled 'Digest of Community Resources Available for Financing Activities of NGOs and other Decentralised Bodies Representing Civil Society in the Fields of Development, Co-operation and Humanitarian Aid'.
8 This is also because DGV has a tradition that the Commission should be represented in parliamentary committees at Chef's level.

9 For an extensive examination of the two traditions see Lloyd (1994).

10 However, the initial establishment of a Migrant Forum, instead of a specific anti-racist network (which as previously mentioned is now on the agenda), could be seen as reflecting a multiculturalist ethos. In the EMF, the criteria for representation in Brussels are election by members of different 'ethnic' backgrounds. Hence the Commission seems to accept that the unit of representation is not only territorial provenance, but also ethnicity. This interpretation is not supported by some activists, who argue, on the contrary, that this Commission's choice also reflects an assimilationist ethos.

11 For a list of successful projects funded within the context of the European Year Against Racism and a description of participating organisations see 'European Year Against Racism: Directory of Projects – Employment and Social Affairs', EUROP (Brussels, 1998).

12 The Civil Liberties Committee was formerly known as the Committee on Civil Liberties and Internal Affairs. Following a reorganisation after the Amsterdam Treaty, it is now known as the Committee on Citizens' Freedoms and Rights, Justice and Home Affairs (LIBE). This deals with civil liberties matters internal to the EU. Human rights in third countries are covered by the Committee on Foreign Affairs, Human Rights, Common Security and Defence Policy (AFET).

13 For instance in recent years SL had a total budget line of about 4.8 million ECU yearly; EMF had 900,000 ECU plus two or three large projects (one on justice and policing, the other on women's economic potential).

14 As Lentin (1998) explains, the European Youth Train initiative involved trains departing in July 1995 from six European cities. Young people boarded these trains and took part in intercultural journeys throughout Europe which concluded a week later in Strasbourg.

15 The experience described and analysed by this activist is in Lentin (1998). The passage quoted is on p. 7.

16 One should also mention the less relevant presence as an interlocutor of the Council of Europe.

17 He pointed out that one of the reasons for limited mobility is that there is nowhere to go after an important NGO position in Brussels. There is no 'revolving door' with government positions as there is in some member states.

5

Ethno-nationalism

Ethno-regionalist coalitions

This chapter discusses a family of EU-level political formations concerned with increasing the power of culturally and linguistically peripheral regions and known by a variety of names which emphasise different aspects: ethno-nationalist, ethno-regionalist, minority nationalist, nationalist and movements of stateless nations. In Brussels as well as in several member states, these political formations are institutionally based in a rich inter-organisational world of movements, parties, federations of parties, Parliament inter-groups, regional offices, cultural associations and local government offices. This is a complex milieu where institutional politics, interest intermediation and the protection of national symbolism closely intertwine. The roots of ethno-regionalist parties often extend into the social movement sector of social movements claiming additional political autonomy if not total independence from nation states. In member states and often in Brussels they are part of a set of advocacy coalitions within which actors in different positions pursue common goals. To a certain extent, these ethno-regionalist coalitions share the common identity of advocating a decentralised Europe respectful of minority cultures and languages. They are critical of the centralising tendencies of member states and accordingly exert some influence at EU level.

These coalitions are associated with a range of recognised movements, such as *Catalanismo* or *Sardismo*, which express long-standing and historically important political cultures and engage in intellectual and protest activities. Coexisting within these traditions is a complex set of views on the relation between specific territories and neighbouring political units – states, other regions and the supranational EU level (Conversi 2002a). This chapter will refer to ethno-regionalism as the ideology of a set of formations ranging from extremist groups to non-institutional separatist ones to regionalist parties, and to the political backdrop of cultural activities such as the politicisation of language use. It will also identify a strong and a weak form of political doctrine. The strong form seeks to achieve the dissolution of states in favour of smaller regional units. It often postulates a coherent set of cultural traits, common economic interests and historical continuity at the regional territorial level, and frequently argues that the historical pursuit of state building and nation building has necessitated the repression of these features, which should be re-emphasised through political mobilisation. This political doctrine is shared to varying extents by the political elites of a number of regions with strong historical identities and by other radical regionalist formations.

In more attenuated form, the language of contentious politics directed against the overpowering dominance of states has also been adopted by a much larger set of regional authorities. The concept of a Europe of distinct and collaborating regions, whose populations are profoundly characterised by unique regional identities has been popularised with the slogan 'Europe of the Regions'.

Given such strong and widespread agreement on regionalism, one would expect to find abundant resources and strong support in Brussels, particularly for the older and culturally more characterised regionalist formations. This, however, is not the case. There is limited funding for cultural and linguistic regionalist initiatives, and limited concern for the issue of regional independence is expressed in official documents. It will be argued here that regional self-determination is discussed only in attenuated form, and that state–region conflicts are often ignored. So-called 'historical regions' are weakly represented in the EP, and they also have only weak functional representation. Only a limited number of regionalist NGOs are able to lobby EU institutions for funding and to exert political advocacy.

This chapter will identify and seek to explain a discursive prominence of regionalism to which this weakness corresponds. The empirical material used consists of institutional documents subjected to content analysis, observant participation at EU-level ethno-regionalist meetings and a set of personal interviews.[1] The field of territorial interests will be examined, and their relations to regionalism as a political philosophy variously embedded in political formations will be analysed. The substantial weakness of regionalists – in the form of scant recognition of their desire for substantial political autonomy or independence – will be connected to a process by which the regionalist discourse has been pre-empted by stronger and less autonomist regions. This state of affairs will be interpreted as a consequence of EU-level regional policy and of the institutional structure of interest representation.

The chapter consists of three sections. Following from a brief historical background, the first section will discuss the framings and political opportunities of ethno-regionalism in relation to state actors. In the second section, the framings of EU policy discourse will be examined, and in that context the differences between the two kinds of regionalism dominant in Brussels: strong regionalism and the weaker kind fostered by EU regional policy, will be discussed. In the third section, the prospects of regionalist lobbies in different policy domains will be examined, with reference to EU policy communities.

Historical background: strong and weak regionalism

There are various kinds of minority nationalism. The main contemporary types are the nationalism of peripheral regions with different cultures and languages, transborder nationalism, the new regionalism of affluent areas, right-wing populist regionalism and combinations thereof. Their origins and the related types of grievance produce different framings in the respective movements and parties. European integration has had a decisive impact on all these various types.

The nationalism of peripheral regions has resulted from the parallel processes of nation building and state building resulting in the cultural and political marginalisation of several European regions, particularly those most distant from the cultural and political centre. For centuries, political marginalisation was bitterly resented in areas such as the Basque and Catalan regions in Spain, Scotland and Wales in the UK, the Breton region and Corsica in France and Sardinia in Italy. In several other areas with minority languages, the process of political translation of sentiments of marginalisation was slower, but a variety of organisations of civil society were culturally uneasy about the efforts at cultural standardisation made by nation-states, albeit with different intensities and in different ways.

Typically, in several peripheral regions the church as a counterpart to the state became a protective bastion of local languages and sensibilities. There is a large body of literature which discusses the consequences of dominance by a strong capital city and points to such political factors as the varying attraction for local elites forced to make a difficult choice between conflicting territorial allegiances. The literature on regionalism has often viewed languages as the visible marker of exclusion. The policy frequently adopted of forbidding their use has resulted in a clear demarcation of identities opposed to the dominant project of nation building.

Explanations that consider the historical genesis of regionalism often focus on the rebellion of elites against capitals. This is the 'internal colonialism' thesis, which argues that particular historical conditions produced accentuated perceptions of injustice (Hechter 1985). These explanations are often applied to regions marked by economic obsolescence and cultural particularism (Harvie 1994). They emphasise that, for a number of reasons, state capitals were no longer able to coopt elites, and this inability produced protest movements supported by disloyal elites.

While latent in a number of European areas, regionalist identities have manifested themselves more prominently in the last few decades. Since the 1970s, there has been a revival of ethno-nationalist organisations in Europe, ranging from terrorist groups to political and cultural movements and to parties, which are now well entrenched in the local governments of some minority regions, particularly the most prosperous ones. The phenomenon has also concerned areas in which language diversity has played a limited role. Explanations for this re-emergence point to such general cultural factors as the collapse of previously dominant all-encompassing ideologies like Marxism.

At EU level, explanations have also stressed the role of the EU in as much as the economic requirements of EU integration, since the Single European Act (SEA), have come to signify the extraction of additional resources from peripheral elites and a halt to deficit spending approaches. These two factors have exacerbated perceptions of injustice in peripheral regions. This approach postulates the emergence of new political opportunities for regionalist movements; and new political opportunities connected with the process of European integration have also emerged from variables of a political economic type. Even small states have become politically and economically viable in an integrated Europe. Separatist movements therefore find fertile ground where they were previously kept at bay by economic considerations.

In addition to this type of historical regionalism, there is a further one also predicated on language and which resulted from transfers of territories as a consequence of state treaties, often following wars. Border areas in which majority languages were spoken were after incorporation re-defined as linguistic minorities, which engendered attempts at internal colonisation by annexing states, discontent in local populations and the emergence of political identities. This was, for instance, the case of German-speakers in Northern Italy after the First World War. Other identities of this kind have had an even longer gestation. Again, the process of integration has had an impact on this kind of regionalism by re-defining the meaning of borders. In a Europe with weak borders, border regions can feel more united and thus create or re-create collective cultural identities. In this sense, the process of European construction constitutes a political opportunity for these ethno-regionalists.

Another, but quite different, type of regionalism has emerged on the basis of economic performance. In recent years, some areas without strong traditions of minority nationalism have performed remarkably well economically. Moreover, national economic dynamics, and dynamics related to processes of globalisation, have increased the economic distinctiveness of regions. This has produced a feeling of common belonging which has sometimes translated into political action. Areas of this kind – for instance, Lombardy, Baden-Württemberg and Rhône-Alps – have been studied under the paradigm of a 'new regionalism' (Harvie 1994). There has sprung up in these areas a family of movements and parties, such as the Northern League and the Veneti d'Europa in Italy, with the populist overtones of a rebellion raised by a marginalised small bourgeoisie against the impact of globalisation and its consequent increase in migration flows.

Member states and the political opportunities of ethno-nationalists

The different historical factors that have stimulated the emergence of regional-ism often still underlie contemporary typologies classifying regionalist tradi-tions in EU member states. For instance, Keating (1998) identifies a conservative regionalism which opposes modernisation, is often associated with Christian Democratic values and celebrates the strength of local affective ties. Secondly, he describes a bourgeois regionalism characterised by the desire of entrepreneurial elites to free themselves from the limitations imposed by often archaic state structures. Thirdly, he identifies a progressive regionalism connected with the libertarian left, ecologist movements and equalitarianism. This is a perspective that can be traced back to the nineteenth century but has re-acquired viability since the 1960s. There is, then, a social democratic regionalism which results from the embracing of regionalism and re-conversion of social democratic par-ties away from centralising statist approaches. Fourthly, a right-wing regionalist tradition has frequently been described. This opposes re-distribution and pop-ulation movements, and can occasionally acquire racist overtones. Finally, there is the nationalist tradition proper, which Keating connects to a pre-state world view in which regions enjoyed great autonomy. On this conception, Europe rep-resents a new mechanism with which to achieve these goals in the modern era. These types of regionalism vary in intensity in different locations, and as public opinion data show, they characterise regions as well-entrenched recipients of territorial identities in Europe (figure 5.1).

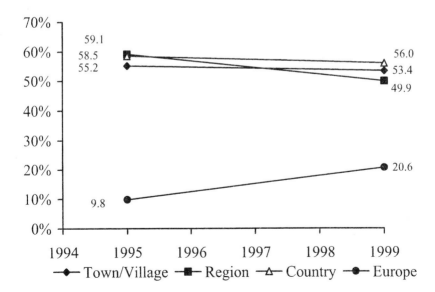

Figure 5.1 Attachment in Europe to town/village, region, country, Europe, 1994–99 (% Very attached)

Source: EB 43.1 Bis (q. 34), EB 51.0 (q. 13)

It is argued here that, in contemporary Europe, the various kinds of territorial regional identity can be classified as two kinds of regionalism: one that is essentially of an activist nature and can be equated to the movement politics familiar with the social movements of the 1980s, and one that is weaker, more generalised and rooted in the dynamics of EU integration and the regional policies of member states. The former is characterised by political formations which expressly articulate demands for independence or quasi-independence. The category includes the minority nationalism of historically peripheral regions and the right-wing populist regionalism of formations like the Northern League and Vlaams Blok. Historic peripheral regionalism defines strong region-alism mainly ideologically, because populist regionalists are of limited influence as regionalist forces and appear not to be cohesive and to be characterised more in terms of their exclusionary right-wing agenda.

The second type of regionalism is a weaker kind which is compatible with the present system. This, as Loughlin (2000) points out, is a regionalism emerg-ing as a consequence of top-down policies by member states. It differs from regionalism as a movement because movement-based regionalism involves mobilisation from below. In terms of acceptance by the population and regional elites, such regionalism is of a weaker kind because it does not reflect long-standing historical and economic cleavages and is less likely to produce advo-cacy coalitions. The other type – strong regionalism – often connects specific social movements and regionalist parties together in broad advocacy coalitions, but also culturally and politically mobilises people from historical regions.

The weaker kind of regionalism has become considerably more significant, given its diffusion and political impact on the relations between the EU level, states and regions in Europe. For years, a gradually increasing amount of power has been transferred to regional authorities in a variety of policy areas. Particu-larly as regards the allocation of structural funds, regional authorities are increasingly free from government control, and in a number of ways bound to policy discourses prevalent in Brussels, such as environmental objectives whose consideration is mandatory in all applications for European funds. Since Ams-terdam, structural funds must also promote mainstreaming approaches for equal opportunities. In its distribution of funds, the EU level is on the one hand freeing regions from member states, and on the other pursuing Brussels-endorsed policy principles.

One of these principles is that of the 'Europe of the Regions', which gives cultural legitimacy to numerous claims for cultural and political semi-auton-omy. Although this policy focus has been extensively used in traditionally inde-pendent areas of distinctive language and culture, it is nevertheless a resource that can be mobilised by other actors, such as new regions and regions with lim-ited identities. It can also be argued that, in a more integrated Europe, standards of appropriateness in public life become more similar, and deviations from them more evident. There is, for instance, growing awareness of the insufficien-cies of public provisions and therefore a radicalisation of regional rivalries based on distributive conflicts. Regionalism thus becomes a widespread strategy to legitimise local competition at the cultural level.

The stronger kind of regionalism, however, is also important. Even if its strongholds – the 'historical regions' or, in the usage of many activists, the stateless nations – are marginal in terms of population size and territorial extension, altogether their elites and their independentist movements constitute a major phenomenon. Even regardless of their aggregated political relevance, they are important as the ideological inspiration of all regionalisms.

One can summarise the issue of types of regionalism by using Loughlin's classification of it into three categories: state citizenship regionalism, moderate autonomist regionalism and radical separatist regionalism (Loughlin 1996). While, as Loughlin points out, the three types can occur together or alternate over time in the same party, they represent ideologically different views and characterise the extreme positions of moderate decentralisation and radical independence for regions.

In contemporary Europe, the specific position of member states on issues of ethno-regionalism are rather different, and they are connected with entrenched conceptions of the state. Positions range between a French model of state centralisation and defence of the state's integrity as a vehicle for shared values and overarching national identities, and a German model of substantial ideological acceptance and practical acknowledgement of the power of regions. These positions are relatively independent from processes of regionalisation, which may even have been promoted while at the same time intentionally hindering the participation of minority nationalists, as evidenced for instance by the case of France (Loughlin 1996). These positions are in part rooted in the accidents of history and culture of the countries concerned, such as the forced regionalisation of Germany after the Second World War and the republican tradition in France, and in part they derive from specific interests associated with the regionalisation process. As instances one may cite the creation of artificial regions and regional structures in small states in order to meet eligibility criteria for structural funds.

In general, the existence of an EU-level regional policy is in part due to the need of states to deal with the increasing complexity and related demands of advanced industrial economies through administrative decentralisation. In part, it has been a response to regionalist identities which emerged as an alternative to declining religious and, later, Marxist ideologies (Ruzza and Schmidtke 1993). It has arisen as a mechanism of internal re-distribution *vis-à-vis* the tensions engendered by the integration of markets, and its presence has legitimated and promoted acceptance of regionalisation in most member states. Over the course of several decades, states have accepted and implemented regionalised structures. However, there are important differences in the power wielded by the regions in member states, and this is reflected in the form and performance of regional representation in Brussels. Some regions are extremely well resourced, politically powerful and organisationally skilled; others much less so. Thus a substantial cleavage has arisen on the basis of the political power accruing from the levels of constitutional entrenchment of different regions (Christiansen 1996). The relation between states and regions is often one of mutual support as regional representatives are often controlled by states, and states tend to be the basis of much political and commercial aggregation among regions in Brussels. Nonetheless, ethno-regionalists also seek to establish direct and independent relations with the EU environment.

Regionalism as a policy principle

For a variety of ethno-regionalist organisations, the EU is both an opportunity and a threat (Lynch 1996; De Winter and Tursan 1998). They are attracted to Brussels by their need to acquire resources, by-pass hostile state policies, link with other minority nationalists and take up the political opportunities provided by the EU environment. Yet, Europe and the process of EU integration are hastening the demise of many of the distinctive cultural features that they want to protect. In addition, there has always been a neo-Marxist component among minority nationalists which views Europe as a club of rich members to be opposed in principle (Loughlin 1996: 145). Because of this ambivalence, and because they have to deal with very different state structures as a mediation factor in their relations with Europe, a variety of stances and behaviours has emerged in the EU institutional environment. These are connected with the different historical origins and types of minority nationalisms.

Generalising by considering the last few decades, one notes that minority nationalists have been relatively pro-integrationist. Parties have taken significantly more pro-European positions than have their bases. This has been due to the low salience of the European issue for electorates and the realisation of the symbolic benefits that come from European integration (De Winter 2001). The EU level has espoused principles of regional self-determination advocated by these parties over and above the degree of acceptance of this principle by national elites. As Loughlin (1996) points out, there is a close connection between regionalism and a EU integrationist agenda. This connection translates into a set of policy principles and support for specific policies – notably cultural policies that embed the claim of self-determination in cultural practices that make it visible to the electorate and the supporters of ethno-nationalist formations. However, establishing a EU counterpart of these formations has proved difficult, while the general regionalist movement has been successful.

The EP, CoR, the Commission (and particularly the Regional Policy Directorate General) and regional offices and delegations of subnational government are indicative of the growing legitimacy of regional representation in the European system of government. The different degrees of acceptance of regionalism in member states has been at the basis of the slow, controversial but until now successful entrenchment of regional policy in the EU. As Hooghe and Marks

(Hooghe and Marks 1996) point out, one consequence of the development of the EU framework has been the proliferation of avenues for subnational representation at supranational level. The process of 'hollowing out' states is encouraging new expressions of regional mobilisation. Regional authorities have become involved in new non-national types of interaction often coordinated by an extensive network of regional offices in Brussels, which notably aggregate cross-nationally along functional lines (Greenwood 1997).

There are substantial differences in the financial resources, organisational abilities, lobbying skills and political autonomy of different regions, and of course in the benefits that EU regional policy can deliver to different regions on the basis of their eligibility for sources of funding. This means that the ability to achieve funding and to exert influence depends on organisation and resources. On the other hand, however, political factors like the specific motivation typical of regionalists to by-pass the state level is still of some importance. For instance, Hooge has connected the timing of the setting up of regional offices in Brussels with the ethnic distinctiveness of regions (Hooghe and Marks 1996).

However, resource factors are considerably more important in predicting regional performance. Thus, in the case of cohesion funds, a pork barrel logic in policy implementation favours better-organised and advantaged groups within regions (De-Rynck and McAleavey 2001). Regional interests may use the language of regionalism for strategic essentialist reasons but they attach little real relevance to it, even if it can be argued that precisely the opportunities that the EU level has created tend over the long period to reinforce real identity claims to regional distinctiveness (Leonardi 1992; Leonardi and Garmise 1992).

Over the years, regional policy has developed within the confines of an expanding set of institutions and a growing number of actors, including over a hundred regional offices, the CoR, the regional DG and the regional committee in the parliament. These institutional spaces are quite closely interconnected but too large to be described as an 'inter-organisational network' in the sense with which the term has been used for other case studies. People working in regional offices tend to know each other; for instance, they meet recurrently in Commission-led consultation exercises. But the wide variety of organisational structures, interests represented and economic specificities make them too diverse to express much more in common than a general belief in increasing regional autonomy. This belief is, however, a taken-for-granted background that cuts across the Brussels institutional world and is reflected in the condensing frame of the 'Europe of the Regions'. It is in this context that some institutions and some regions are known for expressing a stronger political will to increase regional autonomy. Of course, to the extent that this demand radically questions the framework of the nation-state that hosts them, they constitute a challenge to the EU system which only institutionalises weak regionalism.

Nonetheless, despite the effective relevance of the 'Europe *of* the Regions' which many observers see at best as a 'Europe *with* the Regions' (Hooghe and Marks 1996, emphasis in the original), the policy discourse on the regions displays increasingly pronounced autonomist overtones in the statements and documents of the EP, the CoR and several regional offices, although much less so in the Commission. This discursive allegiance of some institutions to regionalism should be explained, and its implications for the supporters of strong regionalism examined.

The European policy discourse on the regions

Content analysis of the institutional documents of regions and regionalism reveals a focus on several distinct frames which differentiate them from OCS. On the one hand, recurrent frames are naturally those such as *development* and *financial instruments* that have spurred the formation of regional policy and are encapsulated in its objective: the need to support economically marginal and de-industrialised regions and enable them to catch up and re-convert where appropriate – and this in a framework that sees the EU construction as enhancing the benefits of functional specialisation which emerges at regional level, while protecting regions against the social exclusion that market dynamics may engender and promoting employment and providing training for future improvements.

On the other hand, an emerging frame focuses on regionalisation as a way of enhancing democracy and addressing the democratic deficit. This focus is evident in the statements of the CoR and could be condensed in the currently emerging concept of *proximity*, which as such, however, appears only occasionally and recently. More frequent in the CoR is the related focus on *subsidiarity*, which as a key EU concept has older origins. In general both proximity and subsidiarity are more central in the discourse of OCS, where *democracy* and *citizenship* also appear frequently.

Weak regionalism stresses subsidiarity concepts but this approach differs greatly from the focus of ethno-regionalists. In order to understand the difficulties of ethno-regionalism at EU level it is useful to clarify this contrast. As regards the first approach, the typical EU understanding of regions is that they are areas of functional specialisation, not depositories of different cultures and nation building projects as the ethno-regionalists maintain. As an employee of a regional office from a minority region pointed out, this is because the structure of EU policy-making favours the fragmentation of problems into discrete sectoral policies. Thus, even minority regions are forced to conceive of themselves in terms of attributes that they share with other politically dissimilar regions: for instance their nature as 'islands', so that they form aggregations with other island regions, or as mountain areas, etc., which undermines the possibility of achieving solidarity at political level.

As for the second understanding of regions, the same respondent said that, despite some 'window-dressing', culture is at best understood as a social activity with a certain number of employed people who need support:

> For the EU 'Culture' means production, which means a number of personnel in a sector like cinemas or cultural initiatives. The history of the peoples that make up Europe is irrelevant and neglected. Look at the East European new entrants. We are about to receive them in the European Union and nobody seems to care about their history or even really wants to know much about them.

This is a far cry from the understanding of regional culture advocated by ethno-regionalists and which has found hospitality in some admittedly weak institutional settings like the CoR. The latter, in a report summarising the CoR's positions on the regional and local dimension in the European integration process, states:

> Europeans' cultural understanding of each other is vital. Knowing other Member States, regions, nationalities and traditions, together with language learning, stimulates public interest in European issues and gives rise to a form of cultural citizenship. This supports the idea that cultural pluralism in Europe and, in particular, minority [less widespread] and regional languages, which are an essential part of the identity of Europe's regions, must be preserved. In this field, local and regional authorities have wide-ranging capabilities, as they are particularly well-placed to act as intermediaries between the European Union and citizens. (CoR, Klär et al. 2000: 7)

As a lever of governance closer to citizens, this conception has come to the fore in recent years in response to the crisis of legitimacy which arose during and after the Maastricht ratification process. There are various ways of defining the concept that empowering regions can address the perception of *excessive distance between citizens and EU policy-making*. One way to condense this concept is to use the policy frame of 'proximity' (CoR, Klär *et al.* 2000: 1), which this report advocates and defines as:

> Proximity is a European policy concept which was devised as a reaction to the inadequate way in which policy is currently practiced. Behind the call for proximity is the hope that a policy, which focuses on the citizen's everyday life and concerns, is best suited to ensure the quality and success of Community measures. For the Committee of the Regions, the local and regional dimension is an integral part of this concept which, if it were taken seriously, would trigger far-reaching reforms in the way the Community works. The traditional ways in which democracy functions are called into question at every level and not just at European level. The involvement of local and regional elected representatives in the Community's democratic process cannot be dissociated from the problems that arise in the consultation process between national governments and regional authorities.

The idea that regions can better interpret citizens' preferences because they are closer to them is put forward in numerous documents of institutions with regional competence. For instance in presentation documents, the Assembly of European regions states that:

> The regions are a pillar for democracy in Europe. They are close to the citizens and are therefore in the best position to meet their aspirations and solve their economic

and social problems. This regional situation fully justifies the regions' participation within State institutions but also in the decision-making process at European level.

Thus, the concept of 'democratic deficit' is extended by regionalists and regional political institutions to include the weak link between regional citizenry and nation states. The dominant frame of regional policy is a weaker form of the 'closer to citizens' frame, and it is encapsuled in the metaphor of the 'Europe of the Regions' seen mainly as administrative and commercial units in healthy competition, together with an element of solidarity reflected, for instance, in Commission documents.

On the other hand, if we take the EP as the reference point, the alternative frame of strong regionalism is often expressed. But it is done so only by a small minority of actors, as it constitutes the ideological background of the EFA coalition of regionalist parties.

The masterframe of strong regionalism

In several interviews, minority nationalists – some based in Brussels and working for parties associated with EFA – argued that Europe must make a radical choice between regionalisation and a radical confederational model, of which they are the proponents and which distinguishes them from others. Various intellectuals and representatives of ethno-nationalist movements interviewed at a coordination meeting of regionalist movements in Brussels in 2001 emphasised that the current definition of politics excludes issues of cultural politics that appeal to large sectors of the population and which if brought into the political arena would generate support for their movements and parties. For instance, the interviewees argued that the recent revival of ethnic music demonstrates people's attachment to their territory, in the broader sense of a distinctive set of traditions, symbols and languages. But they complained that this interest in ethnic music is still non-politicised. It does not translate into policies to foster cultural traditions, nor into cultural institutions, which would in fact be welcomed by a much wider sector of the European population than the inhabitants of peripheral regions. They argued that the desire to revitalise local traditions and identities is strongly felt throughout Europe, which they see as disenchanted with the cultural homogeneity imposed by the last century and a half of intense nation building. But these demands are formulated outside politics, and because they lack the benefit of generalised political reflection they are seen as marginal and particularistic.

The proponents of this concern for local traditions are often keen to connect them to a re-casting of the basis of civil society as a necessary instrument of nation building. The cultivation of shared identities and knowledge is also often an attempt to broaden and deepen citizenship. But this attempt – which they see as emerging naturally in the population – also remains non-political, so that the organisation of the state and the organisation of the civil sphere are distinct, and the current organisation of member states is inimical to the development of their civil societies. They see their role as acting to remedy this self-interested neglect by European states. They view national movements and parties as the only small entities in Europe which merge these two dimensions together, so that the political and the cultural are united.

These minority nationalists set themselves the task of politicising these cultural sensitivities and connecting them to an organic federalist political project. They accept and encourage the regionalisation process that is taking place throughout Europe, but argue that it is not sufficient. To them the principle of delegation that underlies the re-definition of relations between states and regions in the process of regionalisation needs to be replaced with a principle of distribution of sovereignty – of transfer of sovereignty. And they often emphasise the cultural claims of distinctiveness that they connect and use to justify the request of this transfer.

They are aware that other political forces do not see this connection as necessary. As a result, even in marginalised regions, large parts of the population are politically insensitive to the issues to which they are culturally attached. They are aware of their weakness, even in comparison to other movements like the Greens. They argue that this is because their numbers are small but also, as several ethno-nationalists argue, because their views are ignored by increasingly globalised media. The consequence of this state of affairs is that only a weak echo of strong regionalist sentiments feeds into concrete policy making. As will be demonstrated in the rest of this chapter, strong regionalism is nevertheless important because it is a political philosophy which in weaker form inspires a great deal of regional policy.

Frame bridging

It is evident from these considerations that, in the case of regionalism, there is a plurality of concepts in somewhat uneasy coexistence within the EU framework. There is a tension between solidarity and competition well reflected in the conflicts between the Competition and Regional DGs: a tension, that is, between three approaches: one which advocates the functional political division of tasks in order to respond to the challenges of globalisation; one which seeks additional legislative autonomy for regions; and one which calls for full separation – the position of the Council, Regional institutions and ethno-nationalists. A frame bridging emerges in the intermediate position of *subsidiarity* or more recently and less frequently *proximity* and consists in the goal of constructing a 'Europe of the Regions' – a keyword which interprets the moderate reinforcement and re-definition in functional terms of regional autonomy ongoing throughout Europe since the 1970s, and which goes together with the dominant liberal ethos (Greenwood 1997: 222).

The instrumental connection between subsidiarity, cultural and linguistic diversity and European legitimacy has been identified as a key aspect of EU cultural policy (Pantel 1999). It constitutes a bridge between the legitimacy focus of the EU and the diversity aspirations of its citizens. Through its widespread emphasis on subsidiarity and its cultural policy, the EU comes to see itself as a promoter of the diversity that citizens increasingly desire and express in their aspiration for local expressions. Subsidiarity is then seen as achievable by giving a voice to OCS, particularly the OCS of distinctive subnational units. In this context overall diversity is re-interpreted as a guarantee against the dominance of the enforced mono-culturalism of member states and a justification of the process of integration (Commission 1996b). This perspective is entrenched in article 128 of the Maastricht Treaty which establishes that the Council must consult the CoR on cultural action, obliges the EU to take into account the impact on culture in various policies, forbids the harmonisation of national laws in the cultural domain and obliges the EU to respect cultural diversity in its relations with national and subnational units (Pantel 1999: 54–55). This is not sufficient for ethno-regionalists, however, and it is for this reason that their movements continue to be active in several European regions.

The frame analysis shows that a structured contrast also emerges in Brussels between OCS as a whole and EU institutions. They diverge in terms of emphases on the political or economic focus on preferred policy approaches. Thus citizenship, democracy, the importance of civil society and minority rights are almost exclusively stressed by OCS. Conversely, the economic dimension stressed by institutions emphasises development, implementation and re-distribution. In addition, institutions often reiterate their perception of their own importance, which is not, however, shared by OCS.

Institutions and OCS agree on the importance of improving knowledge, exchange of experience and cooperation among actors at different levels of governance. Thus there is substantial agreement on a perception of insufficient information and a preferred policy approach which favours the importance of a non-confrontational approach and cooperation in terms of consultation among different levels of governance – horizontally among subnational levels of governance and between cross-border subnational units.

The regionalist coalition in the EU: one coalition or several?

When addressing the issue of the distinctive character of ethno-regionalism, and in explaining its weakness, it is helpful to frame this family of movements in relation to other movements in Brussels. Although ethno-regionalists share the belief that the power of states must be curtailed in favour of regions, they differ from other movements in the important respect that while they share some ideological tenets with them, a central component of their ideology is allegiance to a specific territory, much less to the totality of minority regions. In this sense, they are different from other pro-inclusion movements which would in principle stress the inclusion of minorities everywhere. They also differ from universalist single-issue movements like the environmentalists whose ideal referents are global. Although they are universalist in the sense that they want to bring benefits to the entire population of specific regions, their overriding concern with territorially delimited populations hinders their ability to form alliances. In Brussels, this particularism is necessarily tempered by the need to form alliances, but the thematic unity of this family of movements is weaker.

The thematic unity of organisations and institutions promoting public-interest causes is accepted by many activists in the broad family of pro-inclusion movements or environmental movements. They may disagree on strategies and tactics, but they all concur on the centrality and interconnectedness of their causes. This taken-for-granted assumption is less self-evident to ethno-nationalists, however, who are ideologically more concerned with their own nation building project than with nationalist causes as such, and may be rivals for the allocation of EU funds. Also, in the broader and fragmented environment of regional policy, historically stateless nations are only a small component, and radical right-wing regionalists like the Northern League and the Vlaams Blok are forces even smaller and more marginalised. Their ideological attempts to construct a thematic unity at EU level are frustrated by their often objectively differing economic interests, traditions of political alignments and lack of incentives to establish relations. All these reasons produce disadvantages in exerting advocacy and obtaining resources, which are connected to a set of institutional mechanisms related to their positioning in the EU system of governance.

Some historic regions have direct access to decision-making at Council level; this is the case, for example, of Scottish ministers in matters of Fisheries. Others are entirely excluded, and their economic and political marginality affects their chances of representation. This is the case of Sardinia, for instance. It is thus difficult to conceptualise ethno-regionalism at EU level as a MAC in the same sense as the other two MACs, although there are important ideological similarities and political alliances between them. Regional policy is a very large, very important and extremely articulated policy area in which ethno-regionalism plays only a minor part; an important part for students of movement-parties and of political discourse but one which should be put in its proper perspective. This said, ethno-nationalism is important because it emerged long before EU regional policy and in many respects has provided the ideological framework for it.

The Parliament

There are a few avenues available for regionalist representation in the EP. The intergroup on minority languages is an important referent, especially for representatives whose parties are not members of the EFA, but come from minority-language regions. Also important is the Committee on Regional Policy, Transport and Tourism (RETT), which deals with regional issues related to cohesion policy and has a political control function on cohesion and structural funds (which cover almost 40 per cent of the Community budget), but also on transport and tourism. The most important expression of ethno-regionalism, however, is the EFA.

The EFA is the main voice for the ethno-nationalist parties in the EP. It was founded in 1981 as an association of nationalist, regionalist and autonomist parties supporting strong decentralisation, and became a federation of parties in 1994. There is also a parallel group – the European Alliance (EA) – in the CoR. The EFA comprises twenty-three political forces (plus two observer groups) ranging in size within their regions from extremely small to quite large. It is represented by ten MEPs and forms a common party with the Greens in the EP. The EFA performs a crucial role of coordination for all the ethno-regionalist MAC. It supports research initiatives, promotes policy issues embraced by all ethno-regionalists and provides information to parties not represented in the EP.

The EFA's programme is based on the radical devolution of power at both the supranational and subnational levels. The EFA argues that the process of European integration should pay closer attention to the specificities of the many small nations making up Europe, and that specific provision should be made to enhance rights concerning languages and culture and 'the recovery of their historic rights'. The rights to self-determination of nations without a state must underpin a more democratic and participatory process of European integration. Thus the EFA advocates the revival of the European integration process but maintains that it should be based on more democratic procedures and a closer involvement of public opinion. Interpreting the interests of several of its member parties and its ideological similarity with the Greens, the EFA pays particular attention to small-scale agriculture. It advocates small-scale farming, which it sees as a strategy to protect the environment and preserve employment in the countryside. The EFA opposes the perception of a united agricultural interest, arguing that at present the Common Agricultural Policy (CAP) supports only the interests of large farmers, interests which are incompatible with those of small ones.

Institutionally, the EFA advocates the strengthening of the regions' role in the Council of Ministers, a clearer separation of powers between the European, state and regional levels, and a stronger role for the CoR, which should be directly elected and have the right of initiative and right of recourse to the ECJ, acting in its own interests or on behalf of regions. In addition to the EP, the EFA calls for a directly elected second chamber consisting of a combination of the Council and the CoR, in which the representation of national minorities would be guaranteed by appropriate electoral laws. This is a clear priority for the EFA, whose statute lists among its objectives 'to give a role in European politics to parties which, by virtue of their own size or the size of the geographical area they represent, would inevitably be excluded from that arena' (article 2 of the statutes). The composition of the EP must thus be re-organised to ensure that the smallest states are properly represented, and that internal nations constitute separate electoral constituencies with their own elected MEPs. Federal and quasi-federal member states should share out their votes in the Council among their federated entities.

The EFA is concerned with social policy, advocating a more interventionist role for the EU level of governance, which it criticises for its excessive concern with economic issues and insufficient attention to social issues. In relation to cultural policy, it advocates a more active EU role in supporting regional and lesser-used languages and proposes their elevation to the same status as the official EU languages. The EFA is concerned with transparency and access to decision-makers and calls for clear rules to guarantee that all interest groups – private and public – have equal access and that responses to public interest consultation should be accessible to the public. It proposes that professional EU lobbyists should be registered with the EU and should record all payments.

The EFA's stable alliance with the Greens was a difficult decision taken by evaluating alternatives: for example, in 1999, whether or not to join a group with the Italian Radical Party. This would have altered features of the EFA, which had to decide between a strict positioning on the left and a more flexible one. The former position was the one long dominant and led, for instance, to the controversial decision not to re-admit the Northern League after it had joined the Berlusconi government, sharing responsibilities with the extreme-right National Alliance. However, this approach is criticised as lacking realism and damaging in the long term. Some activists feel that a rigid centre-left position hinders expansion to include other potential members. A more flexible position seems to be emerging, as revealed, for instance, by the admission in 2001 of the Veneti d'Europa, a formation which, at least at the level of personalities, has connections with the right.

As a whole, the EFA is more critical of the dominance of member states over the EU process than all other parties – not liking the monopolistic role of the Council which may accept regional representation but is not obliged to do so (thus Germany does but Spain does not). Positions on full separation vary, with a few member parties insisting on it while the majority are more ambiguous on the issue, but in any case it demands substantially more autonomy than at present. In general, there is a feeling of exclusion: exclusion from presence and influence in the Commission, penalisation in the EP for small parties and exclusion from the Council are typical grievances of the EFA. It feels that it has contributed to shaping the policy agenda in favour of regionalism, from which every region benefits, but the benefits are too limited for historical nations. As the secretary of the party quipped 'this is just coffee for everybody' instead of a proper meal.

At the political level, the party denies that the fundamental split in resources between poor and rich minority regions plays a role. The policy agenda is one of social solidarity, and to this agenda all members subscribe, including parties from affluent regions. This is in part due to the dominance in the party of Folks Unie, which differentiates itself sharply from the right wing Vlaams Blok and which, because it is located in Belgium, provides essential human resources for a small party like the EFA.

In policy terms, the EFA claims that it exerts a strong impact on specific policy areas. One of these is the protection of minority languages, an area in which an EFA member was the influential *rapporteur* for successful legislation in 1987. The EFA declares that it was no coincidence that a few years later the Commission created a budget line to support minority languages. At a more general level, the issue of participation of regions at EU level has been wholeheartedly supported by the EFA for years. It claims for instance that the 1993 Melis report – bearing the name of a Sardinian nationalist, at that time a member of the EP – has had a strong sensitising impact. There is a perception, however, that the policy agenda which characterises the coalition should be extended beyond linguistic and cultural issues. For instance, some activists advocate closer integration with the agenda of the Greens at both EU level and in member states to produce a joint environmental protection and social justice agenda. This broadening debate has arisen from the realisation that parties in regional governments in an ever more regionalised Europe must often articulate a complete set of policies. The EFA MEPs have also been very active in promoting issues of transparency. For instance Bart Staes, a Folks Unie MEP, was a protagonist of the debates that led to the resignation of the Santer Commission.

The Commission

At EU level, regional policy springs from the joint desire of member states to create policies that put the economy on a better footing to respond to the challenges of globalisation, and from the strategies of EU institutions and territorial interests (Keating 1998; Keating and McGarry 2001). As Tommel (1998) points out, the major role played by the regions in the European policy process during the 1990s was also spurred by the Commission's multifarious strategies to shape regional policy according to its vision through the allocation of structural funds. Although this strategy has not fully produced the quasi-federal structure intended by EU architects, namely a three-tier system, it has stimulated a more decentralised mode of governance and the emergence of a flexible governance system. All the European states have had to develop a regional policy and regional partitions, and they have effectively developed a regionalised structure even where there are substantial internal differences. Possibly only small states like Portugal, Greece and Ireland and the Scandinavian countries are still centralised. To the extent that the Commission as a whole pursues a federalist agenda – an agenda central to the ideological position of the majority of its elites – there is a natural tendency for it to support regionalist perspectives historically and ideologically connected to federalism (Loughlin 1996).

While for all regions the impact of the Commission is of greatest importance for its regional policy (which focuses on social inclusion policy and on support for industrial policy) the EU's impact has also been exerted through cultural policies. These are of particular importance for ethno-regionalists. Recent EU initiatives included a 2001 information campaign aimed at the general public: the European Year of Languages, which was also supported by the Council of Europe and naturally included a focus on regional languages. European regional languages are supported by the European Bureau for Lesser Used Languages. Financial support is also provided for an information network 'Mercator' and projects for the promotion of conferences, cultural events and networking connected to minority languages. Linguistic diversity is recognised by article 22 of the Charter of Fundamental Rights and by a Council Resolution on linguistic diversity of 14 February 2002 (Council 2002). There are about forty indigenous languages within the EU, and they are considered to be an important aspect of European heritage and culture.

The Committee of the Regions

The CoR was created by the Maastricht Treaty as an independent advisory body to defend the interests of local and regional bodies. It aims at enhancing regional subsidiarity by providing other EU institutions with a local and regional point of view on Union proposals and policies. However, because of the rules for selection of its members, the CoR tends to echo the way in which regions are dealt with in member states, rather than reflecting a common regional identity (Christiansen 1996), whose relevance is in any event doubtful. In the EU policy process the CoR provides opinions in various circumstances: in several cases consultations are mandatory (the list of relevant areas has grown with the Amsterdam Treaty) and in some cases are voluntary.

Regionalists are represented in a formation, the EA, which is larger in terms of participants than the equivalent formation – the EFA – is in the EP. This is because in the EP the larger number of parties offers to representatives a choice closer to their domestic parties of reference.

Regional associations

Regions form a variety of associations, and over 200 regions are represented in Brussels. Their peak representative bodies are the Assembly of European Regions (AER) with 250 member regions from twenty-five countries and twelve member inter-regional organisations, which expresses a federal and regionalist agenda, describing itself in presentation documents as 'the main protagonist and animator of the regionalist movement', and the Council of European Municipalities and Regions (CEMR) which unites more than 100,000 local and regional authorities in Europe and forty-two large national Associations of local and regional authorities in thirty European countries. This too has a federalist ethos and supports the process of European construction, being particularly concerned with the objectives of the other MACs previously discussed: environmental sustainability and anti-discrimination policy.

Regional offices

Regional offices are important because in many respects they are the most rapid and frequent form of contact between civil society at regional level and Brussels. Some regional offices act as two-way channels of information, not only relaying local issues to EU institutions but also disseminating knowledge about the EU policy process in regional contexts. Even more broadly, employees of regional offices sometimes use the local press to explain European opportunities and to combat what is often perceived as the negative bias or unjustified apathy shown by the national press towards 'Europe'. In Brussels, the regional offices are part of a large policy community – an inter-organisational field in which, for instance, they may all be consulted by the Commission at large meetings convened to exchange information or air policy proposals, or ones to which all border regions are invited in the context of the INTERREG programme, a Community initiative which aims to stimulate interregional cooperation in the EU.

One would expect to find relevant ethno-nationalist coalitions in the regions. This, however, is not necessarily the case – at least not to any great extent. Regional offices respond to political power at regional level which does not often reflect the views of ethno-regionalists. Regionalists have bases in some of the regional offices, particularly those where regionalist parties have considerable power. From these bases, however, their action is essentially restricted to what the other regional offices do, and this does not specifically advance an ethno-regionalist agenda.

As a regional representative noted, the work done in regional offices tends to be similar for all regions. Some are more oriented to exerting political influence – especially those regions with legislative autonomy – others are more oriented to the economic or technical levels, but as regards the work of contacting institutions and monitoring ongoing events, the cultural or linguistic component does not play a major role. In effect, as Greenwood notes, it is often difficult to distinguish between territorial public authorities and territorially based interests, as the former define their priorities to a large extent in terms of the latter (Greenwood 1997: 218). This said, as a distinct level of governance, regions also have political interests that extend beyond promoting their industries and that may result in interests in all political discourses which legitimise their independent role.

In addition, even the promotion of commercial interests may well require the by-passing of state centrality, so that in these cases, as well, discourses and practices that help business may require additional regional entrepreneurship.

At Brussels level this may, for instance, result in coordination among border regions, where ethno-regionalists may enjoy some advantages related, for example, to their emphasis on bilingualism and their practice of it. A representative from an Italian border region noted that his fluency in another language made him acceptable to two powerful communities and as such was a major advantage. His provincial representation enjoyed ready access to the Cabinet of a same-language Commissioner. He made a similar point regarding ease of contact with Commission civil servants, although he stressed that what really matters is legislative autonomy. This is the important criterion that sets a German or Spanish region apart from an Italian one, and again apart from a British county. Secondly, relationships are developed more on the basis of common interests in specific dossiers than by paying attention to other considerations.

Regionalist concerns with issues of cultural identity and attempts to increase political autonomy are unlikely to figure prominently in the work of regional offices. Important concerns where real resources are allocated are, for instance, agriculture, in which regionalist considerations are irrelevant, and the allocation of regional funds, which are attributed on the basis of belonging to a specific member state and applications for which are, with few exceptions, administered at member state level (Greenwood 1997: 231). The supranational level is not relevant for ethno-nationalists, because it is at this level that decisions are made on which municipalities fall within specific objectives. The cultural ambit is so insignificant that regional offices generally warrant no particular attention. Funding for minority languages is welcomed but it is not a high priority. There are funds available for research and development (R&D) for business purposes, but this is a type of concern that needs particular infrastructures to attract funding – infrastructures that several minority regions do not possess, whilst the rich ones like Val d'Aot and Catalonia do.

Alliances among regions are created on the basis of similar interests, such as protecting certain products, or in order to prevent regional coalitions from establishing quality standards that would have adverse consequences for other regions. But the presence of ethno-nationalism does not have an impact in this regard (for a list of regional aggregations see Greenwood 1997: 233–236). It might, however, motivate cultural re-aggregation in cases of border regionalisms of the kind previously discussed. For instance, the Italian South Tyrol and the Austrian Tyrol share the same space in Brussels, but the union is largely motivated by a similar socio-economic structure and a need of two small entities to join forces. Politically, autonomous regions may form alliances to stop their member states transferring to Brussels issues that they want to keep under close regional control, but again the important variable is the constitutional standing of regions, not the impact of ethno-nationalism.

In a few instances, regional office employees have noted that legislative autonomy – which has grown over the years for several European regions – has made it possible to choose potential partners more freely, so that choices made on the basis of similar cultural and linguistic ambits have emerged to re-enforce regional identities. Identities are thus seen as a product of legislative autonomy rather than as a precondition for political mobilisation. But even in this case the necessary condition for increased contacts is common economic interests. Relations based solely on cultural or political similarities are regarded as unlikely to arise.

As with other lobbyists, interventions span different levels. Technical dossiers are followed by regional offices, but an important role performed by representatives is to act as intermediaries for interventions at political level by, for instance, putting local politicians in contact with specific Commissioners, Parliamentarians or a Director General when necessary. Thus, the MEPs of ethno-nationalist parties collaborate with regional offices in concerted efforts on behalf of the interests of specific locations. But as ethno-nationalist MEPs are frequently not in government in their home countries, and particularly if their representation in the EP is through the EFA, which is a part of a small party, their effectiveness in lobbying at Council level, and in general their direct lobbying effectiveness, is limited. Of course, if decisions involve environmental issues where policy-shaping goes beyond a coalition between the centre-right Peoples' Party and the Socialists, then they may become more important.

Relations between social NGOs and regional offices are generally weak. At times, local social NGOs are skilled in contacting EU institutions directly; more often they find this difficult and rely on their national offices and their connections with EU-level NGOs. Nonetheless, several regional offices occasionally help social and environmental NGOs by explaining the workings of EU institutions and showing them how to set up meetings with relevant civil servants. In any event, the level of funding with which they are concerned is of limited interest to many regional offices, particularly those of the richer regions. For instance, a regional office employee said:

> If there are contacts with NGOs they tend to take place through our politicians. And the funds at Community levels are so little that it is not worth it. With our budget, our local projects we can deal with ourselves. We can finance them ourselves – there is no need to get involved in long bureaucratic procedure . . . to present a project, having to wait for up to a year or two, with all the administrative work and not even be sure whether it will be approved. If we are interested in something we will finance it ourselves, and that's it. That is the quickest way!

However, this approach is more common in regional offices where the political referents are right of centre and less supportive of social NGOs. In other situations, even those of affluent regions, relations between the regional office and NGOs take place more frequently. This is particularly the case of regionalist issues. For instance, grant applications successfully submitted in 2000 by the Val d'Aot minority languages associations (reflecting the concerns of a Northern Italian area with a substantial French-speaking community) were coordinated and renewed with the assistance of the relevant regional office. In this and similar cases, employees stressed the importance of knowing the procedures.

Other interviewees emphasised the importance of personal contacts in the Commission.

When choosing their agendas, regional offices are directly oriented by the priorities of the ruling coalition. Thus, to the extent that regionalist parties have power, their respective regional offices will act on behalf of regionalist causes. They have contacts with political regionalist formations like the assembly of European regions (AER), regions with legislative power and associations of maritime or mountain regions. In these contexts, ethno-regionalist concerns may play an important role, but they do so in a broader context of economic or linguistic similarities.

Discussion

Different movements have their strengths in different institutions, and their objectives differ according to the manner in which various institutions operate, and according to the rules governing the areas of policy that they address. In terms of institutions, as the EP gains in influence it is attracting greater interest as a target for movements. This is particularly the case of regionalists, as their threat to nation states deprives them of some of the leverage available to other movements. The EP's resources, however, cannot be restricted because they are grounded in the democratic process and are therefore automatically available to the winners of seats from minority nationalist parties.

As regards the policy environment of ethno-regionalists, examination of the entire set of interacting organisations within which activists collaborate shows substantial differences with other families of movements at the EU level. As previously seen, a set of movements is operating in Brussels connected to the field of social policy and which advocate the inclusion of social groups subject to discrimination, such as women, racial minorities, the disabled and gays. There is also a prominent sector of environmental movements. There is only a weak legal basis for action in the case of social policy, because the EU has generally refrained from undertaking a prominent role in this area. In the environmental sector, however, there is a strong legal basis. Institutional changes alter the role of movements in Brussels. Thus, as long as social policy remained largely a national area, the concern of movements in Brussels was mainly to obtain resources; with the approval of article 13 they have become more closely engaged in advocacy. Having enjoyed a legal base for EU environmental policy for a longer period, environmentalists have traditionally been as interested in shaping policy as in acquiring resources.

The equivalent referent for regionalists is a regional policy that has rapidly gained ground in recent years, an EP that has a long-standing regionalist representation and a huge amount of resources available through the structural funds. There is also a limited Commission research budget which regionalists can utilise to further their emphasis on symbolic issues such as minority languages.

However, in all these institutional realms, the regionalists constitute only a small minority and their influence is consequently limited. This is the case in the EP where, as previously pointed out, there is a party – the EFA – that groups national regionalist organisations from all the categories described above: the ethno-regionalists, the economic regionalists and the border regionalists (and the very small and ineffective regionalists of areas in which there is generally no regionalist political culture). However, not all the parties expressing regionalist concerns belong to this group.

In the Commission, the regional DG has an interest in promoting the process of regionalisation, but no specific concern for minority regionalism. The CoR is still a weak institution, and it is similarly not particularly concerned with ethno-regionalism. There are a large number of regional offices, and those from rich minority regions have often been instrumental in helping regionalists obtain EU resources, but many areas of minority regionalism are relatively poor and their limited means are reflected in their inadequate lobbying activities.

By comparison, the anti-exclusion social movements and the environmental movements have their basis distributed across the entire EU institutional spectrum. They are represented in the EP – the environmentalists through Green parties and the anti-exclusion coalition through its entrenchment in the parties of the left. But they are also crucially present in viable NGO networks which are financially sustained and incorporated in certain decision-making fora (Ruzza 1996, 2000b). For this reason, they are able to enter other policy areas and exert an ideological agenda-setting role (Ruzza 2000b). The ethno-nationalists are virtually confined to majoritarian politics. Their NGOs are weak; and unlike the environmentalists they do not have a dedicated institutional basis in a DG that can push for the centrality of their concerns. Nor do they have the advantage of the multiple set of alliances that benefits the broad family of anti-exclusion movements.

Conclusions

This chapter has argued that some institutional factors connected to the process of European integration and national regionalisation have started to engender the construction of quasi-ethnic cultures and political movements in areas that were never peripheral before.[2] In various and usually weaker ways, a general emphasis on a regional dimension has emerged on a wide scale in Europe. Corresponding to this weak regionalism is a stronger variant which is residual in traditionally peripheral regions.

While weaker regionalism accompanies the conflicting phenomena of either the emergence of a new bourgeois particularism grounded in a collapse of ideals of social solidarity (Harvie 1994) or a stress on social democratic ideals of solidarity and re-distribution, the stronger version remains circumscribed and marginal. Bourgeois and social democratic regionalisms have become the mainstream in European political cultures and can be set in relation to the cultural dominance of a particular European brand of technocratic liberalism. They exhibit a clear connection with the processes of European political and to some extent cultural integration. This includes a largely but not completely instrumental use of the regionalist idiom, whereby identity claims are flaunted for instrumental reasons. This has been referred to as the 'strategic essentialism' thesis (Achleitner 1997; Conversi 2002; Spencer and Wollman 2002: 169–172). Strategic essentialism is a justificatory strategy in which territorial identities are manufactured *ex novo* or emphasised in order to argue for the exceptionalism of specific areas which would justify claims for additional resources or decision-making power from other levels of governance.

To the extent that mobilising identities can be politically profitable, all political formations can and often do attempt to use the regionalist discourse. However, there is another kind of strong regionalism documented in this chapter which, although marginalised at EU level, retains strong roots in peripheral populations and has some EU-level impact.

Clearly the boundary between the instrumental assertion of ethnic identity in its absence on the one hand, and the magnification of territorial identities and its substantial shared acceptance on the other, is difficult to determine, and it varies over time and among individuals. There are reasons why in recent years local territorial belonging has acquired fresh importance for everybody: in particular, a general decline of nation-states as the dominant source of identity has been noted since the end of the division of the world into opposed blocs (Alonso 1995). But this re-definition does not have the same significance for historical regions. Historical nations have constructed these identities over centuries and their long-standing political mobilisation has an importance that sets them apart in typological terms, regardless of instrumental utilisation by political actors in other contexts which remain of a weaker kind. This weak variant is connected to the development of regional policy at EU level, and it is generally regarded as part of a pervasive structural tension between interacting units – states and regions – in a multi-level decision-making structure.

Summary

This chapter has argued that there are two types of regionalism operating in Brussels: one which is radicalised but marginal and has arisen from three historical trajectories; and one which is weaker but dominant. It has been argued that these different types of regionalism have different relations with EU institutions, which have coopted the weaker form in order to provide legitimacy for the process of EU construction but have marginalised the stronger form, while nevertheless adopting elements of its political philosophy.

Notes

1 Interviews were conducted in 2000, 2001 and 2002 with five MEPs; three Commission officials – one administering language programmes; support personnel in the EP; language-protection NGOs; EFA non-elected activists and supporters; and six employees in a sample of regional offices of regions with minority nationalist movements and parties and two in those of ordinary non-historical regions.
2 For instance, Spanish regions are emulating the Basques and the Catalans by emphasising local identities and demanding more power, and a connected set of cultural and political movements has emerged in areas with no real distinct historical background. Similarly, small and very small regionalist movements are emerging in Italy, such as the Lega Emiliana in a region – Emilia Romagna – which has never previously had distinct territorial movements. This phenomenon is connected to a process broader than the one affecting stateless nations.

6

Europe and movement advocacy coalitions

On the basis of the three case studies, this chapter draws general conclusions on the role of MACs in Brussels and presents a model to frame the interaction between MACs and EU institutions. Because MACs exert their influence in several different ways, this model will be of necessity a complex one encompassing dynamics at all three of the levels considered – political and social dynamics as reflected in domestic, EU institutional and policy community arenas. The relationships between these may produce inconsistencies, tensions and unexpected events that affect the impact of MACs. By looking simultaneously at the three arenas of member states, policy communities and EU policy communities, this chapter will examine the processes that have determined such impact, but first this must be assessed in comparative terms.

MAC outcomes and the Gamson scheme

A useful scheme with which to consider cases simultaneously was proposed by William Gamson in his seminal *The Strategy of Social Protest* (Gamson 1975). Gamson examined a sample of movements and evaluated their impact on policy in terms of the integration of activists in decision-making structures – a variable that he named 'acceptance' – and the fulfilment of movements' demands – a variable which he named 'new advantages'. Briefly, Gamson cross-referenced these two sets of variables, noting that movements can be accepted or rejected by institutions, and that they can be successful or unsuccessful in producing one of four possible outcomes. These four outcomes can be categorised as follows: full response for accepted successful movements, cooption for accepted unsuccessful movements, pre-emption for non-accepted successful movements and collapse for non-accepted unsuccessful movements.

Gamson sought to determine the features shared by successful movement groups, identifying a set of variables that explained the outcomes of challenging groups. The variables he identified and examined were generally related to the unequivocal social movement character of the groups that he examined – that is, their role as disruptive forces and political challengers, one which does not similarly apply to advocacy coalitions. However, some of the variables that he examined will be considered later in this chapter, while several further ones will be added.[1]

Looking back to the case studies, their success can now be assessed in terms of the following two dimensions: the ability to achieve policy objectives and the ability to gain recognition as a legitimate policy actor, i.e. as a source of valid policy ideas, and therefore be included in decision-making. This classification will provide a framework within which to explain the outcomes of the three coalitions. However, before applying this organising scheme to the case studies, the outcomes must first be considered globally across the three arenas considered. This is not difficult because the three arenas are integrated by the EU multi-level governance structure, which gives rise to discrete outcomes that can be classified in terms of the quantity and quality of legislation acting in the direction advocated by movement advocacy coalitions.

Considering all the cases, it appears that no coalitions fall within the doubly negative category of exclusion from institutions and absence of advantages. There are no coalitions unsuccessful in terms of policy achievements and whose activists are rejected in Brussels. Coalitions of this kind would be irrelevant in the EU institutional context. For instance, there are groups in Europe constituted by radical anti-globalisation activists which achieve only very limited acceptance and policy success but are still able to maintain a public presence through their media visibility. But they are unlikely to be represented in Brussels because they would be screened out by the lack of Commission funding, by lack of access and by their ideological refusal to engage with mainstream policy actors. For this reason, this category is not covered by this study.

Of the remaining MACs, the environmental coalition was rapidly incorporated, and soon achieved advantages, even before it had a legal basis. Analysts have pointed out that in the 1967–87 period alone the Commission successfully introduced over 200 directives, regulations and decisions in a manner relatively unaffected by political events and in a period of general de-regulation. The impact of this coalition has subsequently grown and has been noted by several scholars (Judge 1992), even if interviewees have recently reported that it is undergoing a period of retrenchment. It should therefore be placed in the category of full response. The other two MACs have been less clearly accepted and differ in terms of advantages. Anti-racism was for long the subject of supportive statements by all EU institutions but with very modest policy results (Ruzza 2000a). Anti-racist institutional activists had established a base in the EP and the Commission, and anti-racist campaigners had easy access to them, but the absence of a legal basis, a development blocked by several member states, hindered progress. Thus, until the approval of article 13, the anti-racist coalition could be classified as a clear example of cooption. However, in recent years a flurry of activities has re-defined the outcomes of this coalition and gradually changed it into a 'full-response' model.

The regionalist coalition has remained marginal throughout the period in question. Despite the importance of ethno-regionalism in several of the large member states, its expression in Brussels is restricted to a base in a few regional offices, a small party in the EP, and a very limited presence in the NGO sector. This MAC's achievements are therefore modest. Some of its cultural demands – notably for additional resources and for status to be given to minority languages – have met with a measure of success, but its more political ones, such as the demand for a proper regional second chamber, have not been fulfilled. Yet the language of regionalism has been appropriated by most regions – often more powerful ones without a reasonable claim to cultural exceptionalism but with a propensity to use these claims strategically, as the literature on strategic essentialism suggests (Achleitner 1997). Throughout the period, we can therefore classify the outcomes of this MAC as 'pre-emption' in the Gamson scheme.

Why, if taken over the long period, has the trajectory of the three movement advocacy coalitions positioned them as they are? The answer to this question depends on the one hand on choices made by the MACs – that is, internally driven action on issues such as how to frame their grievances or what organisational structures to put in place – and on the other hand on external factors such as the political opportunities made available to MACs by wider political structures and changes.

Each MAC has encountered different problems, in terms of being uniquely located in terms of political opportunities, and in being framed differently in terms of ideas. Problems, politics and ideas have been defined in different ways at the three levels of decision-making considered. As distinctive policy systems, each of these three levels has reacted to the combination of problems that has emerged over the years, the political calculations that have induced actors to frame them in particular ways and to emphasise or downplay them and the ideological baggage that has similarly conditioned their readings of the situation.[2] In this chapter, the three arenas which impact on movement advocacy coalitions will be considered in turn. The hypotheses put forward in chapter 2 will be returned to. Each level of government will be addressed directly, prior to a consideration of the ideational aspects of the various coalitions at each level. This will involve a review of their framing strategies and their outcomes, and of the political opportunities that they have enjoyed in specific environments. Thus, a simultaneous assessment will be undertaken of the structures and processes that advance and hinder movements' goals, the level of access open to different movement advocacy coalitions, questions relating to the type and quantity of resources available and to the motivation of both activists and institutional actors and questions relating to MACs' impact on policy-making.

On the basis of interviews and documentary analysis, it will be argued that institutional dynamics pertaining to elites' preferences and institutional set-ups have had a decisive influence on outcomes. It will be demonstrated that public opinion has had a role in shaping the context of decision-making and that the interaction between MACs and public opinion has oriented the strategies of several actors. These outcomes suggest a model that is in part based on a pluralist view of politics where public opinion determines outcomes, and in part on an elite view of the political process in which the preferences of institutional actors are important. In the words of Giugni and Passy, this is an interactive model of movement outcomes:

> We think that social movements do shape the general public's preferences, which in turn influence public policies and that political alliances do provide crucial opportunities in the institutional arenas. Yet, in order to force the powerholders to engage in substantial policy reform, it is necessary to have the joint and simultaneous presence of a strong social movement and either a favourable public opinion or the action of a major political ally in the institutional arenas. (Giugni and Passy 1998b: 8)

This model should be further elaborated to take account of the complexity of the EU environment; for it is an environment, it is argued, in which framing processes acquire particular importance. This model will now be presented visually and then illustrated in the rest of the chapter.

Briefly, this model posits that there are three sources of influence through which MACs affect EU-level policy. The first consists of the member states, whose actors exercise their advocacy on the basis of electoral considerations – considerations which include which policy areas to Europeanise, which orientating policy principles to select and which institutional set-ups to push. The second source of influence is the action taken by EU elites to stimulate the process of European construction through the selection of which areas to prioritise, and attempts to re-orient sectoral policy principles. The third source is dynamics taking place within policy communities. Here the impact of MACs comes about through the advocacy of bureaucratic units, which in turn relates to the bureaucratic politics of specific policy units, the ethical considerations of institutional activists and the specific impact of MAC opponents. As was pointed out in detail when discussing the case studies, such opponents differ according to the policy area: they are typically sectors of industry in environmental policy, coalitions of member states and sectors of the Commission like DG Competition for ethno-regionalists and neo-liberal sectors of the Commission opposed to social policy for anti-racists.

When presenting the results, a useful distinction to be drawn is between cultural factors relating to the content and salience of public opinion on the policy issues raised by MACs, or the framing of issues, and the political filtering imposed by actors on the basis of institutional dynamics (figure 6.1).

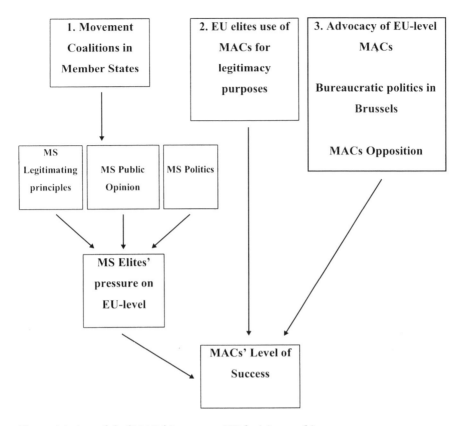

Figure 6.1 A model of MACs' impact on EU decision-making

MACs and influences from the member state level

The hypotheses set out in chapter 2 in relation to the first arena (the choices of governmental actors and the impact of public opinion) concern the role of movement ideas embraced by European public opinion, which were connected to the electoral considerations of policy-makers (H1). It was also posited that certain ideas are important for the self-definition of states (H1a, H1b), for the economic interest of regulating issues at European level – that is, why and when states have decided to Europeanise specific policy areas – (H1c, H1d), and for the possible impact of regulating an area without having to formulate redistributive policies, which was mentioned in the context of both the national and EU level. These variables have influenced the framing strategies available to advocacy coalitions and the political opportunities engendered, which will also be considered.

Public opinion
As pointed out, the importance of advocacy coalitions has varied significantly at the domestic level. A vast array of social concerns, controversies and crises

agitate the political and media agendas at any point in time, and they are likely to be reflected in public opinion and possibly be transposed to international and supranational arenas. Public opinion is generally regarded as a key factor in determining movements' impact. Some scholars have claimed that it is the strongest predictor of the impact of movements (Burstein 1998). Others see the impact of movements as related to the structure of the state. For instance, where policy networks are state-dominated their impact is presumably less marked than in society-dominated policy networks (Risse-Kappen 1994; Risse, Ropp et al. 1999). But it is nonetheless related to movements' popularity.

Public opinion was a significant factor in the success of the environmental coalition but a less important one for the anti-racist coalition, and one difficult to use for ethno-regionalist coalitions as these have widely different saliencies in different contexts. This finding needs to be explained with reference to the specific nature of EU-level dynamics.

One should emphasise that the environment – the focus of the most successful MAC in terms of activists' acceptance and movement-inspired legislation – is also the main concern for European public opinion.[3] Environmental advocates elicit more trust than governments as a reliable source of environmental information. A sizeable proportion of Europeans are preoccupied by environmental issues and they have faith in environmentalist organisations. The relevant factual events are those that have triggered an EU-level policy crisis justifying successful attempts to Europeanise this policy area. The environmental movement has been boosted by a series of environmental crises which have attracted international attention and highlighted the need to tackle environmental issues at the supranational and international levels. Notable examples include the 1986 Chernobyl disaster and the 1995 Shell Brent Spar episode. These and several similar events have caused great concern to European publics over the years.

When migration and racism became controversial with the massive influxes of the 1990s, free circulation among the Schengen countries and increasing attacks against migrants, the EU produced the legislation that had been unsuccessfully advocated for years and began the process of Europeanising the policy area. Nonetheless, anti-racist issues are not particularly popular with EU publics. It has been argued that low-level racism is dominant in both public opinion and in the media representation of migrants and minorities (Van Dijk 1992; Bell 2002). Yet, new legislation has emerged in the area, anti-racism has acquired discursive salience in the declarations of heads of states, and anti-racist campaigners have been included in decision-making fora. This reflects the issue salience that the policy area has acquired, and as will be argued below, its direct connection with dominant human rights discourses. In addition, the rapid Europeanisation of the area and the emergence of anti-discrimination law in the absence of supporting public opinion is also evidence of a strategy by member states to Europeanise unpopular issues which would cause difficulties if regulated at national level.

As for regionalism, despite the recurrent political violence that marks ethno-regional conflicts, regionalist issues have never been put forward as global European problems by the media or political forces. Public opinion has not mobilised in favour of radical regionalist policies, partly because there has been no perception of a policy crisis to which it was imperative to respond. Despite general acceptance of devolution throughout Europe, the field has evolved largely by neglecting the claims to exceptionality advanced by 'historical nations'. It should be noted here that on the one hand the existence of regionalist policies may have pre-empted the formation of both a strong body of public opinion in favour of ethno-nationalism and the consequent cultural and social policies. On the other hand, unlike the environmental and anti-racist movements which tend to address pan-European problems, such as environmental crises and large migratory flows, regionalist issues arise in relative isolation from each other, defeating attempts to Europeanise the field. Thus, for instance, a common EU approach to regionalist parties with links to radical organisations has not emerged.

To summarise the point, differences in public opinion on the three MACs in terms of their differing saliencies, if not of favourable attitudes towards MACs, shape the political opportunities made available to them by state actors. But this happens counter-intuitively, with salient but very unpopular and very popular issues more likely to be Europeanised, but for different reasons. Evidence from the case studies suggests that, in the case of the environment, Europeanisation was a precondition for the effective action demanded by voters, and a consequence of the political pressure applied by industry, which will be considered later.

A separate consideration pertains to the salience of issues. Here it should be also noted that environmental issues are in principle of concern to the entire European population, and with globalisation so are migration issues, while ethno-regionalist issues are limited to pockets of public opinion. In terms of voters, environmental concerns are a potential motivator for the entire population, anti-racist concerns for non-white citizens and for a conscience constituency, and ethno-regionalism for a relatively small portion of the population.

Member states and politics

While events like the Chernobyl disaster, attacks on migrants and ethno-nationalist protests and terrorist activities have had a profound impact on European public opinion, their political consequences and their EU repercussions have been mediated by national political factors. As the social movements literature points out, national protest movements are dealt with differently by different ruling coalitions (see Kriesi, Koopmans *et al.* 1995: 55–81). Different political cultures – some more open to external challengers and some closed to them, some more oriented to formal incorporation and some less so – react differently to movements, promoting or hindering their institutionalisation in the conventional political realm (see Kriesi, Koopmans *et al.* 1995: 215).

At EU level, several of these national factors have been evened out by the different priorities assumed by ruling coalitions in the EU at any point in time. However, the threat of a veto is sometimes sufficient to enable even one single government to block achievement of objectives dear to a particular movement. For instance, the example has been cited of the UK's role in hindering progress of article 13 of the Amsterdam Treaty, and the subsequent set of anti-racist initiatives which were made possible only by a change of government. National differences are also minimised by the EU's typical strategy of tackling problems by stimulating their resolution in debating fora, by 'technicalising' them and, as noted by one interviewee, by 'throwing money' at them. Thus political controversies provide political opportunities for MACs by making their causes appear worthy of funding, research and institutional debate. However, as anticipated, the salience of issues in national politics and their immediate relevance for voters ultimately has a decisive impact, as has also been argued in relation to the conditions that induced France and Germany to support article 13 (Bell 2002), or as the popularity of environmental concerns with the electorate suggests.

On the basis of these considerations, the politics of environmentalism, with its immediate relevance for large numbers of voters, has achieved key and unequalled impact. The fact that environmental issues are more of a general concern than issues of social exclusion or regional marginality has a political significance which is reflected by the importance of environmental regulation at EU level, and it has also had an enabling impact on the environmental advocacy coalition, which found an earlier and stronger institutional basis in DG Environment, greater openness and resources than the other coalitions.

With the growing impact of migration, the anti-racist coalition has grown in importance, but one essential and enduring difference between the coalitions is that anti-racism has been generally embraced by the left, from which it has received resources but is also a marginalising factor. Thus, to the variables 'issue salience' and 'public value orientation' one should add the political framings of issues in relation to electoral politics. Similarly to be noted is that ethno-nationalism has been confined to peripheral areas which have similarly remained marginalised. Conversely, environmentalism has been able to span – in different forms – the left–right divide. Not only has it been accepted and used instrumentally by sectors of business and the service industry, but it has been widely framed as a central political concern. This is a prime reason why environmentalism has been more easy to institutionalise throughout Europe: it has not caused Council splits on the left/right divide in the same way as anti-racism has done. To sum up the point, elite state actors channel issues to the European level in view of short-term considerations which include the necessity to respond to a perception that problems are escalating. But as they do so, they bear in mind the impact of this channelling on electoral politics.

There are further factors that stimulate the Europeanisation of issues and result in the possible impact of transnational MACs. Internationally debated problems are more likely to be transposed at EU level – one thinks, for instance, of the discussions on the Kyoto summit, and the way in which they resonated within EU institutions. Natural disasters or social crises like the recurrent attacks against migrants in the mid-1990s push an issue up the political agenda. Europeanisation also takes place in areas where governments must make choices unpopular with their electorates. This again is the case of environmental issues, where strict environmental standards encounter significant internal opposition raised by vested interests. This consideration may also help to explain anti-racist policy which, to the extent that it is not fully approved by the electorate but is necessary for the reasons previously mentioned – notably labour market and international legitimacy considerations – is most conveniently dealt with at supranational level (Bell 2002).

In relation to both environmental and anti-racist coalitions, a key role has also been played by principles affirmed globally as components of state identities. These two coalitions have supported ideas embedded in international regimes and, as revealed by text analysis of UN documents, whose supranational treatment can be considered a logical extension of their international status.

The political considerations that induce member states to support MACs at EU level must be supplemented by economic ones, and in this context with the role of political opponents, a factor which also concerns the amount of re-distribution that different policy areas require. The three coalitions have been successful to different extents in re-defining interest competition so that it is compatible with their goals. As mentioned in the case studies, the environmentalists have been more successful, partly because the structure of environmental policy is crucial to a broad array of organised interests and political forces. Environmental policy is a fully horizontal policy in that it permeates the deliberations – notably the economic considerations – of communities and business. Economic concerns exert direct influence through interest associations and indirect pressure through public opinion. The success of environmental policy has also been due to the nature of the field, which permits the achievement of higher environmental standards while leaving many power relations unchanged and simply passing additional environmental costs on to consumers. Also, as noted, the business community is split on environmental regulation, with a sizeable component advocating it and then utilising it for first-mover advantage, product standardisation, etc. The strategy has proved less viable for the other coalitions because, as said, anti-racism involves a reallocation of resources among social strata, and regionalism among territorial areas. There is indeed a cost in allowing racism to proliferate in the job market, as anti-racist advocates point out. However, it is a cost which is difficult to quantify, which does not result in systematic organised pressure by vested interests, and which is often borne by the weakest and least represented sections of the population.

Economic concerns are paramount for regionalism. Operating in Brussels is an extended network of regional offices engaged in cooperation and competition which, as mentioned, may use some of the principles dear to regionalists for instrumental purposes. The contribution of regionalists in this field is at best limited, given that it is diluted in a wide and important system of regional interest intermediations, and even for historic regions the participants in this field are only rarely committed regionalists.

All the strategic choices on how and whether to support an EU-level MAC have been made by member states at specific points in time. Electoral considerations, economic considerations and the diffusion of unpopular policies at EU level are all variables heavily affected by timing.

The arena of EU policy formulation

As in previous chapters, when considering the second arena, the focus here will be on the framings and political opportunities of EU elites and the impact of other actors on agenda-setting and policy formulation. Weiler (Weiler, Haltern *et al.* 1995) has described this arena as concerned with the primary legislative agenda of the Community (enabling legislation and principal harmonisation measures), and as involving Community institutions together with governments. As previously noted, in terms of actors at this level, special attention should be paid to the work of policy shapers. European institutions, and particularly the Commission, are hierarchical organisations in which only a minority of actors are specifically involved in policy development – estimated as the order of a few percentage points (Stevens and Stevens 2001). At this level, analysis has also concentrated on the ideational content of policies in relation to MAC pressure.

There is an overlap between this level and the subsequent one of detailed policy-making of an implementing nature proposed by Weiler in his typology. Nonetheless, it is useful to keep the two levels separate, differentiating like Weiler (Weiler, Haltern *et al.* 1995) the sociological level of interactions and networking in the policy environment from law-making having the more direct impact of member state influence and EU legitimacy considerations. Empirically, aspects of the policy design function are shared by, for instance, heads of units who also have management and lower- level policy functions.

There are thus two aspects to be discussed separately: the framing of policies and the attitude toward MACs of EU institutional architects. As regards the first issue, specific attention will be paid to whether the EU policy machinery tends to select policies functional to a goal which it is institutionally charged with pursuing: the advancement of the European dimension.

Selection and frame bridging

As reported when discussing the case studies, in-depth interviews were conducted in the areas of environmental, anti-racist and regional policy at EU level, the aim being to examine the interaction between MACs and EU institutions. For each of these three areas, various actors involved in interaction were considered, with a focus on their framings of issues. Each of the MACs had wide resonance in European societies and comprised a set of social movements recognised for their main claims – masterframes in the language of frame analysts – which articulate the following concepts: that the environment is neglected in modern society and 'environmental sustainability' is essential; that racial prejudice is rampant and damaging to minorities; and that regional cultures are marginalised by nation states.

The processes by which these claims were made relevant in specific institutional settings (frame alignments for frame analysts) were examined in order to determine how emerging framings of movements had helped or hindered their institutionalisation and their impact. In particular, the masterframe of each movement was considered, particularly the extent to which this frame was incorporated by state actors (and therefore how it played a role in their electoral calculations), EU elites and Brussels-based policy communities. Particular attention was paid to which specific institutional domains were able to utilise dominant frame bridges, and whether new emphases and reinterpretations of existing frames emerged. On the basis of the findings derived from this, it is now possible to consider the process of framing as a process of discursive selection in which EU institutions incorporate and modify the approaches of certain movements while marginalising others. It will be useful to begin with a brief summary of the findings yielded by the frame analysis of the three movement advocacy coalitions conducted in the case studies.

Environmentalism

The case studies showed that this movement had many key objectives and approaches, ranging from an anti-modernist ethos through environmental aspects in relation to social justice to a focus on environmental lifestyle commitment. All these components were subsumed by the term 'environmental sustainability' – a goal pursued by a variety of small movement-parties, epistemic communities and NGOs. The components most easily institutionalised in the politics of member states were those whose objectives were well encapsulated by the key term 'sustainable development'. The latter is a condensing metaphor, a social utopia of a society that, while continuing to progress economically, prevents fundamental damage to the environment.

In part because of its very ambiguity,[4] the concept of sustainable development has permitted the movements, together with sectors of industry, to put themselves forward as legitimate partners with governments in the development of solutions to environmental problems. The idea of sustainable development can thus be considered to be an instance of frame bridging in which the concept of environmental protection supported by the environmental movement has merged with the concept of development crucial in the policy language of European states. 'Sustainable development' also resonates well within EU institutions. This bridging has been crucial in creating the cultural and structural conditions necessary for a set of accommodations resulting in a powerful environmental MAC at Community level (Ruzza 1996).

For EU elites it has been a way to carve out a special role for European-level policy-making that takes account of the need for legitimate areas of intervention. The EU has stressed the pan-European dimension of environmental threats, emphasising that much environmental regulation has emerged from European institutions in a situation where environmental policy was virtually absent in several southern member states, and therefore the EU was able to produce something that citizens wanted and needed and which states were not providing to a sufficient extent. In other words, the framing of environmental regulation gave rise to a discursive attempt to achieve a measure of output legitimacy (Scharpf 1999). Furthermore, the legitimating role of environmental policy has continued over the years, remaining a popular and legitimate area for EU intervention (Flynn 2000).

Thus, in terms of frame bridges, merging *sustainability* and economic *development* was one possible frame bridge that made a social movement discourse appealing to a new range of actors and in fresh institutional contexts. These included EU policy-makers with a pro-industry ethos and business actors who could accept a type of environmentalism compatible with economic and technological development, while rejecting 'back to nature' and 'small is beautiful' approaches.

Several processes and structures facilitated the emergence of frame bridges at all levels. Environmentalists, together with actors from industry, were included in a number of fora at local, subnational and national level, particularly in Northern countries which both led on environmental issues and had a tradition of involvement of civil society in decision-making. At the EU elite level, the abundance of environmental discussion groups and workshops provided opportunities to develop new environmental frames. In consultative committees the voice of OCS was influential in policy debates, and in policy communities the presence of committed institutional activists brought movements' views within the realm of comitology. An important role in developing frame bridges has also been played by expert committees where different national policy ideas – which experts are expected to represent fairly faithfully – are debated in a deliberative atmosphere more than in the light of scientific rationality (Flynn 2000: 87–88). To be stressed here is that the heyday of environmentalism has long passed, but basic policy structures are now in place, and to understand these one should refer to the initial stages of development of environmental policy. While movement activism and its impact on Brussels policy-making has now considerably diminished, and Commission officials report the greater impact of industrial lobbies and governments hostile to environmentalism, the frame-bridging influence of movements is by now institutionalised and pro-active environmental policy ideas remain available as tools in policy deliberation.

Regionalism

Demands for more regional autonomy are a constitutive element of a family of regionalist movements to be found in most EU member states, including the Basque, Catalan, Breton and Welsh movements. This is a long-established family of social movements, which are particularly strong in regions with minority languages and cultures. Their masterframe involves contesting the equivalence of nation and state ideologically inscribed in the political culture of European nation-states. For minority nationalists, their regions are nations and should be recognised as such; they should be granted the necessary political authority and their culture should be protected.

These movements are represented in EU institutions in several ways. There are umbrella parties and inter-groups in the EP which support regionalist parties and minority languages. There are Commission programmes that finance the protection of minority languages. And there are NGOs and regional offices of minority regions that promote regional cultural initiatives. At member state level, throughout Europe a process of regionalisation corresponding to the devolution of political authority has been in progress since the 1970s. One outcome has been a network of regional offices in Brussels and relatively powerful political institutions in some member states, such as regional parliaments and assemblies, which are often supportive of these movements' goals. Member states have accepted but re-defined the movements' claims by opposing all aspirations to statehood though supporting claims for autonomy. The strong version of regionalism espoused by movements of minority nationalists has been re-defined in terms of the emphasis by states on the emerging values of responsiveness to local specificity.

Thus re-defined, regionalism has become broadly appealing. As the literature on strategic essentialism shows,[5] strong regional identities can be claimed for opportunistic reasons even when their historical bases are weak or non-existent (Achleitner 1997). Demands for fiscal and administrative autonomy have permeated all regions, which have increasingly come to utilise the language of minority rights regardless of the historical foundations of their alleged distinctiveness. This is a political discourse that not infrequently joins an economic and a cultural claim to distinctive identity in order to legitimise demands for increased political influence. These developments are seen as positive by EU elites, which can use regional demands and EU-mediated regional financial empowerment to erode state power from below. The bridging metaphor of 'Europe of the Regions' and the connected issue of subsidiarity has acquired wide currency in EU circles but it is mainly limited to regions conceptualised as actors like any other interest group, not to regions-cum-nations as advocated by 'strong regionalists'. Strong regionalism with its cultural claims remains marginalised, despite the weak initiatives in the cultural policy field to support a 'Unity in Diversity' vision (Pantel 1999).

There is thus an objective dilution of the demands put forward by these movements, but in this context there has been a limited institutionalisation.

Regionalism has been re-defined from separatist self-determination and an emphasis on conflict with nation-states into a frequently proclaimed model of nested territorial identities able to coexist harmoniously.

Anti-racism

Racism is a problem that anti-racist movements have tackled using various approaches which reflect differences in national political cultures. These range from assimilationist approaches in which racial differences are subordinated to unifying concepts (such as the concept of 'citizen') to multicultural ones in which a cultural understanding of 'race' is inscribed as a component of a rich cluster of attributes that each culture possesses and whose respect is normatively stressed. In member states, reaction to attacks against immigrants has promoted the institutionalisation of anti-racism within the electoral left. Various areas have been singled out for attention. Particular focus has been trained on education, labour markets, trade union participation, social security, health and access to goods and services.

Anti-racism plays a role at EU level, where the concept of mainstreaming of anti-racism – defined as the pursuit of a racism-free society through a better *implementation* of existing legislation, an *increase of knowledge* of the causes and consequences of discrimination and a better involvement of *civil society networks* – acts as the dominant condensing metaphor that guides regulatory discourse. These concepts imply the normalisation of anti-racism and its inscription in a broad set of policies as a necessary if not taken-for-granted element – a horizontal policy to be entrenched in all common policies. The focus on implementation is connected to the concept of mainstreaming as stressed by connected MACs in order to combat other forms of discrimination, such as discrimination against gays and gender discrimination (Mazey 2001).

One of the main areas in which the EU has concentrated its efforts is the labour market. Its recognised ability to improve the functioning of labour markets is therefore applied to something different – the fight against discrimination. In this sense, 'mainstreaming of anti-racism' constitutes a frame bridge in which the EU applies its consolidated skills in the diffusion of horizontal principles across policy areas to the field of anti-racism – which is relatively new to Community action. By stressing the similarity of this area to other policy areas, the European nature of the threat, and the need to intervene so that racism does not hinder the freedom of movement of individuals in labour markets, the EU espouses a framing of anti-racism that is institutionally appealing and congruent with efforts to enhance European integration.

As noted, this preoccupation with popular acceptance has on occasion been criticised by NGOs in the field. For instance, an EU-level cadre from a Commission-sponsored network dealing with issues of discrimination noted that the Commission tends to encourage the participation of 'respectable' citizens' representatives in consultations to the exclusion of more radical ones. This has, for instance, resulted in the perception of an excessive inclusion of non-white affluent businessmen who are not representative of poor and discontented members of minority communities. Episodes like this explain some of the processes that underlie the formation of frame bridges.

The credibility of frame bridges depends on their political viability. Anti-racist frames remain difficult to bridge in a period of widespread preoccupation with the impact of migrations. Yet, the recent successes of the extreme right constitute a political opportunity for the anti-racist MAC, as some of the core values of Europe are called in question and political responses become necessary. Anti-racism is somewhat less usable, and less institutionalised in both member states and at Community level, but its importance is growing. At member state level it directly affects smaller constituencies, but it is entrenched in the values of the electoral left. It is discursively connected to the category of 'human rights' increasingly used by member states for self-definition, which gives it growing relevance. The concept of mainstreaming has resonated with the EU focus on freedom of movement, which is necessary for an effective integrated market. But when connected to migration it refers to an area still largely under state control. As Geddes notes in the case of migration policy, the consequence of 'lowest common denominator' decision-making is that a preoccupation with control overwhelms a concern with the integration of migrants (Geddes 1999: 181). This indicates another type of structure that orients the direction in which frame bridges tend to develop. The power of anti-racism as a mobilising metaphor at policy community level is restricted by the limitations of EU social policy.

Frame bridges and its structural determinants

There are several types of process and structure by which frame bridges occur within policy environments and between policy environments and general culture. Here only some of those most frequently apparent in the cases examined can be summarised. In addition to low-intensity modifications and re-definitions of policy discourses in which cross-fertilisation occurs between political institutions (and this is typically the case of consensus formation), frame bridges can arise as responses to crises, as a consequence of the multiple roles that institutional actors may come to play, and as a consequence of the role of movement sympathisers working in institutional environments.

Policy crises are thoroughly discussed in the literature and often related to social controversies in which a nexus of interactions emerges between the media, social movements and policy-making institutions. Public debates on social issues tend to focus on a limited number of issues at any one point in time. A few remain central for several years and result in articulated political and social controversies. Themes such as the environment, regional devolution and racism have attracted sustained attention and controversies, giving rise to social movements which in turn have contributed to magnifying them. In normatively charged issue areas such as these, specific events like environmental disasters or large influxes of asylum-seekers may give rise to the perception of a policy crisis – the widespread idea that a policy sector has gone adrift and that a radical change of direction is necessary. Crises compel interested actors to propose new policy ideas and structures, and they force debate. Thus policy crises are a general stimulus to construct frame bridges. The range of potential solutions varies, but the extent of the involvement of social movements and of the media are key variables in the diffusion of this debate and its articulation into distinctive and recognised positions.

The impact of crises varies according to the sector. One can distinguish between highly institutionalised sectors with long-standing policies and relatively new ones which are relatively non-institutionalised and characterised by wide-ranging debate. Processes of administrative and political personnel selection and the differential attrition of policy units shape frame bridges in these sectors. When a new policy area emerges – that is, when a previously under-thematised issue becomes politically salient, like the environment in the 1970s – policy-making institutions select new personnel. In some circumstances, such as a scarcity of qualified staff and pre-existing epistemic communities, the available personnel tends to share a common ideational framework. Secondly, there are processes of selective attrition. Participants in emergent and contested policy communities tend to remain involved to the extent that they have a normative commitment or an interest. This reduces the number of frames available at any point in time and promotes stable fields with similar negotiations over policy ideas (Ruzza 2000).

More established sectors face a dilemma between the preservation of existing practices and responsiveness to political challengers. The outcome may be institutional rigidity or negotiation over policy ideas and structures, trial-and-error approaches and purely reactive policy-making (Alink, Boin et al. 2001). All these mechanisms constitute structures for frame bridging. Policy frames emerge from negotiation with stakeholders, including MACs, from the subsequent justification of emerging practices in 'garbage can'[6] processes where problems and solutions are tossed in and taken out by different institutions, and from path dependent approaches (see several contributions in Steinmo, Thelen et al. 1992). In both old and new sectors, by straddling the tension between preservation and responsiveness, policy-makers select and import from society those ideas that are *most compatible with existing approaches*. Institutionalised social movements and MACs are accordingly in a strong position to offer viable policy discourses.

All sectors face special challenges when regulated at the EU level, where the value pluralism of national government must be reconciled. This is achieved not only through specific policy decisions but also through agreements on common framings – often appropriately encapsulated in 'framework' programmes – which may still be internally ambiguous and contested but which nonetheless constitute a reference point in which dominant national and partisan frames are bridged through key ideas such as 'mainstreaming' or 'sustainable development'. On the one hand, the bridges possible at EU level are those that prevail in member states at decision-making time, as governments want to minimise the cost of adopting new policies. Also, because of the EU's stringent decision-making rules, only policy ideas compatible with all members tend to be supported. This orients frame-bridging activity towards a minimum common denominator. On the other hand, there also emerges a specific type of EU crisis management that has been characterised as reformist (and therefore proactive in promoting frame bridges) but of low effectiveness (Alink, Boin *et al.* 2001).

A second structure that, particularly at EU level, facilitates frame bridging is the multiplicity of institutional roles that actors come to play. This refers, for example, to the case of civil servants who take early retirement and work for lobbies, or scientific experts selected to represent their governments, and the multiple role that straddles the divide between member state and EU functions. These persons can be referred to as 'boundary personnel', reflecting the fact that personal and institutional needs for coherence stimulate frame bridging (Ruzza 1996). A related category, which is pertinent to MACs, comprises institutional activists – institutional personnel whose first normative commitment is to a social movement (Ruzza 2000b).

To summarise, the processes by which frame bridges occur are processes of *institutionalisation* and of *selection*. Once publicly affirmed, dominant frame bridges underlie the creation of new institutions, and this has been evidenced by the case studies, where even in recent years a new set of institutions has been created with a mandate to actualise the policy ideas of dominant frame bridges. One might consider for instance the European Monitoring Centre in the case of anti-racism, or the CoR. In a period of multi-level governance, successful frame bridges are unlikely to remain confined to one policy environment. They will diffuse throughout the integrated policy system. There could, however, well be competition for framing issues between policy actor and levels of governance. Intentional frame bridging takes place at all the three levels considered. Heads of state represent activists' demands that are not strongly opposed by other interests. European elites favour proposals that imply more power for Europe. EU institutional actors operating on the basis of bureaucratic politics and normative concerns favour compatible policies. Unintentionally, frame-bridging processes emerge in the three sectors as taken-for-granted approaches connected to path dependency and 'garbage can' processes which become 'naturalised' in specific policy communities or in the culture at large.

Frame bridges can then be seen as a 'dilution' of social movements' ideas which make them acceptable to key social institutions; but the extent to which they succeed, and the reactions of political institutions, are highly variable. Several other variables come into play in the exercise of actual influence, and outcomes may differ widely: from full response to rejection, and from pre-emption to ritualised acceptance (Gamson 1975). Nonetheless, the acceptability of social

movements' ideas to broad social sectors plays a key role in the causation of outcomes. Re-defined environmentalist ideas such as sustainable development are
more acceptable to one of the main actors of environmental policy, namely industry. Re-defined regionalist ideas appeal to regional authorities and re-defined
anti-racist ideas appeal to welfare state regulators in a way that the original social
movement ideas did not.

At EU level, the institutional locations where processes of frame bridging
resulting from consensus formation may occur are the consultative fora whose
abundance characterises the EU system of governance. All the three policy
areas examined are likely to produce an interaction of EU and movement
actors, and a merging of frames which can empower these movements as well
as a set of actors connected to these movements for normative or purely instrumental reasons. However, this influence may be mitigated by the absence of
clear rules for inclusion in the policy process, and the weakness of some MACs
at member state level. Movement-related groups are, however, good test cases
for studying the impact of the transition from 'government' to 'governance' on
OCS. If the challenge of governance consists of a new and broader battle to
accommodate conflicting interests and discover ways to take cooperative
action, then social movements, and particularly institutionalised social movements, are at the forefront of this battle. Their hopes for policy relevance rest
on their ability to stimulate the formation of effective advocacy coalitions and
to feed innovative ideas into the policy process that can enable cooperation
among diverse actors.

Framings and EU institutional architects

The processes of frame bridging that emerged from all the case studies were
facilitated by the political culture of EU policy architects. EU policy-makers
with a pro-industry ethos were in agreement with business actors able to accept
a type of environmentalism compatible with economic and technological
development while rejecting 'back to nature' and 'small is beautiful' approaches.
Similarly, anti-racism and freedom of movement merged in the concept of
mainstreaming, which resonated with the EU focus on freedom of movement as
necessary for an effectively integrated market. Conversely, alternative framings
like anti-capitalist perspectives or re-distributive framings appeared to be marginalised. Regionalism was re-defined away from separatist self-determination
and an emphasis on conflict with nation-states in favour of a model of nested
territorial identities able to coexist harmoniously.

These findings can be extended to other movements which display similar
processes. Pertinent examples of mainstreaming as an alternative to more conflicting political framings are the EWL, where a similar stress on mainstreaming
has emerged, and the gay rights movement, which in Brussels is represented by
the ILGA network. Women activists argue that a focus on rights as individual

attributes and connected to civil liberties tends to prevail over the necessity of addressing the structural causes of discrimination.

As already noted, these frame bridgings can express instances of consensus mobilisation when they are intentionally pursued as a strategy, but they can also reflect consensus formation when they are of the unperceived, taken-for-granted kinds (Klandermans 1988). The distinction is only analytical as there are possible mixes of the two, but it is conceptually important. Consensus mobilisation as an operation which addresses the media and political arenas in strategically useful terms is the conventional concern of movement politics, and some organisations like Greenpeace are reputed to be particularly skilled in its use. In Brussels, activists belonging to all the three movements expressed doubts over the prevailing framing of EU institutions, but were willing to mediate on the way in which principles were framed and these framings were strategically manipulated.

Evidence of consensus formation emerged from interviews with Commission officials, in particular high-level officials whose qualified support for specific MACs was often articulated through its re-interpretation in terms of a dominant neo-liberal ethos and an interest in EU integration, which of necessity in recent years has included a concern for EU legitimacy. As frequently pointed out in the literature, legitimacy considerations are becoming increasingly important for EU elites in a period of seeming weakness and lack of direction in the European project. As the case studies show, this complex situation of interdependence produces mutual support between popular MACs and EU actors, despite substantial differences internal to the two environments – the social movement sector and EU institutions – and between them.

An initial distinction should be drawn between the approaches of policy-makers operating at the core of the thematic areas of concern to advocacy coalitions and of those at the periphery. At the core there is great sensitivity to movement approaches, as evidenced by documentary analysis but also by personal interviews with decision-makers. At the periphery, there is a weaker or even distorted application of the policy principles emphasised at the core. Thus, in terms of full acceptance of MAC policy principles, this concerns at best only a small subsection of EU elites. Generally, in the MAC-sensitive areas analysed, and specifically in the anti-racist and environmental ones, strong ideologies are expressed which are not representative of EU elites in general. While the DG Environment is not infrequently described as populated by 'ecological freaks' (Cini 1996) or as 'a green colony' (Pollack 1997) – though things have changed in recent years – in other areas of EU institutions there is outright hostility towards environmentalists. Similarly, as noted, motivated supporters of MACs perform anti-discrimination work at all levels, and this includes some civil servants, but concern with discrimination is weaker elsewhere.

In particular, the concern shown for environmentalism and anti-racism by committed sectors of the Commission and EP gives rise to a distinctive ethos which accepts the necessity of state intervention in these sectors more than elsewhere in EU institutions, where a relatively neo-liberal emphasis is more typical (Hooghe 2001). Also common is a qualified if not enthusiastic support for the project of European construction. In this sense, several senior officials seem to be engaging in two forms of activism, one pro-European and the other in favour of a specific MAC. In addition, their ideological orientation places strong emphasis on professionalism and pragmatism, which often prompts accusations of ineffectiveness against social movement representatives. EU elites and policy-makers are impatient when dealing with movement actors, whom they regard as lacking the professional standards of high-level information and efficiency that they expect from lobbyists. And the few neo-liberals and pro-marketeers among them are suspicious of ideologies and policies that clash with their neo-liberal credo of market primacy.

The currently widespread negative image of Europe is perceived as profoundly damaging by many civil servants, and accusations of a lack of transparency, of excessive bureaucracy and of remoteness and corruption are often deeply resented. Faced by what is widely perceived as a crisis, the EU elites interviewed were ready to keep an open mind and high accessibility and wanted to be seen as receptive to all representative expressions of civil society. Although, as the literature also suggests, national political cultures influence the kind of relations that officials establish with their clienteles (Hooghe 1997), national traditions more amenable to the involvement of civil society appear to prevail in the environmental and anti-racist policy contexts, with many individuals from Nordic countries involved.

Traditionally, the ideology of top-level decision-makers in Brussels has been at least moderately pro-integrationist (Hooghe 1997). Thus one should not be surprised to find a certain amount of zeal in connecting MACs' policy ideas with an integrationist focus – processes that should be classed as frame bridging. But joint support for EU integration and for MACs is not restricted to elites. It emerged from the three case studies that the Brussels institutional environment tends to develop relatively similar taken-for-granted assumptions about policy principles. Put in the language of institutionalism, in social movement-related fields there is a degree of normative isomorphism between regulators and regulated, advocates and politicians. Movements have a real effect, albeit in limited areas of EU institutions. There are shared evaluations of the relative merits of incorporating certain emerging transnational norms and the movements and lobbies that press to exert impact on policies, and there is even consensus on the long-term institutional goals, such as 'European construction', to which supporting certain movements may contribute.

'Consensus formation' is then useful in describing the 'taken-for-granted' unplanned processes involved in the creation of frame bridges which merge the dominant institutional concepts of the EU with its pro-market, integrationist, neo-liberal ethos and the concern of movement advocacy coalitions with environmental, regional and anti-racist issues. This process results from repeated interaction among different types of actors, some movement-related, others with political, institutional, technical and scientific backgrounds in larger and articulated movement advocacy coalitions, and it epitomises the processes that were observed in Brussels in undertaking this study. In particular, examples of consensus formation were apparent in the statements of institutional activists, who often appeared to join their pro-European values, a neo-liberal ethos and movement concerns together in merged frames.

Processes of consensus formation occur naturally in institutions as emerging frames are re-interpreted in terms of the main institutional ethos. Over time, the ideas of the movement advocacy coalitions have acquired uncontested naturalness – an indication of the success of all these movement advocacy coalitions.[7] These processes are facilitated by the fact that at the ideological level, processes of frame bridging constitute the integration of a well-developed and dominant but normatively challenged ideological system – that of liberalism – and a set of emergent but often under-developed ideological systems, which can acquire a more completed form in the different environments with which they interact. By applying Freeden's conceptual scheme, and with particular reference to the social movements examined in the case studies, it can be argued that the ideological completeness of EU liberalism comes in contact with the under-specified character of green ideologies on which the environmental MAC is based (Freeden 1996) and nationalist ideologies (Freeden 1998) on which the ethno-regionalist MAC is based and produces new ideological formations.

To sum up, the case studies show that movement incorporation – the joint process of acceptance of activists as members of policy communities and of their ideas – emerged as a result of a set of interconnected processes: the instrumental reasoning of EU elites pursuing a strategy to legitimate the European construction project; path dependent dynamics of selective recruitment and the consequent activist background of civil servants; policy learning by civil servants working in movement-related settings; bureaucratic bureau-shaping, budget-maximising strategies and personal self-advancement by bureaucrats.

The politics of EU institutional architects

As has often been pointed out, EU politics is frequently shaped by incrementalism. Once a theme appears on the policy agenda it will grow with time into an escalating set of measures, which may require studies, increasing budgets and stronger policy initiatives. This means that EU architects have often seized on topical issues which provoke strong social concern matched by insufficient governmental action in order to carve out a distinctly EU niche – a reason to justify European intervention (Cini 1996). Once a topic – for instance, environmental regulation, anti-racism or a regional culture – has become part of the EU agenda, a bureaucratic incrementalist logic may take over. Unlike in member states, where a change of ruling coalition may re-define priorities, and dilute the impact of the social events that have sparked policy initiatives, at the EU level social controversies often leave lasting traces. Problems which movement coalitions often label 'social problems' are therefore important in shaping policy agendas and sometimes in activating policy change.

The case studies thus paid special attention to factors that filtered the reception of social controversies by EU institutions. One such factor was the awareness by EU architects that EU publics consider a specific policy area to be of legitimate EU-level competence. There are fundamental differences among the extents to which the Europeanisation of different policy areas is accepted. Survey evidence suggests that environmental policy is consistently considered to be more a legitimate EU competence than the policy areas related to the other two coalitions. On average, this view was expressed by 66 per cent of Europeans over the period 1989–93 (Sinnott 1995: 265). In comparison, the ethno-regionalists' concern for cultural policy was approved as a proper EU area of intervention by only 39 per cent. The case of anti-racism is more complex, because it connects with the broad issue of human rights, in which respect it is supported by 80 per cent of the population, while in other connections it is less popular. As an issue regarding political asylum it is accepted as a legitimate EU concern by only 55 per cent, and as an issue concerned by immigration policy by 54 per cent. Other discrimination-related areas are equally unpopular. Action for women is supported as a European concern by 48 per cent of EU publics (Sinnott 1995: 265).

In addition to the legitimacy accorded to the Europeanisation of different areas, one must also consider their overall salience. Again, environmental protection emerges as more salient than other areas, including those related to re-distribution of resources at territorial level and for specific social groups (Sinnott 1995: 267). These considerations therefore highlight the overall greater importance of environmental policy for EU architects.

Policy communities

As regards this area, the characteristics of different MACs have already been discussed. With reference to the hypotheses raised in chapter 2, the presence of bureaucratic politics and of institutional activism at the level of detailed policy-making can now be evaluated. Specifically, the presence of budget-maximising and bureau-shaping considerations can now be evaluated (Dunleavy 1991) (H3); and in relation to institutional activism, whether or not institutional activists play a more dominant role in policy outcomes for social movements with substantial access to the established political structure can now be considered, as can whether or not the presence of government insiders matters for policy outcomes when the policy in question is highly complex or technical in nature (H3a).

Policy communities: problems and politics

The third level refers to what Weiler (Weiler, Haltern *et al.* 1995) identifies as a more specifically sociological terrain of relations within networks of policy-makers and advocates. It is at this level that most detailed decision-making takes place in specific policy communities, and it is at this level that it is possible to identify a set of reasons for social movement inclusion, or lack of it, that relate to the normative dimension, but also to the career considerations of civil servants. When putting forward the hypotheses here, the possible role of bureau-shaping and budget-maximising strategies is stressed (H3), as is the potential role of institutional activists in matters of high technical complexity and in situations of controlled access (H3a).

In general, all EU institutions are open to lobbying from pressure groups. There is an exchange of resources that differs somewhat among different types of groups and EU institutions. Briefly, pressure groups can provide technical information that would be too time-consuming, expensive or inappropriate for institutions to acquire independently. In performing this function, they are no different from private interests, and as for private groups rules of inclusion remain vague and often depend on personal contacts with EU civil servants (Saurugger 2002). This function was particularly evident for environmental groups.

Public-interest lobbies are also seen as important in all the three MAC fields because they can counter-balance the biased information provided by industry. Here an evidently controversial issue concerns the quality of the information furnished. The policy-making process needs accurate, comprehensive and rapidly available information. Public-interest lobbies find it difficult to acquire sufficient resources with which to perform this information-gathering role effectively. But even the limited information that they are able to acquire usefully supplements and counter-balances the information provided by private interests. In this regard, the kind of technical knowledge that environmental public-interest lobbies are able to furnish proves a very useful counterpoint to private interest representation; and it may be fairly specific, given that environmental groups have undergone a process of division of labour. The information provided by anti-racists and regionalists is of a more political nature. It is to some extent acquired by EU institutions through electoral channels and therefore relies less on help from broad movement advocacy coalitions.

Secondly, interest groups can provide a view of the preferences of specific groups and warnings as to the likely reaction to new policies in member states. This function is problematic for all groups because it is restricted by the associability problems which have been widely studied by the literature (Mazey and Richardson 1994; Greenwood 1997). Movement-lobbies are especially important because, insofar as they represent emergent constituencies and marginalised social groups, they often feed innovative ideas into policy-making. However, it is particularly difficult for movement-related groups to play this role, as their referent is ideologically fragmented, unstable over time and often unable or unwilling to decide on procedures of representation. For instance, some groups reject decisions based on voting procedures and seek instead to achieve consensus through extensive deliberation. As a consequence, decisions may take a long time and may not be considered binding by some members. This is a problem experienced to equal extents by all public- interest EU-level networks and which undermines perception of them as reliable. The lack of clear delegation mechanisms exposes all EU networks to the criticism that they lack internal democracy, and it rebounds negatively on the MACs that incorporate them. It is therefore a problem for environmentalists and anti-racists, but less so for regionalists, who are based mainly in small movement-parties and in regional offices which maintain links with the electoral process. In addition, time constraints on the role of MACs in an advisory capacity forces EU-based organisations to decide on policy positions with little or no membership consultation. This again justifies accusations that they lack transparency and accountability and applies to all movement advocacy coalitions.

A third function of groups is to help with implementation. Generally, EU institutions have no direct implementing role and must mobilise all the help and information they can in relation to implementation. This includes ensuring the transposition of legislation and ensuring the compliance of members. However, public-interest lobbies are often relatively powerless in influencing domestic decision-making at all levels of governance, and therefore have limited importance in the implementation process. They can, nevertheless, mobilise the voluntary sector, and in a period of generalised state retrenchment this may have a substantial impact on the implementation of certain policy areas like social policies. However, this ability varies substantially from movement to movement. The environmental movement has developed a pattern of dialogue which also involves industry, which has learned to avoid head-on confrontation whenever possible. The absence until recently of a legal base for anti-racist policy and the fragmentation of migrants' associations has limited this role, as well as the preference-aggregation role undertaken by the EU-based anti-racist movement. Ethno-nationalists are again in a very different position, because the regionalist organisations that support them in member states have limited implementing relevance.

Interest groups perform other functions as well, such as applying pressure on member states to accept EU policy proposals, but public-interest lobbies are often too weak to play a significant role in this regard. However, they can perform functions that are infrequently undertaken by other interest groups. They can legitimise sympathetic civil servants and political actors who propose legislation which is contentious because it is ideologically controversial, too costly, opposed by private interests, or opposed by other institutional sectors, or when there is a perceived need to legitimise particular institutional policy proposals with reference to civil society.

Additional functions more distinctive of public-interest lobbies concern their use of EU institutions as financial resources. An important and not infrequently central reason for the presence of these groups in Brussels is their ability to attract funding for specific research projects, pilot projects and occasionally for running costs. They can also divert funds from projects to running costs and thereby give substantial continuity to their operations. It is difficult to assess all relevant sources of funding, because for instance ethno-nationalists are able to influence the utilisation of structural funds and gain influence from them. However, once again, environmental budget lines for environmental organisations are, and have been in the past, larger than those allocated to groups working on anti-racism and ethno-nationalism, even if one includes the budget for proximate causes like language protection or migrant concerns (Sluiter and Wattier 1999; ECAS 2002).

In the EU context, pro-MAC politics is typically supported by institutions which 'host' MACs, and by the individuals who have been described here as 'institutional activists'. Institutional activists play a fundamental role in furthering the objectives of certain movement advocacy coalitions. They must deal with both bureaucratic policy-making organisations and social movements.

Even if institutional activists do not derive their commitment to movements from a specific organisation-based collective identity (they are often too busy or too cautious to participate in activist networks), they draw it from other sources which define them as participants in MACs. These consist in the moralisation of certain policy issues advocated by movements, their frequent personal histories of commitment to a movement, and reciprocal recognition of moralised participation in a collective effort against often well-defined opponents.

Civil servants and bureaucratic politics

Like other actors, top EU decision-makers have to decide on the basis of personal career considerations, but also on the basis of the long-lasting, pervasive and quasi-normative character of DG ideologies (Michelmann 1978), so that the difference between instrumental and principled considerations is difficult to discern when the two coincide. This is the case in areas such as environmental policy which are strong in one sector of EU institutions and weak in others.

Among MAC participants, and even among institutional actors, disillusionment with the workings of other areas of the institutions has spurred an interest in establishing a direct relation with civil society and in consensus-forming mechanisms. A traditionally embattled DG like DG Environment finds a certain compensation in the EP and external support for its tensions with other areas of the institutional framework, such as typically with the DG responsible for internal market and cohesion policies (Peterson and Bomberg 1999). Even in the absence of supporters, commitment to MAC causes may be to some extent self-sustaining. For instance, if the views of a Commissioner are at odds with the prevailing ethos of the rest of the bureaucracy, tacit but not ineffective resistance may ensue. Carlo Ripa di Meana, a former Environment Commissioner, pointed out in a personal interview that when a new Commissioner less committed to environmental standards was appointed, he found it difficult to counteract the strong environmentalist ethos of DG Environment. In Ripa di Meana's words, 'the machine just stops working, and grinds on ineffectively', so that 'the machine' would not completely shift in reverse: DGs have strong ideologies that cannot easily be modified, but administrative routines can be stalled from the top (Michelmann 1978). If there is a congruence of views between EU elites and other civil servants, the support of bureaucratic power has a substantial enhancing impact. Thus, both EU leaders and policy communities exert influence and may have reasons to support social movements, although they may not necessarily be the same ones.

Institutional activists

Within movement-oriented policy communities, the interconnection between institutional environments and movements is often close and enduring. Movement coalitions have important institutional advocates – institutional activists – and while their ideas have gained some currency throughout the institutional framework, their impact is stronger in limited institutional niches. They have learned from institutional niches in the Commission and the EP to triangulate across institutions in order to maximise their impact. In these inter-institutional spaces, the core movements' supporters are much weaker than are the complex networks of institutional activists, sympathisers, and sponsoring EU elites. Yet their presence makes a difference, as reported by both pro-movement and anti-movement actors.

The fact that a body of institutional actors supports movements from within institutional realms is important even if they are not in direct contact with activists. Institutional activists inject social movement ideas into institutional contexts through direct channels and have a margin of control over the frame-bridging strategies that emerge – the connections between dominant institutional goals and movements' objectives. In some cases, they are able to operate strategically, actively promoting processes of frame alignment (see Snow *et al.* 1986). Similar considerations on the importance of sustained interaction have emerged in the literature on advocacy coalitions, which also points to the lower information costs when there is close coordination among actors.[8]

Conversely, the incorporation of movements within institutions brought about merely through public opinion is subject to a great deal of distorted interpretation. Policy discourse is still influenced by movements, but it is a much more tenuous connection – one where care should be taken not to 'claim too much' for movements, because there will be so much 'background noise' that movements' ideas will be re-interpreted in terms distant from those posited by the movement.[9] This was the case of ethno-nationalism, which had only limited representation through personnel in policy-making functions.

If an institutional arena comprises no specific interests in maintaining more direct contact with movement framing, it becomes more likely that movements' goals will not be achieved, and that compromises will be less than satisfactory. The way in which the roles of activists and institutional actors overlap is therefore very important. This is an occurrence that is more frequent than social movement theory has so far recognised (an exception is Santoro and McGuire 1997).

Yet the movement cultures display an awareness of the importance, opportunities and limitations of institutional activism. Cadres and militants know, appreciate and often mention the importance of movement insiders in a variety of contexts, even if it is often difficult to identify them, given that in some cases activists will be keen not to be seen as such because their institutional credibility might be undermined. A case in point was the insistence of a director of an anti-exclusion network that the membership of civil servants in organisations like Amnesty International should be treated as strictly confidential.

The role of institutional activists was more clearly evident in the environmental field, whose technical nature made their contribution essential. Without their technical expertise, the NGOs' lack of resources with which to follow all the various stages of the policy process would result in the pervasive affirmation of industry's viewpoint. In less technical fields, their role was still welcomed by movement actors because they were instrumental in facilitating access, acquiring information about funding sources and supporting applications.

To sum up, movement discourse circulates even without a direct involvement of movement organisations, and it is able to reach and unite members of policy networks not directly connected to protest activities. Their commitment, moreover, may be crucial in the EU policy environment. As Majone points out: 'because uncertainty is so pervasive in policy making, the values of administrators and experts inevitably count a great deal' (1989: 26). Of course, the pro-active values of administrators count to the extent that the latter are in a position to promote change. This is so when the policy area in which they operate has a proper legal basis (or is able to operate without one, as was initially the case of environmental policy), adequate resources, a critical mass of committed administrators, etc. This was more the case of environmental institutional activists than of the less resourceful institutional activists in the social exclusion units.

Movement activists and their ideas

Movement advocates are often disenchanted with the limited policy results that they achieve, and the most radical of them are ambivalent about their role in Brussels. As mentioned in relation to Greenpeace, they fear that they may merely be providing legitimacy for a project of EU construction that goes hand in hand with what they see as the inequitable Western-driven globalisation of world culture, economy and politics. Nonetheless, they often express the conviction that their role is not simply one of active advocacy, but more generally serves to encourage policy learning.

On the basis of the case studies, it appears that while clear conflicts of interests are frequent and often involve private interest groups, it would be incorrect to interpret policy dynamics in simple terms of gains and losses.[10] An important function of movement advocacy coalitions – and, as emerges from the interviews, particularly of movement activists – is to help other actors re-consider their interests, or to form new policy preferences in the light of new information. This feature has been reported by activists, particularly Green activists, as one of their fundamental activities in Brussels. Thus, strategic action is helped by a number of considerations, such as the fact that, as Weir (1992) points out, when unexpected events occur, institutional actors do not necessarily know their interests, because the configuration of actions and likely consequences is too complex to evaluate. Faced with this uncertainty, a collective search for ways to respond to events gets under way in institutional arenas. During this process, institutional actors assess their full range of interests on the basis of their taken-for-granted assumptions and produce new frames and new decisions which become the antecedents for a path of connected events and their interpretations. Movement advocacy coalitions can help orient this process. But in other circumstances, processes working in the opposite direction have been recorded. For instance, an industrialist reported that he was ready to support other industrialists' positions even if this hindered his interests. Yet, when re-definitions of interests can be achieved, this counts as a success for the movements. In these instances, movements come to be incorporated by mainstream social actors on the basis of the validity of their arguments. When this happens, movements become a component of collegial formations engaged in policy deliberation. Collegial incorporation is different from the dynamics analysed by neo-corporatist theory. The environmentalists who have been described in the study of environmental policy in Brussels presented here are not being heard simply because they can cause disruption, or because they represent an identifiable constituency. In fact, the EU policy environment is relatively insulated against the direct threat of disruption, which is more effective at the national level.

Conversely, the neo-corporatist inclusion of advocacy groups – which also takes place and is typical of policy events in which no frame bridging takes place – sees interest intermediation as a sort of mere averaging of gains and losses. In corporatist intermediation, actors remain separate: business, labour and government representatives express crystallised social identities and configuration of interests. But this is often not the case in collegial incorporation. As the research undertaken in this study on the EU institutional framework shows, ideal packages emerge that join pre-existing discursive frames, such as the concept of sustainable development, which merges economic and environmental world views and grants environmentalists full participation in the policy process. MACs' demands are not negotiated simply because of their strength, but they are accepted as correct by relevant parts of the policy community. To all policy-community participants this is a form of pressure for normative isomorphism with their institutional environment.

These considerations call into question the issue of the prevalent type of relations among actors at EU level. As Greenwood notes, there is a prevailing view of all euro-interest associations as weak 'federations of national federations', often unable to agree and act upon meaningful common positions (see Greenwood and Ronit 1994). Furthermore, as he also notes, neither corporatism nor pluralism are system-level theories and empirically at EU level no blanket generalisations can be posited. The applicability of these theories has to be referred to specific contexts and, as the case studies document, there is great variation in such federations' ability to organise and perform in a united fashion. This depends on a variety of issues which have been studied in depth by corporatist theory, such as the ability of negotiating partners to control their base, to deliver on their promises, etc. or the state's ability to provide a stable framework in which resource exchanges take place. It is argued that the particular kind of institutional arrangement of EU institutions cannot deliver this stability. Nevertheless, corporatist theory, even in its meso-level version (see Cawson 1985) focuses on considerations of economic rationality which can also be applied to re-definitions of interests. Re-definitions take place because elements in the environment force a re-assessment of costs and benefits for specific categories, re-assessments on whether a particular unit belongs to a category, re-assessment of time uncertainties involved and re-assessments of the ability of representatives to represent. Negotiating partners, according to this perspective, continue to search for selective benefits. However, a different view is that if all partners are called to administer a public good directly they may in some circumstances engage in a search for that public good independently from the search for selective benefits. This would encourage a different stance – a stance that has even been seen as potentially more successful (see Regini 2000: 161). This different stance can be seen as inspired by the ideal-type of collegial interaction (see Waters 1989). The argument is advanced here that in the EU context there are pressures in the relation between public-interest groups and other negotiating partners to take this stand. As public opinion research shows, a fundamental resonance between social-movement views with public opinion and movements' representatives promote interests that are shared by large sectors of society (including business actors and civil servants), it is understandable that, at least to some extent, they may be incorporated in debates oriented by a genuine collegial atmosphere. In any event non-movement actors are aware of the provision of political legitimacy that derives from subscribing to movements' concerns.

Interactions between the three levels

As observed in this analysis of the impact of the three levels of movement, a set of different political actors has transposed the idealism of several previously successful social movements to the EU system of governance and integrated it in a set of complex advocacy coalitions. In addition to movement organisations, a number of conventional political and bureaucratic actors have also contributed to transferring the issues and ideas of social movement politics to Brussels.

All the themes discussed in this volume refer to powerful social controversies: the environment, the protests of regionalist movements and the issue of racism have all aroused and sustained media attention and popular debate. It is only in the course of these controversies that policy innovation becomes possible and the role of movement coalitions more relevant. In the course of these controversies, when new policy approaches become possible because there is a need to respond to a perception of crisis, the interaction between the three levels becomes focused on a search for alternatives. In other words, the 'three usually separate process streams – problems, politics and policy ideas – converge', and it is on the rare occasions when they converge that policy innovation becomes possible (see Majone 1996: 74). The interaction between the three levels is particularly poignant when this convergence occurs in the context of high-profile social controversies, such as those sparked or sustained by movement coalitions.

When this convergence comes about, it gives new relevance to, and may re-define, the way in which policy actors perceive their interests. The environmental disasters of the 1970s, the independentist movements that attracted sustained attention in the 1980s and the racist attacks against a new wave of migrants in the early 1990s were all mechanisms that sparked protracted social controversies and gave innovation opportunities to a range of policy entrepreneurs.

Without the controversies that make new policy ideas necessary, policy innovation would be less frequent. Without the favourable political conjuncture that makes new ideas viable, the new ideas would remain on the fringes of policy-making. The ideational dimension, the normative drive of movement advocates are important but, as Majone (1996) points out, it is the *convergence of problems, politics and ideas* that makes innovation possible – a possibility that the EU Commission in particular is well equipped to utilise in its favour. But, as stressed in all the case studies, effective triangulation between institutions also takes place to foster policy innovations. The EU level is distinctive in that policy innovation depends upon a variety of actors in different arenas.

Policy innovation of the type advocated by movement coalitions is distinctive. It involves a controversial dimension often not present in other policy areas, a normative element and the free donation of time and activism as mentioned before that sparks social controversies, involves a wider variety of actors than do other policy areas, attracts media attention and therefore takes place on a broader pan-European stage. It is of a kind that requires the interaction between the three levels: national politics, EU elites and EU policy communities.

Taken together, these studies demonstrate the existence of a great variety of initiatives on the boundaries between the movement sphere and institutional life. Much movement impact would be invisible if movements were conceived in isolation from their diffusion in institutional realms. Action promoted by movement activists in their role as institutional actors would be taken to be institutional action, and the social movements' contribution would be discounted. Policies internally formulated and institutionally promoted by movements would be regarded as outcomes external to their influence. By broadening the focus to encompass movement advocacy coalitions, a distinctive source of policy change can be identified. This is a type of action that differs from other forms of interest representation in that it is driven by the influential injection of energy, time, knowledge and resources by broad coalitions that last in time, defeating what critics see as the reactive, short-term character of movement politics. For MAC participants, this is an enduring battle, with victories and defeats, but it is one where normative standards ensure that actors remain committed for many years.

Consequently, success cannot be gauged within the narrow confines of a specific policy objective in a single location. Rather, it should be conceptualised as an integrated set of long-term impacts in a variety of cultural, political and even commercial environments, which constitute the background for specific campaigns and the terrain for interaction between EU and national movements. Success is the outcome of multiple interconnected processes of 'institutional housing' which cause movements to be taken for granted in a variety of political and social institutions and gives them institutional breadth and depth – the ability to permeate more than a few circumscribed areas of institutional life and to resonate in the political identities of a variety of actors (Krasner 1988).

Discussion

To summarise the findings of the previous sections, it appears that at all levels, public discourse and legitimacy considerations played a decisive role. Table 6.1 summarises the arguments so far developed in this chapter. Table 6.1 depicts a model of political opportunities which positions different movement advocacy coalitions in relation to their environments. The general importance of legitimacy concerns in relations between OCS and EU institutions, and therefore the importance of the timing considerations that have given so much more weight to OCS organisations in recent years, is evident from table 6.1. On the basis of this model, one can interpret the outcomes of other movements in Brussels. Here one can consider as an example the trajectory of the women's movement.

The EU-level women's movement
In applying the model outlined in table 6.1 to the impact of the women's movement on the EU policy environment one can start by noting that overall the outcomes have been positive for the movement. Specific political opportunities that helped this movement from the 1970s also contributed to its relevance at EU level, and in addition other specific reasons made it relevant at that level. As with previous movement coalitions, one has to differentiate between success in terms

Table 6.1 MAC support, by type of actors, according to the perceived importance of problems, politics and ideas

When are MACs supported?	Problems	Politics	Ideas
Intergovern-mental arenas	When they are EU-wide or there are strong coalitions of member states	When they give short-term advantages in electoral politics (give legitimacy)	When connected to transnational ideas as state-legitimating and constituting, when connected to transnational activists' networks (select)
EU elites' arenas	When they justify a EU role	When they favour long-term pro-EU politics When they refer to new policy issues with weak pre-constituted vested interests (give legitimacy/budget)	When address EU civil society Merge pro-EU, neo-liberal and social movement ideas (select)
Policy communities	When they allow budget-maximising and bureau-shaping strategies	When there is a group of institutional activists who allocate resources. When there are intra-DG rivalries (give legitimacy/ money)	Merge budget-maximising and social movement ideas (select)

of desired outcomes in several member states and processes of Europeanisation of both the policy area and of its advocates. One then has to focus on the extent and outcomes of such processes attempting to identify the specific contribution of the relevant advocacy coalition.

History of the EU women's movement

Gender issues were already addressed in the early days of the Union by article 119 of the Treaty of Rome. They were put on the EU agenda by the womens movement of the 1970s and women's rights received early attention in EU-level social policy (Hantrais 1995: 80). In the period between 1975 and 1992 six important directives were approved which addressed areas such as equal pay, equal treatment in employment and training, and some social security benefits. A series of action programmes then channelled resources and attention to gender equality, ranging from a focus on the workplace to attention to political representation, household division of labour and women's image in the media. A programme of institution building in favour of women was conducted successfully within the EU environment, and led to the creation of dedicated agencies and networks. Geyer stresses the willingness and ability of both the Commission and the Parliament to promote gender policy, and the positive impact of the ECJ (Geyer 2000b: 105).

These structures and initiatives have facilitated the goal of making gender issues into one important horizontal policy focused on the concept of gender mainstreaming throughout all policy areas.[11] These successes can be directly connected to the impact of the movement. Not only was the early EU emphasis on equal opportunities directly connected to the impact of the movement in the 1970s (Geyer 2000b), but the more recent goal of gender mainstreaming also found its original formulation specifically within the movement (Mazey 2001: 11).

In brief, as recognised by the literature, the EU environment has proved particularly favourable to the adoption of this movement's policy goals (Hoskyns 1996; Mazey 1998, 2001). Its ideas have been incorporated within the EU framework. Its structures, increasing legal base and resources have made it into arguably the most successful social policy area at EU level (Geyer 2000b: 9). And its policy initiatives have been an important tool in spreading the movement's goals and vision throughout Europe, particularly Southern Europe where without the movement it might have been more difficult to match the policy changes achieved in Northern countries. Of course, to recognise the important role of EU institutions does not diminish the acknowledgement of the persisting difficulties, rooted in cultural and political resistance but also more specifically in the obstacles to expand European policy to other areas, that it would be necessary to address in order to make a substantial impact on gender discrimination.

These outcomes can be interpreted through the model previously illustrated. In particular, starting with member state actors' approach to the women's MAC in Brussels, one notes that the movement has benefited from states' reaction to the interconnected set of problems, politics and ideas that the women's movement raised at the EU level but also by a set of specific reasons that helped its Europeanisation and its influence at EU level.

In terms of problems, as with the environmental movement, women's issues gained relevance in the agenda of EU countries by benefiting from a multifarious set of policy problems engendered by the changing role of women in society. For instance, as the proportion of educated women grew, and the number of women in job markets mounted, gender discrimination was put on the agenda of several member states, thanks also to the limited but growing entrance of women into political elite groupings.[12] Debates in the 1970s and after on legislation on controversial issues such as abortion rights constituted a political opportunity for this movement in some countries and became reflected in the electoral calculations of broad leftist coalitions. These state-level opportunities translated into EU policies owing to several distinctive factors.

EU-level opportunities

In terms of politics the electoral calculations of key member states which helped this movement early in the history of European integration were also related to a host of economic considerations which had a direct impact on EU-level politics. For instance, in discussing willingness to Europeanise gender issues with reference to the early days of the European construction process, the literature refers to calculations of an economic and electoral nature by the French (Hantrais 1995; Hubert 1998: 52–55; Geyer 2000b: 104) which led them to Europeanise gender measures to diffuse the costs that they had to incur at domestic level. Later, in the 1970s, gender issues benefited from the development of the facilitating structure provided by the 1974 Social Action Programme – a social policy framework in which gender issues played an important role (Geyer 2000b).

Other types of political opportunities can be identified in which electoral calculations of member states' actors have been transferred at EU level. Mazey, for instance, refers to the opportunities related to electoral calculations which emerged at several IGCs (Hubert 1998; Mazey 2001).

In terms of ideas, as stressed by the model discussed here and represented in table 6.1, in its successful transposition at the EU level the movement benefited from the assistance of transnational activist coalitions (Mazey 2001: 20) which promoted the frame bridge between women's rights and human rights more generally. An international moral definition of women issues (Keck and Sikkink 1998) and a cohesive coalition of northern Member States (Mazey 2001: 20) helped this movement to diffuse its ideas. The relative predominance of a socially progressive mood throughout the period of inception of gender-related policies has also been stressed (Hubert 1998; Mazey 2001).

In terms of its relationship to EU elites, as Mazey points out, support for this movement was connected to consolidating the policies and legal support of the EU (Mazey 2001: 22). Secondly, an attempt emerged to use social-policy initiatives to improve the legitimacy of the EU. In other words, as specified in the model, EU elites were attracted to the possibility of establishing a relevant new area of EU intervention and at providing political legitimacy.

In terms of policy communities, as with other movements, a prominent role was played by a cohesive and motivated group of feminist institutional activists. Several were active within EU institutions and were liaising with prominent academic feminists, thereby constituting an effective advocacy coalition at EU level (Hubert 1998; Mazey 2001: 24).[13] A growing number of institutional activists found arenas within the EP, the Commission and the Commission-sponsored EWL network from which they could dedicate time and energy to the movement's goal. As Mazey reports, within the Commission some twenty-five officials work full-time on equal opportunities (Mazey 2001: 27).

The model previously outlined and its possibility of application to other movements such as the women's movement, stimulates a reconsideration of political opportunity approaches when one considers their utility for advocacy coalitions.

An expanded Political Opportunity approach

POS approaches assume the separation of movements and institutions, and the centrality of political change for the expansion/contraction of movements. Both need to be qualified when the focus is not on movements but on movement advocacy coalitions at EU level. First, as the case studies have shown, sectors of movements and institutions tend to overlap with the passage of time. The POS model is effective in explaining the emergence and to some extent the transformation of movements, but it fails to account for their institutionalisation in the latter phases. Movement outcomes are often long-term, intermixed with institutional practices and not easily reducible to a linear causal relation between movement and institution. Essentially, over time, certain movements and institutions tend to merge, and it is consequently impossible to conceptualise them as separate variables: one must look instead at the institutional field and its internal dynamics. Over time, these cease to be separate, so that anti-racist activism increasingly arises from within churches, environmentalism is strong among bureaucrats, ethno-nationalist initiatives are spearheaded by the EP, etc.

Secondly, we may centre the analysis on issues of legitimacy, which have been under-thematised by POS approaches. On adopting an expanded approach to political opportunities which borrows its concern with interrelations among institutional spheres, and the incorporation of emerging ideas by institutions, from neo-institutionalism, the institutional need for political legitimacy can be seen as a crucial opportunity for movements.

The issue of the political opportunities available to movement advocacy coalitions in EU settings can be reinterpreted as a process by which two different political environments – the institutional environment and the movement environment – interpenetrate each other. Put differently, we are witnessing the gradual and reciprocal 'housing' of ideas, activists and policies between parts of the social movement sector and parts of the institutional sector. This is in effect a process of selection whereby certain sections deemed to be more compatible are mutually selected from the entire set of organisations, networks, individuals and ideas that constitute a movement and an institutional environment, so that collaboration thus begins.

Explanation of the willingness of state actors to transpose issues at EU level should not ignore timing considerations. These influence how emerging problems are dealt with. The willingness to Europeanise policy areas and the kind of policy instruments preferred have changed over time. Controversies sparked by the three coalitions have been characterised by the different configurations of possible solutions available when they occurred. Environmental regulation arose as a topical issue when an EU regulatory approach was the one taken for granted. When a legal base for environmental regulation was proposed, the EU was still unaffected by debates about subsidiarity, legitimacy and large-scale negative reactions to EU-level transfers of power. When the issue of racism received wide coverage in the media during the early 1990s the climate had changed, and the rapid institution building and policy development that supported the creation and expansion of DG Environment would have proved unfeasible, not least because of the more partisan nature of anti-racist policy areas (in terms of the left–right cleavage). Instead, the option taken was the rapid creation of an agency, the EUMC, but with restrictions on the institutional expansion of the area.

The crises which have put regionalism on the agenda have occurred on a longer time scale, and a crucial set of events or a period of policy development cannot be so easily identified. The development of regional policy has, moreover, been oriented not by issues of sovereignty and cultural symbolism but by market issues. Regional devolution in all the major member states, the EU's role in helping underprivileged regions and the related debate on subsidiarity have together contributed to the expansion and legitimacy of EU regional policy, not of the EU regionalist MAC. A protracted crisis can also be identified as regards regionalism if one considers the social emergencies provoked by a variety of violent ethno-territorial movements in Europe. But these have been portrayed by the media and by state actors merely as internal problems for which no European solution could be envisaged.

Finally, consideration must be made at this level of the potential direct threats (i.e. petitions, protests, legal threats) raised by advocacy coalitions against power holders. Among the independent variables, Gamson (1975) identified, for instance, the greater success of groups that do not seek to displace their opponents – a variable that also appears pertinent in the context of this study, where ethno-nationalist coalitions are interested in sovereignty and (unlike regional authorities) compete more directly with national political elites than do single-issue movement coalitions, which are often content with a policy advisory role.

If we re-define political opportunities in terms of possibilities of mutual 'housing' between Institutions and MACs, we need to examine at what level there is overall convergence, and the specific discursive content of such convergence. In particular, it is necessary to analyse the emerging views of civil society by the different families of actors as these views shape the 'rules of engagement' between MACs and institutions.

Perspectives on the role of OCS

A first contextual discourse analysis concerns the role of civil society and the type of roles that different actors wish to attribute to NGOs and other associations. More OCS involvement is generally seen as desirable and advocated in a variety of functions. Institutions and OCS organizations generally agree across roles and sectors, even if with some differences of emphasis. This makes it possible to identify a prevalent EU model of shared understanding of OCS ideal features. This model will first be delineated with reference to institutional documents and then integrated with reference to additional elements which are distinctive of the discourse of OCS.

First, both institutions and OCS sees civil society as a necessary and welcome source of participation in policy-making, as it emerges for instance in a DG Social Affairs text:

> In all of this the Commission has paid great attention to the contribution which civil society can make. Much of what has to be done can only be achieved with the contribution of civil society organisations and concerted actions between public authorities and civil society. It is generally recognised that the organisations of civil society can help promote a more participatory democracy, chiefly because they can reach out to the poorest and most disadvantaged population groups and give a voice to those who are debarred from using other channels. Their specific skills and their connections at local, regional, national and international level may also prove useful and contribute to policy design and to the management, follow-up and assessment of actions.

Secondly, among the valued contributions of OCS are frequently stressed its ability to help institutions gather information and communicate with the public. For instance, an environmental document stresses its role in making sure that policy-making 'Involves all stakeholders in the process and are communicated in an effective way'.

Thirdly, OCS is seen in its capacity to disseminate the awareness of desired lifestyles (such as environmental or non-discriminatory ones). This implies that OCS is given a rather direct role in implementing policy objectives related to attitudinal change, which are frequently described in relevant action plans and programmatic documents of the three policy sectors, such as those pertaining to attitudinal changes towards more environmental or multiculturalist or anti-discriminatory awareness.

Fourthly, OCS is seen as supporting aggrieved citizens – such as local victims of pollution incidents – against more powerful social actors such as business and governments. These objectives are connected with the needs of engendering more transparency and accountability in politics and, as for instance indicated in a DG Environment presentation, 'the empowerment of citizens' and more generally to improve representation.

Fifthly, all actors see OCS as necessary partners for dialogue with societal forces. The listing of these desirable attributes sometimes occurs jointly. For instance the Fifth Environmental Action Programme (5EAP) states:

The active involvement and participation of non-governmental organisations [NGOs], both environment and consumer oriented, as well as trades unions and professional associations will be crucial to the general process of awareness-building, to the representation of public interest and concern, and to the motivation and engagement of the members of the general public themselves.

Other frequently made points are references to the need to redress the imbalance of resources between OCS and other actors. For instance, a Commission document reviewing the 5EAP notes:

The problem with NGOs is that they do not have the resources to contribute to the legislative process (for example, with respect to the Chemicals–IPC Directive). Dialogue cannot succeed at a technical level without an equality of resources, but dialogue and partnership should definitely be the road.

Policy documents stress the transnational character of OCS as a means to reach a broader constituency. For instance an institutional document in the field of anti-racism states:

The Commission encourages their role of independent information providers supporting organisations taking part in combating and preventing discrimination, enabling them to compare and contrast their approaches with experience in other regions of the Community.

This transnational character which might be understood in terms of attributing OCS a role of coordination in vertical governance is also supplemented by reflections on the role of OCS in terms of horizontal governance. As recognized in the 2001–6 action programme to combat discrimination, the Commission emphasises the 'networking character' of policy-making and in this respect the specific role of OCS. A Commission document, for instance, advocates 'the promotion of networking at European level between partners active in the prevention of, and the fight against, discrimination, including non-governmental organisations'. This benefit of reaching 'distant regions' is also stressed in relation to OCS' role in reflecting local knowledge into the policy-making process. The Commission and OCS claim that associations are a source of local knowledge, as for instance evidenced in a DG Social Affairs communication, which states that: 'NGOs are essential partners in the fight against racism and play a vital role in combating that scourge on the ground.'

The theme of local knowledge is stressed not only in relation to improving implementation – that is, in terms of a relation that emanating from the centre reaches the periphery – but also in terms of decision-making and representation flowing from the periphery to the centre. For instance, a Commission document in the anti-racist sector reviewing the relevant action plan notes:

As for civil society organisations, the added value of their participation in decision-making, and during the design and evaluation of projects, centres around their capacity to question programme goals and methods on the basis of a different and legitimate perception of needs. The target groups' own organisations, in particular, achieve good results because they know and understand needs and aspirations on the ground, they provide sustainable long-term services and are gaining legitimacy in dialogue with politicians.

As in this quotation, the concept of legitimacy is frequently mentioned in advocating the involvement of civil society.

The role of civil society in OCS documents

The same objectives stressed by institutions are indicated by OCS organisations. In addition they put forward demands for additional accessibility and a wider role at both EU and at national level, as evidenced in this quotation from an ENAR position paper: 'NGOs, unions and other civil society groupings should be actively consulted in the formulation, implementation and assessment of a national action plan.'

OCS organisations also see themselves as having an impact at community level. For instance, a website presentation of BirdLife International states:

BirdLife International works to help local communities to address the links between environmental problems and human welfare. This approach aims to enable local people to become self-sufficient through: increasing their sense of ownership and responsibility, allowing local people to learn new skills, ensuring local people's needs are taken into account. Creating a sense of empowerment in the community results in more positive and sustainable biodiversity conservation.[14]

A general willingness to engage does not prevent frequent criticism of EU institutions. For instance, criticising the Commission a joint EEB/WWF/FOE document states:

While the Commission recognises the role business has to play, it does not refer to the existence of a civil society that expresses itself in different interest groups, including environmental, workers' and socially oriented organisations. Its only reference is to consumer organisations at one point.[15]

The criticisms typically raised against OCS are sometimes re-directed towards the EU institutions. For instance, a joint EEB/WWF/FOE document reverses the typical criticism of lack of accountability of OCS organisations, which is re-defined in terms of a duty of the Commission to be accountable for the input it received from OCS:

proposals include early warnings on new policy initiatives and legislation, invitations for input in early stages of the process and, very importantly, an explanation on what the Commission has done with the input.[16]

Finally it is important to note a general divergence from the neo-liberal and market-oriented ethos of the Commission. This is evidenced, for instance, by an emphasis on the role of the state that does not appear in Commission documents. An EEB proposal for an environmental action plan notes: 'As this inequity is structural, the EEB is not in favour of a withdrawing state, it sees the state as having an important role in steering society and bringing balance between stakeholders.'[17]

A strong state is also a precondition for a proper acknowledgment of the role of OCS. The same document continues by noting that: 'This is also a matter of democratisation, as citizens organisations usually can count with more confidence with the public than governments or business.'[18]

To sum up, institutions and OCS are in agreement in delineating some key features that they would like to encourage in the relation between institutions and OCS but there are also some disagreements. On the basis of these observations a general model of EU–OCS relations can be described.

A model of EU–OCS relations

Several social theorists have attempted to classify views on civil society (see, for instance, Walzer 1995; Cohen and Arato 1999). There are different views as to the type of associations to be consulted (NGOs, non-profit organisations, foundations, social movements, trade unions, churches, families, etc.) and the confines of the term in relation to prevalent organisational forms in politics (Delanty 2000; Crouch, Eder *et al.* 2001). Theorists have produced typologies which emphasise similar criteria but are not directly comparable as they focus on a variety of issues. Some focus on the territorial scale at which civil society is to be considered (local communities, nation-states or cosmopolitan civil society).[19] Others focus the debate on the benefits of a well-developed associational sector for institutional efficiency (Putnam, Leonardi *et al.* 1993; Putnam 2000), or for third-sector effectiveness (Anheier 2001), or for addressing the democratic deficit (Scharpf 1999; Schmitter 2000; Warleigh 2001). There are authors who have discussed civil society in relation to the public sphere (Calhoun 1993; Habermas 1996; Cohen and Arato 1999). The foundations of civil society are differently conceptualised, connecting civil society to various valued outcomes. Liberals typically stress single individuals connected in free associations (Held 1987; Dahl 1989). Communitarians examine the community roots of individuals in characterising the role of civil society and its connection to the good life (Walzer 1995).

Other again stress the role of civil society in selecting leaders, in promoting solidarity and trust, in limiting political power through society-based checks and balances, in decision-making (mere information functions versus participation in collective deliberation with state actors, and versus legally sanctioned inclusion in decision-making procedures with voting rights) (see, for instance, Gellner 1994). And there are mixed typologies – for instance, the distinction between pluralist and corporatist inclusion relates both to a typology which focuses on role (aggregating interests or not) and on type (umbrella organisations or not). Civil society has a different centrality in different normative views (see, for instance, Habermas 1992, 1996; Hirst 1997) and is sometimes connected to the changing dimension of the political sphere over time (Mayer 1987).

I will limit this analysis to delineating a model that best describes the EU approach to civil society as it emerges from the documents and interviews discussed above. This model can be described in general terms, and is only weakly connected to the above-mentioned approaches in the literature, with the exception of the debate on the theories of democracy. In these terms, there are dominant and converging elements that allow one to define a EU model of civil society involvement from which there are some deviations. This model is characterised by an overarching emphasis on participation which is actualised mainly in terms of a consultative role (reflecting an awareness of the consequences of proposed legislation rooted in NGOs' first-hand knowledge of their communities' needs) and an information-providing role (which reflects NGOs' technical knowledge). To a lesser extent there is evidence of a desire to include OCS in debates on the merits of proposing legislation in a dialogical role inspired by models of deliberative democracy. There is little evidence of a desire to include or requests to be included in autonomous unencumbered decision-making. In addition, an EU model of civil society also includes an emphasis on its role in connecting different levels of governance and in relating to other non-state actors in horizontal network governance.

Deviations from this model include the perspective of several OCS associations which emphasise a stronger state as guarantor of their inclusion in deliberative fora and as guarantor of their role as provider of information and as provider of resources. Similarly, deviations from this model, but in the opposite direction, are expressed by institutional actors who dissent from any interventionist agenda to redress the imbalance between private and public associations, and occasionally from institutional actors (mainly in non-social-policy roles) who dissent from any perspective that promotes the inclusion of non-state actors in policy-making. These are, however, infrequent approaches, particularly in relation to the issues of social inclusion discussed in this volume where keywords such as the 'open method of coordination' are repeatedly employed, possibly indicating a desire to see the role of OCS go beyond a mere information-providing role to a more participative role (Armstrong 2002, 2003).

The structure of organised civil society and EU expectations

Some general reflections on the structure of MACs are now possible. As we have observed in all the cases, MACs extend over institutional boundaries, and processes of triangulation between actors based in different institutions are common. In general, OCS in all its various forms, which include churches, public-interest groups and social movements, is well integrated in the EU system of governance. In addition, there are loose boundaries between people belonging to different categories of organisations, with occasional changes of roles and frequent inter-institutional and inter-organisational alliances; and there are cross-organisational identities, of which MACs are an important expression. The important implication of the presence of loose boundaries is that as a unit of analysis the inter-organisational space is as important as single organisations of different nature and functions. It is at this broader level that policy cultures are formed and action is legitimated. The more public decision-making is, the more the legitimatory function of public discourse becomes relevant. We can effectively distinguish a public level of discourse on the MACs' themes of concern – the environment, regional self-determination and racial discrimination – from detailed policy-making on specific issues. Because of the presence of boundary-spanning personnel previously examined, and the permeability of institutional domains to activists, the inter-organisational space emerges as an important construct within which processes of frame bridging take place. In this space, as visually represented in figure 6.2, operate institutional activists to inject particular policy domains with moral relevance, as boundary-spanning personnel operate to diffuse policy frames.

As noted in all the cases, we can effectively distinguish a public level of discourse on MAC themes from detailed policy-making on specific issues. It is at this public level that key moralised concepts such as 'mainstreaming anti-racism' and the 'Europe of the Regions' and 'environmental sustainability' emerge as key concepts. They emerge in key Commission documents such as 'Towards Sustainability' (1992) or 'An Action Plan Against Racism' (1998a), and in conferences, study groups and advising fora such as those created by the

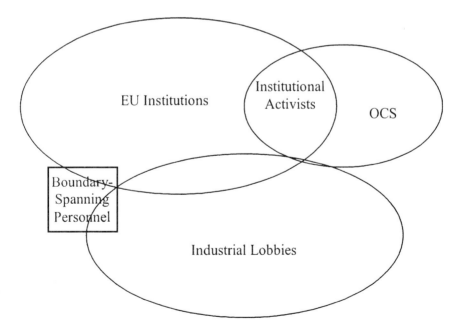

Figure 6.2 The EU policy arena as an interorganisational space

Commission after the 5EAP. At the level of policy deliberation these concepts do not often find direct resonance. However, as noted, their institutionalisation in the inter-institutional space of EU debates is important as it fixes the standards of acceptable policy deliberation.

Within the agreed general frames already identified, there are variations that different actors espouse. For instance, in the regionalist sector the economic dimension tends to be stressed more frequently by institutional actors who mediate between the concerns of public-interest lobbies and of private pressure groups and reflect the dominant ethos. General frames such as 'subsidiarity' retain enough ambiguity that they can accommodate many of the interests of different actors.

In specific policy deliberation much of the ambiguity of the concepts espoused by MACs becomes apparent. However, the fact that they are not infrequently considered a device for public consumption does not lessen thir importance. As legislative initiatives are taken in their name, those actors who are committed will to an important degree be able to hold all participants accountable to the principles to which they publicly subscribe. Over time, public statements trickle down to specific policy-making criteria. The main limitation of the power of these concepts is that overall their supporters are rather powerless, in some MACs more than in others.

The way that these concepts become institutionalised is often only a weak reflection of what the advocates pursued. It is in fact a compromise between the aims of the three kind of actors involved: intergovernmental, EU elites and policy communities on the one hand and civil society – particularly the OCS of social movements and public-interest groups – on the other. The various constituencies interact selecting those policy ideas that maximise their goals.

Conclusions

In this chapter, it has been argued that the presence and increasing popularity of collegial forms in politics, and the EU's concern for transparency and the participation of civil society, foster frame-bridging processes. Consensus formation processes arise whereby existing political ideologies and those emerging in social movements are merged. Social-movement ideas are thus incorporated through movement lobbying and their impact upon policy-making and movement resource acquisition strategies but they often come to be re-defined and expressed in a modified form that is compatible with institutional goals. In relation to framing processes, the importance of debating arenas in which consensus on preferred policy approaches develops and then trickles down to specific policy events has been highlighted, although at times there is a distance between the principles that emerge in policy debating arenas and those utilised in concrete policy-making. This contributes to the new politics of persuasion and advocacy by bringing together under one frame actors who used to oppose each other, thereby shaping both the ideational context and the content of EU policy.

Throughout the case studies those variables which make social movement politics more acceptable were examined, and the types of political systems, policy processes and policy domains conducive to social-movement politics elucidated. In this context, it is argued that public discourse has a major impact which is filtered differently by different policy environments: some are more receptive than others to social-movement ideas channelled through institutional activists and media discourses. It is also argued that environmental domains are particularly open, for a number of reasons: among them domain-specific ones, such as the first-mover advantages that pro-active environmental regulation can provide, and the consequent acceptance of a wide range of actors, and reasons concerning the extreme versatility of the moralised policy frame 'environmental sustainability' which induces institutional actors to adopt it in a variety of contexts. But in the absence of sustained control by institutional activists and public discourse, the outcome is cooption of the movement. Conversely, ethno-nationalist movements encounter substantial obstacles in the public discourse and institutional framework that supports the nation-state, and some of them as subcultural movements are fairly irrelevant, as their weak organisational structure deprives them of an anchor that fixes their identity and assists them in the negotiation of institution–movement exchanges.

Taken together, the three case studies point up the fact that movement activists and institutional actors differ in their general ethos, policy styles and personal backgrounds. Yet, as the case studies have shown, a measure of mutual dependency has developed. This chapter has reviewed the nature of the interconnection among resources and ideal motives that characterises the field of advocacy coalitions in Brussels as a whole, emphasising the strong links that have developed within MACs. It is argued that the field is in part informed by bureaucratic politics, but also by an attempt to legitimise the project of European construction – a goal which many political and bureaucratic actors in Brussels espouse – and by joint engagement in promotional causes with social-movements representatives. Normative behaviour therefore plays a significant role in the social-movement-inspired advocacy coalitions that have been examined. Also important were considerations of appropriateness, since these pressured actors into subscribing to approved cultural values and practices – a form of behaviour that can be characterised as mimetic in that it re-enacts practices and expressions considered appropriate and legitimate. Finally, the studies pointed to the coercive component in the relations between resource holders and other members of policy communities.

Summary

This chapter has examined those elements of the EU socio-political and institutional context which facilitate or hinder the work of social-movement-related public-interest associations. Considering the three cases simultaneously, an assessment was undertaken of how social movement ideas are taken up by public-interest associations and in EU institutional realms, how their priorities are adopted or re-interpreted and their activists incorporated. To this end, the processes that shape their ideological mix have been stressed, and the ideal and instrumental reasons that induce institutions to pay attention to movement-related organisations examined.

A key concept employed has been that of selection. This has been applied to the way in which the EU governance level filters pressure from civil society. This happens at the structural and at the discursive levels. At the structural level, rules for inclusion and exclusion of activists and the expectations from OCS as formalised in EU documents have been considered. At the discursive level, the role of 'frame bridging' has been stressd. This is a cultural mechanism by which a synthesis between the dominant ideas of social movements and institutions is achieved.

Reflecting contextually on the complex picture that thus emerges of change and permanence within each of the coalitions, the various coalitions have been considered jointly. This has enabled an examination of the political and organisational dimensions of movement advocacy coalitions in EU institutions in relation to the three levels of intergovernmental actors, EU institutional architects and EU policy communities.

Notes

1 It should be stressed that policy *success* refers to movements' goals, not to their organisations. Thus, a pre-empted movement will see its goals fulfilled but its organisations marginalised.

2 For a classic approach to policy analysis which emphasises the interconnection of problems, policy and ideas see Wilson (1983).

3 See Appendix B regarding data on the popularity of different concerns.

4 See, for instance, Redclift (1992).

5 This term refers to the instrumental use of identity concerns in a number of policy areas, including regional policy.

6 For the concept of the 'garbage can' in organisational behaviour, see March (1988).

7 In terms of the neo-institutionalist (and realist) Krasner, these re-interpretations are instances of *institutionalisation*, where a newly emerging institution such as a social movement acquires links with specific institutional environments. It becomes deeply embedded in the identity of institutional actors and structurally connected with other institutions. The breadth and depth of connections is Krasner's measure of institutionalisation (Krasner 1988).

8 The importance of relational channels has been shown by Schlager (1995) and Sabatier (1998), who place it as a central hypothesis of the advocacy coalition framework. Sabatier notes: 'Actors who share core policy beliefs are more likely to engage in short-term policy co-ordination if they (1) interact repeatedly, (2) experience relatively low information costs, and (3) believe that there are policies that, while not affecting each actor in similar ways, at least treat each actor fairly.'

9 This is the accusation made by Ann Swidler against the work of William Gamson (see her (1993) review of *Talking Politics*). Swidler points out that Gamson's endeavour to

show the impact of social movements in society is to some extent thwarted by the evidence for the unexpected pastiches and substantial re-interpretations that movement themes undergo in the public at large.

10 As previously mentioned, conflicts of interests are also shaping relations among public pressure groups, particularly those active in different domains, even if alliances are normal and long-lasting. On conflicts in the social policy sector, see also Geyer (2000a).

11 For a discussion of the concept of gender mainstreaming see Rees (1998).

12 This, and other structural conditions are, for instance, emphasised in connection with the women's movement by Geyer (2000b).

13 Agnes Hubert, in addition to her scholarly role (Hubert 1998), has been a EU civil servant in prominent institutional positions for several decades. In a personal interview she confirmed the crucial role of feminist civil servants.

14 Birdslife (2002), Web Site Presentation, www.birdlife.net/people/index.cfm.

15 Green 8 (2001), Position on EU Sustainable Development Strategy, www.eeb.org/publication/Response%20to%20SDS.pdf.

16 Green 8 (2001), Position on EU Sustainable Development Strategy, www.eeb.org/publication/Response%20to%20SDS.pdf.

17 EEB (2001), EEB Proposals to strengthen the Environmental Action Programme, www.eeb.org/publication/6th%20EAP%20Final.pdf.

18 EEB (2001), EEB Proposals to strengthen the Environmental Action Programme, www.eeb.org/publication/6th%20EAP%20Final.pdf1.

19 There are differences related to the scale at which civil society is seen as operating. In general terms, civil society has been defined in correspondence to the territorial borders of the state by almost all analysts with the exception of those working on transnational civil society (Keane 1988, 1999; Streeck and Schmitter 1991).

Appendix A: methodological approaches

In chapters 1–6 I have examined the relationship between OCS and EU institutions and examined the mechanisms of influence. With reference to the relationship between the two fields, my main methodological approach consisted of key actor interviews in the field of EU institutions and in OCS. In addition, a comparative analysis was undertaken of themes emerging in the policy documents of the two fields. This analysis has contributed to guiding my interpretation of the relationship between OCS and EU institutions and is therefore reflected throughout all the chapters, particularly with reference to the second level of analysis. However, it is useful here to provide a more structured report of the methodology of theme analysis adopted and of some of the findings. This methodological appendix aims at this clarification.

The following appendix (appendix B) will focus on the role of public opinion. In discussing the impact of movement advocacy coalitions on institutions I have identified several sources of influence. These sources have been explored using three distinct methodological approaches corresponding to the three levels of analysis. Appendix B will discuss in more detail the methodology pertaining to the first level, which stressed the impact of public opinion on the three MACs considered. A summary of relevant survey data will provide a comparative picture of the relevance of the three MACs discussed in the text.

Relations between OCS and EU institutions: frame analysis

The methodology of content analysis of policy documents responded to the need to examine systematically the relationship between the policy agenda advocated by MACs and the EU agenda. Performing this analysis implied a dynamic exploration of strategic framings and re-framings by competing policy actors diagnosing problems and proposing solutions – a process in which not infrequently a situation emerges of 'solutions chasing problems and problems chasing solutions in the absence of a fixed agenda' (Mazey and Richardson 1997). This dynamic analysis has been discussed in the text (one can consider, for instance, the instrumental re-definitions of sustainable development in terms of merging sustainability and development). In addition there is a more static and long-term competition whereby OCS and EU institutions produce contrasting and self-serving framings or even congruent framings. This process has been examined through a comparative exploration of themes present in programmatic documents. My analysis focused on identifying aspirations, examining the perception of problems to be addressed by policies and the criticism of actors involved in the policy process and of normative political principles with a guiding impact on policy making.

To analyse these dimensions I opted for a type of content analysis known as 'frame analysis' and described in chapter 2. This methodology attempts to identify and classify recurrent concepts in policy documents and to relate them to specific kinds of actors. It also attempts to identify how these concepts change, merge or differentiate over time and across different types of actors. In practice, the analysis was performed with the help of a small team of six researchers and focused only on the years 1990–2000 and on the aggregate difference between OCS and institutions.

The frame analysis is also meant to supplement and validate, with the involvement of additional analysts, the longer-term documentary analysis that this author performed in the three policy sectors.

Methodological considerations about the frame analysis

As previously mentioned, the adoption of the technique of frame analysis comes from a central tradition in social movement research and also in policy analysis (Snow *et al.* 1986; Schon and Rein 1994; Benford 1997; Triandafyllidou and Fotiou 1998; Alink, Boin *et al.* 2001; Cooper 2002; Ruzza 2002). The selection of the frames resulted from our underlying hypothesis that there is a correspondence between the issues raised by the movement sector and those stressed by the EU. To be easily identifiable, the ideological packages of the MACs had to be defined in a clear and concise way. To produce such a list of frames a team of five researchers and a general coordinator was assembled. The team examined various activist materials and EU documents and websites. Handouts summarising the political goals of movements, programmatic documents and reaction to official EU positions were particularly helpful. We formulated several frames which reflected the crucial points of the MACs and EU policy visions and programmes.

It was essential to minimise the measurement problems which necessarily arise in the evaluation of the contents of texts. This meant first of all that those involved in the frame analysis had to identify frames consistently. Problems of reliability were addressed with a two-step strategy. First, in the initial phase of the project, before the actual review of the material, I sought to achieve the best possible clarification of the meaning of concepts such as *sustainable development* or *mainstreaming* anti-racism, and by which criteria they were to be defined in a text.

The scoring of documents was then performed. In the initial phase, following the methodology of grounded theory (Glaser and Strauss 1968; Strauss and Corbin 1998) the team concentrated on identifying frames as they emerged in the course of the analysis. Subsequently, especially in the first few sessions, we discussed uncertain cases, and in doing so reformulated the definitions in a more appropriate (i.e. easily identifiable) way. A subset of the same texts was analysed independently by scorers and the results were compared.

When the framing grid appeared sufficiently stable, all documents were re-considered utilising it, and a set of new documents was added. The team realised that in order to ensure homogeneous classification it was necessary that there was supervision to check for consistency in the identification and application of frames. In ambiguous cases prompted a re-consideration of classifications by analysts. This amounted to a mechanism to increase both *validity* and *reliability*. Validity was increased because this process forced a re-thinking of the appropriateness of the labels. Reliability was improved as different analysts' conceptions of coding specific frames were discussed in weekly meetings over three months in order to achieve convergence. The resulting list of frames then constituted an inventory of the main themes that characterised the different policy fields.

Sample selection

The document sources utilised for the EU field included a wide selection of documents prepared by the different institutions. We then considered web presentation pages of relevant institutions. These consisted of DG web pages presenting the specific policy remit (DG Environment, DG Regional Policy, DG Employment and Social Affairs – Section on Anti-racism); agencies and consultative institutions (environmental agency, CoR, EUMC); and the EP (web pages describing the thematic areas).

Secondly we considered the Commission's programmatic action plans and institutional evaluations of action plans. For institutions we considered recent action plans in the various fields and the main reactions by the institutions. In the field of environment we examined the last two action plans (5AP and 6AP), one in anti-racism (1AP) and programmatic documents in regional policy. We also considered reaction to APs by the EP in the form of resolutions, other resolutions indirectly connected to APs and the opinions of all consultative bodies on the action plans.

For OCS the primary materials consisted of reactions to EU APs by EU networks as well as large OCS organizations established in Brussels and submissions to the European Convention on the Future of the European Union, programmatic documents and web presentation pages of these organisations. For the Environmental sector we considered the EEB, Climate Network, WWF Europe, Greenpeace Europe, Birdslife, Friends of the Earth Europe and International Friends of Nature, Transport and Environment.

For the Regionalist sector we considered the EBLUL, AER, Association of European Border Regions (AEBR), Council of European Municipalities and Regions (CEMR) and Congress of Local and Regional Authorities (CLRAE). We also considered associations of regions and a sample of regional offices from the type of regions examined in the text – regions with prominent ethno-nationalist advocacy coalitions such as Sardinia, Veneto, Catalunya and Pays Basque.

For the anti-racist sector we classified documents produced by ENAR, the SL Group and MPG. A balanced number of similar sources were considered in each sector.

The selected texts constitute a sample which indicates the issues which are of concern to many policy-makers and activists, agenda-setting efforts and preferred policy solutions.[1]

As mentioned, the task of the coders was to read the texts, decide whether a text matched one or more of the frames and apply the frames identified using a software package (Atlas.Ti). This task was at times ambiguous. In such cases scorers discussed the attribution in frequent telephone conversations with the general coordinator and in weekly meetings with other scorers. In this manner a convergence of scoring criteria was achieved to a satisfactory level. Paragraphs were our unit of analysis. A paragraph was classified into one or more of the frames when it matched the central statement of one of our categories. Thus, when two or three frames were present in a text two or three occurrences were counted. A total of about 1,000 paragraphs per sector were coded (ENV=1000, REG= 998, AR= 1074). They thus constitute our unit of analysis, which refers to a total of approximately 134 documents (AR: 44, REG: 43, ENV: 47).

In addition to the frames identified other variables were coded. These are: policy sectors (AR, ENV, REG), type of actor (the various OCS organisations or institutions), type of document and year of selected texts. We also produced a set of modifiers, which we called performative codes and were coded as separate variables. These refer to the relational content of the actions referred to by the specific frames utilised. In other words, through our grounded theory approach we observed that the actions most recurrent in the texts were criticisms (coded as 'to criticise'), requests for political intervention in favour of a specific cause (coded as 'to advocate') and analytical evaluations of specific states of affairs of issue areas (coded as 'analysis'). This was useful as it allowed the analysts to achieve a specification of the action context in which certain themes emerged.

The interpretation of findings is based on a consideration of the absolute number of frames. Given the limited size of the sample only general and approximate comparisons are reasonable. Differences of a few frames are not interpretable. Nonetheless even with these limitations, some relevant findings emerge. They integrate the key-actor interviews and the more interpretive work done on the documents and also discussed in the text.

Relations between OCS and EU institutions

In this analysis, EU institutions and OCS constitute two fields which at times share a common policy agenda but often present different emphases. In the following sections I will examine the findings. The codes identified and measured by coders are indicated in bold. The analysis focuses on the one hand on the global relationships between OCS and EU institutions, and on the other on the specific policy domains: the environmental (ENV), anti-racist (AR) and regionalist (REG). I will start with a global consideration of differences between the EU and OCS fields and then proceed to examine specific policy sectors.

A few different types of content emerged from the analysis: themes that pertained to all the different policy sectors and actors, which were called common codes, domain-specific themes, called domain-specific codes and themes that expressed actions to be performed which, as mentioned, were called performative codes (to criticise and to advocate) and were applied to sector-specific codes to give evaluative content when necessary.

Thus an example of a performative code is 'to criticise' which can be applied to several specific themes such as the theme of sustainable development, thereby providing them with interpretable content. Therefore an environmental organisation would for instance criticise the concept of sustainable development (as ideologically loaded or inadequate, etc.). This would be scored as the joint code of 'criticise sustainable-development'.

Additionally, new codes were devised after the analysis on the basis of an examination of results. These supercodes merged single codes. The codes of emphasising 'market instruments', stressing 'development' were subsequently aggregated in the supercode 'economic dimension'.

Findings

The findings consist first in the identification of the dominant frames (here only a quantitative report on the dominant frames is provided as a discussion of the qualitative internal variations of the frames identified is in the text – see in particular the discussion of the frame named 'importance of civil society', which refers to the reasons why civil society is considered important by OCS organisations and by EU institutions). Secondly, there is information on relations among frames across sectors and within each sector.

In tables A.1–A.8 is a list of all the codes that emerged (whose meaning is self-explanatory). They constitute the discursive universe of policy-making in these sectors in Brussels. First there is a list of sector-specific codes (table A.1), then of the transversal codes that are emphasised by all sectors (tables A.2–A.3).

In table A.1, the following frames were also identified and appeared with a frequency below 5 per cent: Impact on environment, Technological environmentalism, Coordination and planning, Application of public policy/principles, Voluntary agreement, Importance of citizens, Transboundary, Sharing responsibilities among actors, EU enlargement process–EU integration, Development.

Table A.1 **Frames identified in the environmental sector, their percentage over total number of paragraphs scored and percentage within OCS and EU institutions**

	Total	*OCS*	*EU*
Sustainable development	21.8	24.5	16.7
Horizontality	16.3	14.5	19.0
Implementation	15.0	12.7	17.4
Importance of Civil Society	14.9	18.0	10.3
Market driven approach	14.1	6.2	7.5
Effectiveness of public policy	10.2	8.5	11.7
Sustainability	9.8	11.3	7.1
To improve knowledge	9.7	2.7	15.9
Nature conservationism	8.1	7.8	8.0
Dissemination	8.1	2.2	13.4
Timing	7.6	9.4	5.2
Institutional effectiveness	6.4	6.8	5.9
Monitoring system	5.4	6.0	4.8

In table A.2, the following frames were also identified and appeared with a frequency below 5 per cent: Horizontality, Importance of local dimension, Control, Ethnic inequality, Different but equal, Lobbying, Integration of sector-specific objectives into other policy areas, United Nations, Affirmative action, Repression, Institutional racism, Multiculturalism, Violence, Re-distribution.

In table A.3, the following frames were also identified and appeared with a frequency below 5 per cent: Deeper understanding, Exchange of practices, Sharing responsibilities among actors, Rights, Proximity, Minority, Citizenship, Solution, Governance, Integration of sector-specific objectives into other policy areas, Effectiveness of public policy, Integration, Participation, Inequalities, Control.

In addition to sector-specific codes, there are codes that have been identified in all policy sectors. As there are interesting differences of emphasis between EU institutions and OCS, the respective values are also listed in table A.4.

Table A.2 Frames identified in the anti-racist sector, their percentage over total number of paragraphs scored and percentage within OCS and EU institutions

	Total	*OCS*	*EU*
Implementation	32.7	33.2	32.3
Discrimination	24.8	29.4	22.4
Application of public policy/principles	22.6	24.2	24.0
Cooperation–Partnership–Networking	18.2	14.8	19.2
To improve knowledge	18.0	16.9	18.7
Member states' responsibility	15.2	22.1	11.1
Analysis	14.7	15.1	14.5
Equal opportunities	13.3	15.8	11.6
Importance of civil society	13.2	15.1	12.1
Dissemination	12.6	13.0	12.4
Human rights	10.5	10.4	10.4
Solution	10.5	8.1	12.2
Effectiveness of public policy	10.2	8.6	11.4
Importance of member states' dimension	8.4	10.1	6.3
Deeper understanding	7.8	7.0	8.7
Combat	7.5	7.5	10.0
Valuation policies and practice	7.4	9.9	5.3
Employment	7.3	7.0	7.0
Funds	6.6	4.2	7.7
Civil rights	6.2	9.6	4.8
Market	6.2	5.7	6.0
Group specificity	6.0	11.9	2.8
Europe is useful	5.9	3.9	7.0
Visibility	5.8	3.9	6.6
Mainstreaming	5.7	3.1	7.1
EU enlargement process–integration	5.2	5.5	4.6
Exchange good practices	5.1	2.3	6.0
Women	5.1	6.2	5.3

On the basis of these most frequently appearing frames it has been possible to identify distinctive configurations of policy discourse in each sector. The same frames appear in both the EU and the OCS fields and their configuration has been named respectively sustainable development, mainstreaming and subsidiarity/proximity, as discussed in the text. In addition, the discursive field of EU institutions and OCS stresses implementation, the horizontal diffusion of these policies and the valuable contributions of civil society.

Cross-sectoral findings

The first important finding is that there are commonalities in the policy frames identified within European policy documents which, while allowing for overall convergence on the masterframes identified, distinguish EU discourse from OCS documents. In general, EU documents stress the economic dimension more than OCS (EU = 58.1 per cent, OCS = 41.9 per cent), and focus on a smaller number of frames. We can note that whilst a common discourse has developed within EU institutions, the themes emerging from

Table A.3 Frames identified in the regionalist sector, their percentage over total number of paragraphs scored and percentage within OCS and EU institutions

	Total	OCS	EU
Horizontality	18.4	10.4	28.0
Development	16.8	14.2	21.9
Cooperation	16.5	18.0	12.4
Subsidiarity	14.3	18.2	8.7
Financial information	14.2	12.1	16.3
Analysis	13.2	12.3	15.3
To improve knowledge	12.5	10.8	13.8
Coordination and planning	12.1	6.4	19.6
Implementation	11.6	8.9	14.0
Importance of civil society	11.0	21.4	0
Supporting	10.3	11.7	9.1
Application of public policy/principle	9.4	7.6	10.3
Dissemination	8.4	8.5	8.0
Europe is useful	8.0	3.0	15.5
Democracy	7.1	8.1	4.1
Cohesion	6.1	4.9	8.2
Multiculturalism	5.9	10.0	2.5

Table A.4 Common codes identified in all policy sectors (percentages)

Frames identified	Total	EU	OCS
Implementation	20.1	22.5	17.7
To improve knowledge	13.5	16.4	10.6
Horizontality[a]	12.8	16.0	9.6
Importance of civil society	13.0	8.1	19.6

Note: [a] This refers to the diffusion of a policy principle throughout two or more policy sectors.

OCS are more varied. The fact that this has not happened within OCS may hinder its ability to coordinate tactics and strategies.

Common frames that characterise EU institutions and OCS in the three policy sectors are horizontality (that is, the integration of sector-specific objectives into other policy areas), implementation, improving knowledge and importance of civil society. These are general frames that are fairly uniformly shared by EU and OCS documents such as the frame of civil society, which refers to the desirability of involving civil society. This diffusion also refers to the balance among sectors, as emerges from table A.5.

Table A.5 Percentage of 'importance of civil society', 'implementation', 'horizontality' and 'improve knowledge' frames in the three sectors

	Importance of civil society	Implementation	Horizontality	Improve knowledge	N
AR	13.2	32.7	4.4	18.0	1074
ENV	14.9	15.0	16.3	9.7	1000
REG	11.0	11.6	18.4	12.5	998
TOT	13.1	20.1	12.8	13.5	3072

This finding shows that there is in Brussels a general agreement that civil society is important and should be more involved in the policy process. The environmental sector shares with the regional sector an emphasis on the frame of horizontality, which is less marked in the case of anti-racism, as shown in table A.5. This is possibly due to the fact that anti-racism has largely defined itself in the realm of social policy where the EU common policy is limited and no diffusion is easily attainable and cannot therefore be claimed. However, one should note that a decision was taken to differentiate horizontality from mainstreaming (5.7 per cent), which in fact does contain the concept of horizontality, but is more complex and also contains a host of other dimensions. This complexity of the concept of mainstreaming is also often under-scored by scholars researching the women's movement.[2] If one adds the values of horizontality and mainstreaming in the anti-racist sector one finds that the total percentage (10.1) is nonetheless still below that of the other two sectors. It is worth noting that mainstreaming is much more used by the institutions than by OCS (EU institutions = 80.3 per cent, OCS = 19.7 per cent).

The anti-racist sector is a newly emergent sector where the powerful article 13 and the related AP need to be implemented at all levels. Thus, discursively this sector is principally concerned with the issue of implementation.

As a theme, implementation is, however, understood differently in the three sectors. In the environmental sector the main emphasis is on the effectiveness of implemented policies[3] (10 per cent) and on the monitoring system (6 per cent), while the anti-racists and regionalist actors stress the need for the application of policies. Moreover anti-racists ask for the implementation of principles (rather than policies)

However, in general terms, implementation remains a crucial concern of all movement-related areas where reluctant governments and hostile sectors of EU institutions can delay or avoid implementation. This emerges clearly in the anti-racist sector where we can observe that all actors taken together criticise the implementation of policies.

The relative novelty of the anti-racist sector is also reflected by its emphasis on improving knowledge. This frame has two different meanings: dissemination of knowledge and deeper understanding, which refers to the necessity to acquire information for a better understanding of problems. The main emphasis is on the first meaning in all sectors.

Tendency to advocate and to criticise

EU institutions and OCS also express a different propensity to advocate and to criticise. This difference varies in different policy sectors. This emerges clearly from table A.6.

Table A.6 shows that the social movement character of NGOs is reflected in their generally more critical stance and advocacy attitude. In absolute terms, the most critical stance is expressed by environmental OCS organisations, thus revealing their unequivocal social-movement character. If we compare the overall level of criticism across the three sectors, we note that there is a substantial difference, with regionalism (1.6 per cent) being far less likely to express criticism that the other sectors (ENV 14 per cent and AR 11.6 per cent).

With reference to the common frames, table A.6 shows that EU institutions stress implementation more than OCS in the anti-racist sector. The opposite takes place in the environmental sector. This suggests that while implementation is a crucial concern of anti-racists who have recently seen the approval of a set of important initiatives connected to article 13, such concern with implementation is more relevant for environmentalists who have achieved the implementation of environmental regulation to a much higher degree over the years.

Table A.6 EU institutions and OCS emphasis on expressing criticism and advocacy in different policy sectors (percentages within sectors)

	To advocate			To criticise		
	EU Inst.	OCS	Tot. (N)	EU Inst.	OCS	Tot. (N)
Anti-racism	55.0	45.0	100 (369)	31.9	68.1	100 (116)
Environment	39.2	60.7	100 (130)	27.6	72.3	100 (141)
Regionalism	33.4	66.5	100 (206)	12.5	87.5	100 (16)

The importance of civil society is emphasised by OCS in the environmental and regionalist sectors (in fact, in the regionalist sector it is stressed only by OCS) while in the anti-racist field the distribution is more balanced. The need to improve knowledge and horizontality are emphasised most frequently by EU institutions (table A.7).

Table A.7 Policy sectors by type of common frames 'to advocate' (percentages)

	EU advocate	OCS advocates
Implementation		
Anti-racism	55.1	44.9
Environment	42.3	57.7
Regionalism	52.2	47.8
Improving knowledge		
Anti-racism	57.8	42.2
Environment[a]		
Regionalism	51.4	48.6
Importance of civil society		
Anti-racism	53.2	46.8
Environment	18.2	81.8
Regionalism	0.0	100.0
Horizontality		
Anti-racism	50.0	50.0
Environment	61.1	38.9
Regionalism	60.0	40.0

Note: [a] few instances were identified.

There is a frequent usage of the concept of 'to criticise' in the environmental and anti-racist sectors, we note that it mainly refers to the sector-specific codes (sustainable development and sustainability of the environmental sector, mainstreaming of the anti-racist sector and cohesion or proximity of the regionalist sector) rather than the 'modes of operation' that we codified in common frames (implementation, importance of civil society, improving knowledge and horizontality). Therefore, common frames refer to shared and approved concerns. The only exception in this regard is represented by the frame implementation in the anti-racist field: as we noted above OCS and EU institutions criticise implementation (OCS: 68.1 per cent, EU institutions: 31.9 per cent). This makes implementation the most important concern in the anti-racism field, differentiating it from environmental and regionalist sector.

Sectoral frames

There are also differences across policy sectors.

Anti-racism
In the anti-racist field a clear finding is the high degree of isomorphism of the discourse of Institutions and of OCS. This emerges from table A.8, in which most important frames are listed. There are some differences of emphasis.

Table A.8 Percentage of anti-racist sectoral frames by type of actor and by performative codes

	To advocate		To criticise	
	EU inst.	OCS	EU inst.	OCS
Importance of discrimination	15.7	34.9	18.9	29.1
Cooperation, networking	14.2	12.0	10.8	3.8
Role of member states	27.1	34.3	29.7	24.1
Market	28.1	2.4	16.2	17.7
N	203.0	166.0	37.0	79.0

Here one should note that the code importance of discrimination in association with 'to advocate' has been utilised to indicate an emphasis on anti-discrimination, or it indicates the need to fight discrimination.[4] Moreover we can specify that EU institutions use the frame 'to combat' which generally refers to the explicit utilisation of the word 'combat' much more than OCS to stress this aim. The frame 'to combat' is almost always utilised by institutions (88 per cent) and occurs in EU documents in association with the word 'discrimination', illustrating the adoption of what one may regard as a movement-inspired metaphor by the institutions. Interestingly, OCS does not use it, as it does not use 'mainstreaming', revealing a preference for moderation in the language utilised.

Significant stress also emerges on the importance of cooperation and forming networks (18.2 per cent over the total of paragraphs) among the relevant actors in combating racism. This is particularly evident from the recurrent emphasis on information exchange and exchange of good practice (5 per cent). Institutions focus on combating discrimination and do so with particular attention to the economic dimension which includes combating the markers of discrimination in the labour market, such as unemployment (7 per cent). Conversely, OCS pays markedly less attention to economic issues while sharing the rest of the policy agenda.

In terms of differences, in table A.8 we also notice that OCS emphasises the role of member states more than EU institutions (34.3 per cent against 27.1 per cent). Role of member states is a supercode (a conjunction of two codes) which encompasses importance of member states and member states' responsibility, and refers to their responsibility (particularly for implementing EU legislation) or to their importance as a distinctive level of government to whom an attribution of responsibility for effectiveness is made. In addition, OCS also stresses the role of local authorities (4.4 per cent).

Other recurrent frames are: equal opportunities (13 per cent), which is linked with 'advocate' (6 per cent) and 'human rights' (10 per cent). These are sector- specific frames, like affirmative action (3 per cent), 'different but equal' (3.4 per cent) that is a catchphrase adopted mainly by EU institutions.

The juxtaposition between a multiculturalist and an assimilationist policy frame often appears unclear as both are no longer easily identifiable, possibly because the necessity of a combination of both approaches is now taken for granted.

Regionalism

In the field of regionalism, the most frequently used sectoral frames are cooperation (16.5 per cent) among actors at different levels of governance, subsidiarity (14.3 per cent), coordination and planning (12.1 per cent), exchange of practices (4.9 per cent) and sharing responsibilities among actors (4.7 per cent). There is thus substantial agreement on a perception of insufficient information and a preferred policy style which favours a non-confrontational approach and cooperation among different levels of governance – that is, horizontally among subnational levels of governance, and between cross-border subnational units.

However, as represented in figure A.1, EU institutions and OCS diverge in terms of different emphases on political or economic areas of concern. Thus democracy (7.1 per cent), the importance of civil society (11.0 per cent) and minority rights (8.6 per cent) and citizenship (3.8 per cent) – all political concerns – are almost exclusively stressed by OCS. Conversely, the economic dimension stressed by institutions emphasises development (16.8 per cent), implementation (11 per cent) and financial information (14.2 per cent).[5] Proximity, despite being mentioned in a key policy document as an overarching EU concern appears very seldom (4 per cent). It might be that this is still an emerging frame integrating and replacing the consolidated emphasis on subsidiarity (14.3 per

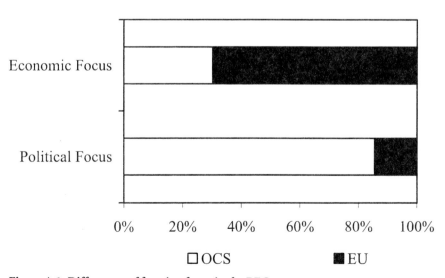

Figure A.1 **Differences of framing focus in the REG sector**

cent) which is particularly stressed in connection to civil society (65.3 per cent versus 34.7 per cent). In this domain institutions often reiterate their perception of their own importance (Europe is useful: 7.5 per cent) which, however, is not shared by OCS (93.8 per cent versus 6.3 per cent).[6]

Environmentalism

In the environmental field institutions and OCS agree on the importance of the frame of sustainable development and sustainability, which are, however, slightly more central to the concerns of OCS actors, as represented in figure A.2.

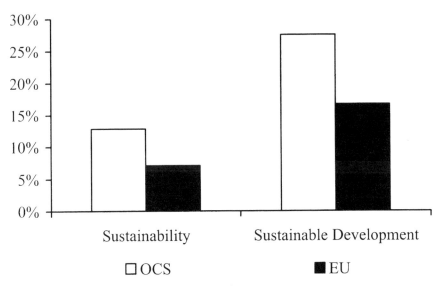

Figure A.2 Differences of framing focus in the ENV sector

The market-driven approach (14.1 per cent) occurs frequently in this field, and refers, for instance, to the perceived necessity to remove public subsidies and achieve a better environment through market-driven policy instruments. It also refers to voluntary agreements and specific measures such as eco-tax and eco-audits which incorporate environmental costs in financial reports.

In this field, OCS expresses a recurrent critical stance of institutional approaches, which on second-level documentary analysis[7] appears particularly strong and technically informed. In addition, it is notable that OCS criticises member states and the ineffectiveness of institutions (6.4 per cent), particularly the Commission.

Conclusions

This appendix has examined the discursive claims of EU institutions and OCS. In general, we have observed a substantial convergence of themes among the actors. At the level of EU policy formation I examined the strategic considerations of EU actors and how they were reflected in the ideational component of policy-making. This included the discursive justifications employed in processes of agenda-setting and identification of preferred policy solutions. In line with the present focus on civil society, on the one hand the relations between the preferred policies of EU institutions and their goals and on the other the goals of OCS were explored. On the basis of a frame analysis comparing EU and MAC documents it was argued that mechanisms of frame bridging mediate EU willingness to incorporate MAC policy frames.

Summary

The objective of this appendix has been to provide framing data illustrating discursive strategies and agenda-setting dynamics. I examined processes of frame diffusion and showed that policy frames of interest to EU architects are merged with frames that are of importance to advocacy coalitions.

Documents analysed

AEBR, 2002, Proposals of AEBR to the European Convention
     www.are-regions-europe.org/
AEBR, 2002, The Added Value of Cooperation
     www.aebr.net/index.php
AEBR, 2002, Recommendation of AEBR
AEBR, 2002, Web Site Presentation
     www.are-regions-europe.org/INTERREGIONAL/GB-AEBR.html
AEBR, CEMR and CPMR, 2003, Proposals to the Convention
Assembly of European Regions – AER, 1996, Declaration on Regionalism in Europe
     www.are-regions-europe.org/GB/A4/A41.html
Assembly of European Regions – AER, 2002, Web Site Presentation
     www.are-regions-europe.org/GB/A1/A1.html#convictions
Assembly of European Regions – AER, 2002, AER Action Plan 2002
     www.are-regions-europe.org/GB/A2/A21.html
Birdslife, 2002, Web Site Presentation
     www.birdlife.net/people/index.cfm
Birdslife, 2002, Web Site Presentation: How We Work www
     www.birdlife.net/work/index.cfm
CAN Europe, 2001, Open Letter by Environmental NGOs to EU Minister
     www.climnet.orgmatthias@climnet.org
Catalunya Regional Boureau, 2002, Web Site Presentation
     www.gescat.es/
Catalunya Regional Boureau, 2003, Web Site Presentation
CEMR, 2002, Web Site Presentation
     www.ccre.org/site.html
CEMR, 2002, Proposals to the Convention of the Future of Europe
     www.ccre.org/site.html
CEMR, 2002, Web Site Presentation: Governance
     www.ccre.org/site.html
CEMR, 2002, Web Site Presentation: Statements
     www.ccre.org/site.html

CLRAE, 2002, Web Site Presentation

Committee of the Regions – CoR, 1999, Opinion of the Committee of the Regions on the 'European Action Plan Against Racism' cdr 369/98 FIN, Official Journal C 198, 14 July 1999 p. 0048

Committee of the Regions – CoR, 1999, Web Site Presentation: Regional Authority
www.cor.eu.int/en/pres/pres_rol.html

Committee of the Regions – CoR, 1999, Web Site Presentation: Summary
www.cor.eu.int/en/prss/prss_cdr.html

Committee of the Regions – CoR, 2002, Web Site Presentation
www.cor.eu.int/en/prss/prss_5qu.html

Committee of the Regions – CoR, 2002, Web Site Presentation: On Commission for Constitutional Affairs and European Governance – Work Programme
www.cor.eu.int/en/pres/pres_com05.html

Committee of the Regions – CoR, 2002, Web Site: COTER Work Programme
www.cor.eu.int/en/pres/pres_com01.html

Committee of the Regions – CoR, 2002, Web Site Presentation: Commission for Sustainable Development – Work Programme
www.cor.eu.int/en/pres/pres_com03.html

Committee of the Regions – CoR, 2002, Web Site Presentation: ECOS – Work Programme
www.cor.eu.int/en/pres/pres_com02.html

Committee of the Regions – CoR, 2002, Web Site Presentation: Culture and Education – Work Programme
www.cor.eu.int/en/pres/pres_com04.html

Committee of the Regions – CoR, 2002, Web Site Presentation: Commission for External Relations – Work Programme
www.cor.eu.int/en/pres/pres_com06.html

Committee of the Regions – CoR, 2002, Web Site Presentation: Structural Funds

DG Employment and Social Affairs, 2001, Web Site Presentation: Community Action Programme to Combat Discrimination 2001
europa.eu.int/comm/employment_social/fundamri/prog/intro_en.htm

DG Employment and Social Affairs, 2002, Web Site Presentation
europa.eu.int/comm/dgs/employment_social/intro_en.htm

DG Employment and Social Affairs, 2002, Web Site Presentation: European Year Against Racism
europa.eu.int/comm/employment_social/fundamri/eu_racism/eyar_en.htm

DG Employment and Social Affairs, 2002, Web Site Presentation: Mainstreaming Anti-Racism
europa.eu.int/comm/employment_social/fundamri/eu_racism/main_en.htm

DG Employment and Social Affairs, 2002, Web Site Presentation: Introduction on Racism and Xenophobia
europa.eu.int/comm/employment_social/fundamri/racism/intro_en.htm

DG Employment and Social Affairs, 2001, European Commission Contribution to the World Conference Against Racism, Racial Discrimination, Xenophobia and Related Intolerance, Durban, South Africa, 31 August–7 September 2001
europa.eu.int/comm/external_relations/human_rights/wcar/index.htm

DG Environment, 2001, 6th Environmental AP: Executive Summary
europa.eu.int/comm/environment/newprg/6eap_xsum_en.pdf

DG Environment, 2002, Web Site Presentation
  europa.eu.int/comm/dgs/environment/directory.htm
DG Regional Policy, 2001, Regional Policy Action Plan 2001
  europa.eu.int/comm/regional_policy/intro
DG Regional Policy, 2002, Web Site Presentation
  europa.eu.int/comm/regional_policy/intro/regions3_en.htm#gen
Economic and Social Committee, 2001, Opinion on 6th Environmental AP
Economic and Social Committee, 1998, Opinion of the Economic and Social Committee
  on the 'Communication from the Commission: An Action Plan Against Racism',
  Official Journal C 407 , 28 December 1998 p. 0183 – 0187
EEA, 2002, EEA Brochure
  www.org.eea.eu.int/documents/brochure/brochure_index.html
EEA, 2002, Web Site Presentation: Who We Are
  www.org.eea.eu.int/documents/who_we_are
EEB, 2000, Main Activities: Sustainable Development
  www.eeb.org/activities/sustainable_development/main.htm
EEB, 2001, On European Action Programme
  www.eeb.org/activities/env_action_programmes/main.htm
EEB, 2001, Sustainable Development: Making It Happen: A Crucial Role For the European Union
  www.eeb.org/activities/sustainable_development/EEB%20Barcelona%20Position
  %20Paper%20.pdf
EEB, 2001, EEB Proposals to Strengthen the 6th Environmental Action Programme
  www.eeb.org/publication/6th%20EAP%20Final.pdf 1
EEB, 2001, Work Plan 2002
  www.eeb.org/publication/WORKPROGRAMME-2002.pdf
EEB, 2001, The Use of Environmental Information by Civil Society
  www.eeb.org/activities/General/eea-11.28.pdf
EEB, 2001, EEB as Stakeholder
  www.eeb.org/sds
EEB, 2002, Making the Economy Work for Sustainable Development
  www.eeb.org/activities/sustainable_development/final-joint-text.pdf
EEB, 2002, Web Site: General Activities
  www.eeb.org/activities/general.htm
EEB, 2002, Web Site Presentation: Mission
  www.eeb.org/about/mission.htm
EEB, 2002, A Nice Start but a Tough Race
  www.eeb.org/activities/sustainable_development/eeb-esc-13-09-02.pdf
EEB, 2002, Web Site: On Transparency
  www.eeb.org/activities/transparency/main
EEB, 2002, Web Site Presentation: Working Methods
  www.eeb.org/about/working.htm
ENAR, 1999, ENAR Position Paper: Racism is not an Opinion
ENAR, 2000, ENAR Communication on the Green Paper on a Community Return
  Policy on Illegal Residents
ENAR, 2000, Web Site Presentation: Reunion Family
  www.enar.eu.org/en/campaign/

ENAR, 2000, Web Site Presentation: World Conference
    www.enar.eu.org/en/campaign/wcar
ENAR, 2000, Position on European Conference 'All Different, All Equal: From Principle
    to Practice'
ENAR, 2001, Web Site Presentation: Campaigns 2001
    www.enar.eu.org/en/campaign/3
ENAR, 2002, Web Site Presentation: About Us
    www.enar.eu.org/en/about
ENAR, 2002, Web Site Presentation: Mission
    www.enar.eu.org/en/mission
ENAR, 2002, Web Site Presentation: Principal Campaigns
    www.enar.eu.org/en/campaign
ENAR, 2002, Web Site Presentation: EU-Citizenship
    www.enar.eu.org/en/campaign/citizenship
ENAR, 2002, Web Site Presentation: Legal Protection
    www.enar.eu.org/en/campaign/
European Bureau for Lesser Used Languages – EBLUL, 2000, EBLUL Final Document 2000
    www.eblul.org/klaskpajenn.asp?yezh=saozneg&rumm=document+final
European Bureau for Lesser Used Languages – EBLUL, 2000, EBLUL Final Document
    Charleroi 2000
    www.eblul.org/klaskpajenn.asp?yezh=saozneg&rumm=document+final
European Bureau for Lesser Used Languages – EBLUL, 2001, EBLUL Final Report 13
    October 2001
    www.eblul.org/klaskpajenn.asp?yezh=saozneg&rumm=document+final
European Bureau for Lesser Used Languages – EBLUL, 2002, EBLUL Press Release 8
    February 2002
    www.eblul.org/klaskpajenn.asp?yezh=saozneg&rumm=document+final
European Bureau for Lesser Used Languages – EBLUL, 2002, EBLUL Final Report 12
    October 2002
    www.eblul.org/klaskpajenn.asp?yezh=saozneg&rumm=document+final
European Bureau for Lesser Used Languages – EBLUL, 2002, EBLUL Final Report 15
    June 2002
    www.eblul.org/klaskpajenn.asp?yezh=saozneg&rumm=document+final
European Bureau for Lesser Used Languages – EBLUL, 2002, EBLUL Final Report 9
    February 2002
    www.eblul.org/klaskpajenn.asp?yezh=saozneg&rumm=document+final
European Bureau for Lesser Used Languages – EBLUL, 2002, Web Site Presentation
    www.eblul.org/pajenn.asp?ID=40&yezh=saozneg
European Commission, 1998, An Action Plan Against Racism. Communication from
    the Commission (COM(1998)183 Final) of 25 March 1998
    europa.eu.int/comm/employment_social/fundamental_rights/Publi/pubs_en.htm
European Commission, 2000, Commission Report on the Implementation of the Action
    Plan against Racism January 2001
    europa.eu.int/comm/employment_social/fundamental_rights/prog/origin_en.htm
European Commission, 2000, Contribution to the European Conference: 'All Different,
    All Equal: from Theory to Practice', 17 April
    europa.eu.int/comm/employment_social/fundamental_rights/pdf/pubdocs/ecwc
    _en.pdf

European Commission, 2000, Web Presentation: European Conference Against Racism and Intolerance 'All Different, All Equal: from Principle to Practice'
europa.eu.int/comm/employment_social/fundamental_rights

European Federation for Transport and Environment, 2000, Environment: Towards Meeting the Challenges of Sustainable Development

European Monitoring Centre on Racism and Xenophobia – EUMC, 2002, Web Site Presentation: About Us.txt
www.eumc.eu.int/about/index.htm

European Monitoring Centre on Racism and Xenophobia – EUMC, 2002, Web Site Presentation: Mission Statement
www.eumc.eu.int/about/mission/htm

European Monitoring Centre on Racism and Xenophobia – EUMC, 2002, Web Site Presentation: Why a Centre to Combat Racism
www.eumc.eu.int/about/background.htm

European Parliament, 1998, European Parliament Resolution A4-0478/1998, Resolution on the Communication from the Commission 'An Action Plan Against Racism'

European Parliament, 1998, Resolution on Racism, Xenophobia and Anti-Semitism and the Results of the European Year Against Racism, Official Journal C 056, 23 February 1998 p. 0035

European Parliament, 1999, Resolution on Respect for Human Rights in the European Union, Official Journal C 098, 9 April 1999 p. 0279

European Parliament, 1999, Resolution on Racism, Xenophobia and Anti-Semitism and on Further Steps to Combat Racial Discrimination
www.europarl.eu.int/en/discrimi/ssi/race/default.shtm

European Parliament, 2000, Report on Public Access to Environmental Information,

European Parliament, 2000, European Parliament Resolution on 'Acting Locally for Employment – A Local Dimension for the European Employment Strategy',
www.3.europarl.eu.int/omk/omnsapir.so/pv2?PRG=GENECRAN&APP=PV2&LANGUE=EN&TYPEF=TITRE

European Parliament, 2000, European Parliament Resolution on Lesser Used Languages
www.3.europarl.eu.int/omk/omnsapir.so/pv2?PRG=GENECRAN&APP=PV2&LANGUE=EN&TYPEF=TITRE

European Parliament, 2001, 6th Environmental AP: Position of the European Parliament

European Parliament, 2001, Resolution on Integrating Environmental Issues with Economic Policy, A5-0172/2001

European Parliament, 2001, Resolution on Environment Policy and Sustainable Development – Minutes

European Parliament, 2002, Environment Policy: General Principles

European Parliament, 2002, Report on Environmental Inspection

European Parliament, 2002, Resolution on Environmental Noise, PE-CONS 3611/2002 -C5-0098/2002 – 2000/0194(COD)

European Parliament, 2002, Environment: Standardisation and Rationalisation of Reports, P5_TA-PROV(2002)0388

European Parliament, 2002, Environment: Public Participation in Respect of the Drawing up of Plans and Programmes, P5_TA-PROV(2002)0405

FOE Europe, 2002, Web Presentation
www.foeeurope.org/about/english.htm

Friends of the Earth Europe, 2001, Globalisation, Ecological Debt, Climate Change and Sustainability
    www.foeeurope.org

Friends of the Earth Europe, 2002, Reaching a Sustainable Europe
    www.foeeurope.org/press/fith_env_action_plan.htm

Green 8, 2001, Position on EU Sustainable Development Strategy
    www.eeb.org/publication/Response%20to%20SDS.pdf

Green 8, 2003, Proposals to the Convention

Green 8, 2003, The Future of the European Union and Sustainable Development

Greenpeace Europe, 2002, Web Site Presentation: Mission,
    www.greenpeace.org/extra/?item_id=4265&language_id=en

Greenpeace Europe, 2002, Web Site: About Us
    www.greenpeace.org/aboutus/

IFN, 2000, European Strategy for Sustainable Development Launched

IFN, 2002, Positions of the Friends of Nature on European Unification

IFN, 2002, Europe and Sustainable Development

IFN, 2002, Web Site Presentation

IFN, 2002, Europe Must not be Reduced to a Self-Service Shop

IFN, 2002, Web Site Presentation: Who, What,

Inforegio, 2002, Web Site: Presentation of European Regional Policy,

Migration Policy Group – MPG, 2000, MPG Speech, Brussels
    www.migpolgroup.com/publications/default.asp?action=publication&pubid=83

Migration Policy Group – MPG, 2002, Web Site Presentation: About Us
    www.migpolgroup.com/aboutus/default.asp

Migration Policy Group – MPG, 2002, Web Site Presentation: Implementing European Legal Standards
    www.migpolgroup.com/programmes/default.asp?action=displayprog&ProgID=13

Migration Policy Group – MPG, 2002, Web Site Presentation: Specialised Bodies
    www.migpolgroup.com/programmes/default.asp?action=displayprog&ProgID=15

Migration Policy Group – MPG, 2002, MPG Speech, Copenhagen
    www.migpolgroup.com/publications/default.asp?action=publication&pubid=86

NGO platform, 1999, Response to the Commission's Discussion Paper on Article 13

NGO platform, 2000, Report from the Forum of Non-Governmental Organisations: End Racism Now
    www.coe.int/T/E/human_rights/Ecri/2-European_Conference/
    3-NGO_contributions/01-ONG_Reports.asp

NGO platform, 2002, Combating Racial and Ethnic Discrimination: Taking the European Legislative Agenda Further
    www.migpolgroup.com/publications/default.asp?action=publication&pubid=20

Regione Veneto, La Sede di Bruxelles – Sito ufficiale della regione Veneto
    www.regione.veneto.it/settori/settore.asp?cat=763

Sardinian Regional Boureau, 2002, Web Presentation
    www.regione.sardegna.it/europa/europa.html

Scottish Regional Bureau, 2002, Scotland Europa
    www.scotlandeurope.com

Scottish Regional Bureau, 2002, Web Presentation: Networking Scotland in Europe
    www.scotlandeuropa.com/sp_index.htm

Scottish Regional Bureau, 2003, Web Site: Europe and the Regions
www.scotlandeurope.com
Starting Line Group, 1998, Campaigning Against Racism and Xenophobia: From a Legislative Perspective at European level
www.migpolgroup.com/publications/default.asp?action=publication&pubid=47
WWF Europe, 2002, Web Site Presentation
www.panda.org/about_wwf/where_we_work/europe/what_we_do/policy_and_ev ents/epo/index.cfm

Notes

1 All classified dcuments and database files are available on the web, at www.soc.unitn. it/users/carlo.ruzza

2 See the chapter on mainstreaming in Rees (1998).

3 Implementation was considered too internally differentiated to be considered as a self-standing code. It was therefore specified into two dimensions: *effectiveness of implemented policies,* which refers to the necessity to increase the effectiveness of already implemented measures and *application of public policy,* which refers to the observation that already decided norms and regulations had to be implemented.

4 The first type of sentences would include for instances advocacy for anti-discrimination measures – for instance, 'new anti-discrimination policies are needed', the second refers to the emphasis on eliminating instances of perceived discrimination, such as in 'there are high level of racist incidents and discrimination'.

5 Financial information has always been understood in its meaning of information on available financial resources for regional development.

6 As mentioned we included documents from regional offices. We deemed it important to differentiate our sample of OCS from our sample of regional offices which is of a different kind and also of necessity much more limited and therefore somewhat arbitrary. Only a very few regional offices were examined – mainly to see whether their discourse differed substantially from other organisations. However, we did not note relevant differences between regional organisations and regional bureaus.

7 This refers to the grounded theory concept of constantly re-examining primary sources.

Appendix B: MACs and public opinion

Public opinion and the environment

Environmental attitudes have changed over time but they have shown fairly similar trends in most member states (cf. EB 29, q.242, 1988; EB 37.0, q.74, 1992; EB 43.1 bis, 1.15, 1995; EB 51.1, q.3, 1999). Attachment to environmental values generally showed an upward trend in the first part of the 1990s. The highest level was reached in 1992, when 86 per cent of interviewees saw the environment as an immediate and urgent problem, while only 14 per cent saw it as a non-problem or a problem for the future. The average level stayed relatively constant until the mid-1990s, and then decreased, until in 1999 it fell below the 1988 level once again (see chapter 3). Nevertheless the environment appeared to be one of the greatest concerns (57 per cent in 1989, as compared to 63 per cent in 1997), whereas in the same period the fight against racism lost its importance (from 56 per cent to 22 per cent). The fact that all countries exhibited similar trends, although with significantly different average values could be connected to the relatively lower concerted opposition and veto threats that one finds in other policy areas. Figure B.1 shows the values observed in the five largest member states. I have also included the values demonstrated by Greece (the highest of the member states) and Belgium (the lowest).

Public opinion and discrimination

Considering the surveys conducted since 1990 (cf. EB 37.0, q.73, 1992; EB 39.0, q.36, 1993; EB 42, q.85, 1994; EB 48.0, q.44, 1997; EB 53, q.46-48, 2000), which aim at documenting Europeans' attitudes towards racial, national and religious diversity, one finds fairly discontinuous trends. The indicators utilised were essentially a mix of xenophobia and racism. Interviewees were asked whether they perceive people of other nationalities, races and religion as a disturbing factor. As we can see from figure B.2, the average trend in the EU essentially shows a phase of diminishing propensity to consider diversity as a disturbing factor during the early 1990s. In the second half of the decade, we can see a new period of growth in the number of people regarding such diversity as a disturbing

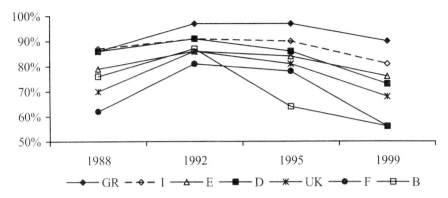

Figure B.1 Importance of environment protection, 1988–99 (% in the five main EU countries, plus Greece and Belgium)

Source: EB 29 (q. 242), EB 37.0 (q. 74), EB 43.1 bis (q. 15), EB 51.1 (q. 3)

factor. In 1998, 10 per cent of the interviewees said that they approved of racist movements, or of the position of racist organisations in relation to immigrants (*EUMC Annual Report*). Moreover, while 70 per cent of European citizens approved of the movements against racism, every fifth European disapproved of them. In 2002 (EB 56.1) 66 per cent of European citizens said that they were afraid of ethnic conflict in Europe, while 30% were not afraid of it and 10 per cent 'didn't know'.

While there is a consistent average decline in opposition to xenophobia (and, implicitly, in support for anti-racism), there are, however, very different trends in different EU countries. Countries like Belgium, Germany and Denmark are more tolerant towards national differences. The UK, Ireland and Austria are tolerant towards religious differences. The Scandinavian countries (Denmark, Sweden and Finland) are less tolerant towards religious diversity. In any event it appears that, as noted in the text, the recent policy success of the anti-racist coalition has taken place in a general climate of growing intolerance and decreasing size of anti-racist public opinion. For example, two special

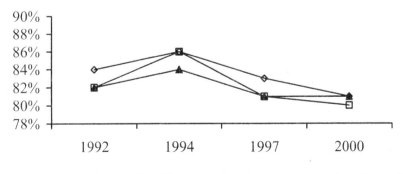

Figure B.2 Positive attitudes towards people of another nationality/race/religion, 1992–200 (%)

Source: EB 37 (q. 73), EB 39.0 (q. 36), EB 42 (q. 85), EB 48.0 (q. 44), EB 53 (q. 46–48)

surveys conducted by Eurobarometer on behalf of EUMC in 1997 and 2000 (EB 47.1, Ebs 138) measured support for the statement that 'it is a good thing for any society to be made up of people from different races, religions and cultures'. If we compare the proportions of those supporting this argument in 1997 and 2000 we note that support decreased from 66 per cent to 64 per cent at the EU level. At the same time, agreement with the opposite statement increased from 21 per cent to 24 per cent (figure B.3).

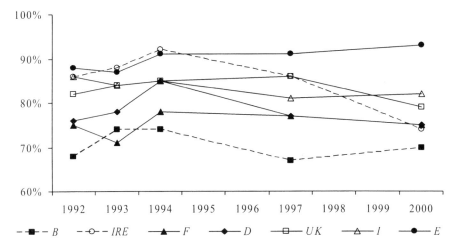

Figure B.3 Positive attitude towards people of another race, 1992–2000 (% in the five main EU countries, plus Belgium and Ireland)

Source: EB 37.0 (q. 73), EB 39.0 (q. 36), EB 42 (q. 85), EB 48.0 (q. 44), EB 53 (q. 46–48)

Public opinion, regionalism and local attachment

In relation to the localised pressures, expressed in terms of attachment to own locality (within village or city), to own region, to own nation and to the EU, evidenced in the surveys carried out in the course of a decade (cf. EB 36, q.64, 1991; EB 43,1 bis, q.34, 1995; EB 51,0, q.13, 1999; EB 54,1, q.8, 2000), it is necessary to emphasise that, in the period under consideration, there is a notable continuity among the surveys regarding the sense of strong or moderate attachment to each of the local, regional and national levels (see figure B.4), though a moderate diminution of the sense of belonging to the own region is recorded.

But if we observe the figures related to declarations of 'strong attachment to', it is possible to observe a marked decrease in the sense of belonging to the region (a drop of 13 percentage points from 1995 to 2000). In parallel to this, there has also been a gradual diminution in the sense of strong belonging to the locality (involving a fall of 6 percentage points over the ten-year period, though half of this fall occurred between the 1999 and 2000 surveys). In the most recent survey, carried out at the end of 2000, eight out of ten individuals declared a strong or moderate allegiance to the local level. In member states, this sense of local belonging exceeded 75 percentage points. There are, however, national differences among the EU member states. Southern European countries,

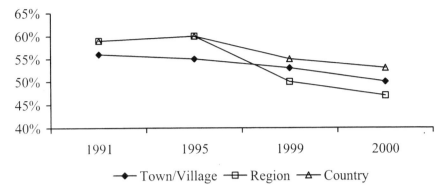

Figure B.4 People's strong attachment to their town/village, region, country, 1991–2000 (EU % average)

Source: EB 36 (q. 64), EB 43.1bis (q. 34), EB 51.0 (q. 13), EB 54.1 (q. 8)

together with Austria and Ireland, are particularly keen on local belonging. If we concentrate only on the portion of the sample that expressed strong belonging, we can see that in twelve out of fifteen member states, over 50 per cent of interviewees are strongly attached (figure B.5).

Over time, regional belonging is gradually decreasing in the five large member states. In most Northern European countries (UK, the Netherlands, Scandinavia, France), there is a prevalence of attachment to the national level, whereas in most central and southern European countries (Germany, Belgium, Italy, Spain, Portugal), there are stronger local belongings.

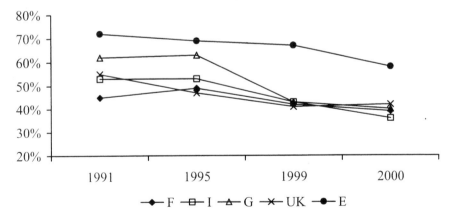

Figure B.5 People's attachment to their region, 1991–2000 (% in the five EU main countries)

Source: EB 36 (q. 64), EB 43.1bis (q. 34), EB 51.0 (q. 13), EB 54.1 (q. 8)

References

Achleitner, F. (1997). 'Region, ein Konstrukt? Regionalismus eine Ertfindung?', in F. Achleitner, *Region, ein Konstruct? Regionalismus eine Pleite?* Basel, Birkhäuser: 101–111.

Alink, F., A. Boin, *et al.* (2001). 'Institutional Crises and Reforms in Policy Sectors: The Case of Asylum Policy in Europe', *Journal of European Public Policy*, 8 (2), 286–306.

Allen, C. and J. S. Nielsen (2002). 'Summary Report on Islamophobia in the EU after 11 September 2001', Vienna, EUMC and Centre for the Study of Islam and Christian–Muslim Relations, University of Birmingham: 62.

Alonso, W. (1995). 'Citizenship, Nationality, and Other Identities', *Journal of International Affairs*, 48 (2): 585–600.

Anheier, H. (ed.) (2001). *Global Civil Society 2001*, Oxford, Oxford University Press.

Armstrong, K. A. (2002). 'Rediscovering Civil Society: The European Union and the White Paper on Governance', *European Law Journal*, 8 (1): 102–132.

Armstrong, K. A. (2003). 'Tackling Social Exclusion Through OMC: Reshaping the Boundaries of EU Governance', in T. B. and R. Cichowski, *The State of the Union: Law, Politics and Society*, 6, Oxford: Oxford University Press: 170–194.

Banchhoff, T. and M. P. Smith (1999). *Legitimacy and the European Union*, London, Routledge.

Bates, S. (1998). 'EU Lifts Blocks on Aid Funds', *The Guardian*, 18 July: 15.

Bell, M. (2002). *Anti-Discrimination Law and the European Union*, Oxford, Oxford University Press.

Bellamy, R. (2001). 'The Right to have Rights: Citizenship Practice and the Political Constitution of the EU', in A. Warleigh, *Citizenship and Governance in the European Union*, London, Continuum.

Benford, R. D. (1997). 'An Insider's Critique of the Social Movement Framing Perspective', *Sociological Inquiry*, 67 (4): 409–430.

Ben-Tovim, G. (1997). 'Why "Positive Action" is "Politically Correct"', in T. Modood and P. Werbner, *The Politics of Multiculturalism in the New Europe: Racism, Identity and Community*, London, Zed Books.

Bleich, E. (1998). 'From International Ideas to Domestic Politics: Gatekeepers, Priors and Educational Multilateralism in England and France', *Comparative Politics*, October: 81–100.

Boli, J. and G. M. Thomas (eds) (1999). *Constructing World Culture: International Non-governmental Organizations since 1875*, Stanford, CA, Stanford University Press.

Bonnett, A. (1993a). 'The Formation of Public Professional Radical Consciousness: The Example of Anti-Racism', *Sociology*, 27 (2): 281–297.

Bonnett, A. (1993b). *Radicalism, Anti-Racism and Representation*, London, Routledge.

Bonnett, A. (2000). *Anti-Racism*, London, Routledge.

Burstein, P. (1998). 'Bringing the Public Back In: Should Sociologists Consider the Impact of Public Opinion on Public Policy?', *Social Forces*, 77 (1): 27–72.

Burstein, P. (1999). 'Social Movements and Public Policy', in M. Giugni, D. McAdam and C. Tilly, *How Social Movements Matter*, Minneapolis, University of Minnesota Press: 3–21.

Burstein, P., A. Eaton *et al.* (1997). 'Why do Social Movement Organizations, Interest Groups and Political Parties Seem to Have So Little Impact on Public Policy?', American Sociological Association Conference, Toronto.

Buttel, F. and P. Taylor (1994). 'Environmental Sociology and Global Environmental Change: A Critical Assessment' in M. Redclift and T. Benton, *Social Theory and the Global Environment*, London, Routledge: 228–255.

Calhoun, C. (1993). 'Civil Society and the Public Sphere', *Public Culture*, 5: 267–280.

Cawson, A. (ed.) (1985). *Organized Interests and the State: Studies in Meso-Corporatism*, London, Sage.

Checkel, J. (1997). 'International Norms and Domestic Politics: Bridging the Rationalist–Constructivist Divide', *European Journal of International Relations*, 3: 473–495.

Checkel, J. (1999a). 'Norms, Institutions and National Identity in Contemporary Europe', *International Studies Quarterly*, March.

Checkel, J. T. (1999b). '(Regional) Norms and (Domestic) Social Mobilization: Citizenship Politics in Post-Maastricht, Post-Cold War Germany', ARENA Working Papers, WP 99/3, University of Oslo.

Chopin, I. and J. Niessen (1998). 'Proposal for Legislative Measures to Combat Racism and to Promote Equal Rights in the European Union', London, Starting Line Group and Commission for Racial Equality UK.

Christiansen, T. (1996). 'Second Thoughts on Europe's "Third Level": The European Union's Committee of the Regions', *Publius: The Journal of Federalism*, 26 (1): 93–116.

Christiansen, T. and E. J. Kirchner (eds) (2000). *Committee Governance in the European Union*, Manchester and New York, Manchester University Press.

Cini, M. (1996). *The European Commission*, Manchester, Manchester University Press.

Cini, M. (1997). 'Administrative Culture in the European Commission: The Cases of Competition and Environment', in N. Nugent, *At the Heart of the Union: Studies of the European Commission*, London, Macmillan: 71–89.

Cobb Roger, W. and H. Ross Marc (1997). *Cultural Strategies of Agenda Denial: Avoidance, Attack, and Redefinition*, Lawrence, KS, University Press of Kansas.

Cohen, J. L. and A. Arato (1999). *Civil Society and Political Theory*, Cambridge, MA, MIT Press.

Commission (1992). 'Towards Sustainability: A European Community Programme of Action in Relation to the Environment and Sustainable Development' (Fifth Environmental Action Programme), COM (92), 23 Final, 27 March 1992, vol. II, Brussels.

Commission (1993). 'An Open and Structured Dialogue between the Commission and Special Interest Groups', JOC, 63/2 (5 March 1993): 2–7.

Commission (1995). 'Communication from the Commission on Promoting the Role of Voluntary Organisations and Foundations In Europe – DG Enterprise', Brussels, DG Enterprise.

Commission (1996a). 'Commission Communication Concerning the Development of the Social Dialogue at Community Level', COM(96) 448 Final, 1996/475 (18 September 1996): 1–34.

Commission (1996b). 'Premier rapport sur la prise en compte des aspects culturels dans l'action de la Communauté Européenne', COM(96)160, Brussels.

Commission (1997a). 'Communication from the Commission on Promoting the Role of Voluntary Organisations and Foundations in Europe', COM 97 (241) Final (18 January 2000): 1–88.

Commission (1997b). 'The European Institutions in the Fight Against Racism: Selected Texts', Brussels, Employment and Social Affairs.

Commission (1998a). 'An Action Plan Against Racism', Brussels.

Commission (1998b). 'Adopting and Promoting the Social Dialogue at Community Level', COM 98 (332) (20 May 1998).

Commission (1998c). 'Racism and Xenophobia in Europe – Eurobarometer Opinion Poll no. 47.1', Luxembourg, OOPEC.

Commission (1999). 'What Do Europeans Think about the Environment ? The Main Results of the Survey Carried out in the Context of Eurobarometer 51.1', Luxembourg: OOPEC, 1999, DG XI – Environment, Nuclear Safety and Civil Protection in Conjunction with DG X Information, Communication, Culture and Audiovisual Media.

Commission (2000a). 'The Commission and Non-Governmental Organisations: Building a Stronger Partnership', COM(00) 11 Final (18 January 2000): 1–26.

Commission (2000b). 'Developing New Modes of Governance. Brussels', Forward Studies Unit, Notis Lebessis, John Paterson, Working Paper.

Commission (2001a). 'Environment 2010: Our Future, Our Choice', COM(2001) 31 Final – Sixth Environment Action Programme of the European Community, Brussels.

Commission (2001b). 'European Governance: A White Paper', COM(2001)428.

Commission, M. Preston *et al.* (2001). 'Report of Working Group "Consultation And Participation of Civil Society"' (Group 2a), Brussels, European Commission.

Commission and N. Thogersen (2001). 'White Paper on European Governance Work Area No. 1, "Broadening and Enriching the Public Debate on European Matters"', Brussels, European Commission.

Commission on Global Governance (1995). *Our Global Neighbourhood*, Oxford, Oxford University Press.

Conversi, D. (2002a). 'Conceptualising Nationalism: An Introduction to Walker Connor's Work', in D. Conversi, *Ethnonationalism in the Contemporary World*, London, Routledge: 1–23.

Conversi, D. (2002b). 'Resisting Primordialism (and Other -isms)', in D. Conversi, *Ethnonationalism in the Contemporary World*, London, Routledge: 269–90.

Cooper, A. H. (2002). 'Media Framing and Social Movement Mobilization: German Peace Protest against INF Missiles, the Gulf War, and NATO Peace Enforcement in Bosnia', *European Journal of Political Research*, 41 (1): 37–80.

CoR, Klär *et al.* (2000). 'Report on Proximity by the Committee of the Regions', Brussels: 1–18.

Council (2002). 'Council Resolution of 14 February 2002 on the Promotion of Linguistic Diversity and Language Learning in the Framework of the Implementation of the

Objectives of the European Year of Languages 2001', *Official Journal of the European Communities*, C (050): 0001–0002.

Cram, L. (1993). 'Calling the Tune without Paying the Piper? Social Policy Regulation: The Role of the Commission in European Community Social Policy', *Policy and Politics*, 21 (2): 135–146.

Crook, A. (Member of ECAS Executive Council) with assistance from the Charities Aid Foundation (CAF) (2000). 'Listening To Civil Society: What Relationship between the European Commission and NGOs?', Brussels, ECAS.

Crouch, C., K. Eder *et al.* (eds) (2001). *Citizenship, Markets and the State*, Oxford, Oxford University Press.

Dahl, R. A. (1989). *Democracy and its Critics*, New Haven, Yale University Press.

Delanty, G. (2000). *Citizenship in the Global Age*, Milton Keynes, Open University Press.

Delwit, P., E. Külahci *et al.* (eds) (2001). *Les fédérations européennes de partis. Organisation et influence*, Collection 'Sociologie politique', Brussels, editions de L'Université de Bruxelles.

De Rynck, S. and P. McAleavey (2001). 'The Cohesion Deficit in Structural Fund Policy', *Journal of European Public Policy*, 8 (4): 541–557.

De Winter, L. (2001). 'The Impact of European Integration on Ethnoregionalist Parties', Barcelona, Institut de Ciències Politiques i Sociales – Universitat Autònoma de Barcelona: 1–43.

De Winter, L. and H. Tursan (eds) (1998). *Regionalist Parties in Western Europe*, London, Routledge.

DG Research (1996). 'Rules on Lobbying and Intergroups in the National Parliaments of the Member States', Brussels, Directorate-General for Research, Working Document, National Parliaments Series.

Diamantopulos, A. (2000). (Commissioner) *The National and European Role of European Social Welfare Organizations*, Athens.

Diani, M. (1992). 'The Concept of Social Movement', *Sociological Review*, 40 (1): 1–25.

DiMaggio, P. and W. Powell (1991). 'The Iron Cage Revisited: Institutional Isomorphism and Collective Rationality', in P. DiMaggio and W. Powell, *The New Institutionalism in Organizational Analysis*, Chicago, University of Chicago Press: 63–82.

Dunleavy, P. (1991). *Democracy Bureaucracy and Public Choice*, New York, Harvester.

ECAS (2002). *A Guide to European Union Funding for NGOs*, Brussels, ECAS.

Eder, K. (1996). 'The Institutionalization of Environmentalism: Ecological Discourse and the Second Transformation of the Public Sphere', in S. Lash, B. Szerszynski and B. Wynne, *Risk, Environment and Modernity: Towards a New Ecology*, London, Sage.

Eder, K. and B. Giesen (2001). *European Citizenship: Between National Legacies and Postnational Projects*, Oxford and New York, Oxford University Press.

Eder, K. and M. Kousis (2000). *Environmental Politics in Southern Europe*, Dordrecht, Kluwer Academic.

Edwards, G. and D. Spence (1994). *The European Commission*, Harlow, Longman.

Edwards, M. and J. Gaventa (eds) (2001). *Global Citizen Action*, London, Earthscan.

ESC (1999a). 'Opinion of the Economic and Social Committee on "Transparency and the Participation of Civil Society Organisations in the WTO Millennium Round"', *JOC*, 1999/368 (20 December 1999): 43–46.

ESC (1999b). 'Opinion on "The Role and Contribution of Civil Society Organisations in the Building of Europe"', *OJ C329*, 17 November 1999: 30.

ESC (2000a). *The Civil Society Organised at European Level*, First Convention on the Civil Society Organised at European Level, Brussels, ESC.

ESC (2000b). 'Concise Report of the Debates of the First Convention of Civil Society Organised at European Level', Brussels.

ESC (2000c). 'Opinion of the Economic and Social Committee on the Commission Discussion Paper, "The Commission and Non-Governmental Organisations: Building a Stronger Partnership"', *OJC 268*, 15: 267–273.

ESC (2001a). 'Opinion of The Economic and Social Committee on "Organised Civil Society and European Governance: The Committee's Contribution to the Drafting of The White Paper"', Brussels, CES 535/2001 Fr-De/Mev/Jkb/Ym Sub-Committee on Governance.

ESC (2001b). 'Organised Civil Society and European Governance: The Committee's Contribution to the Drafting of the White Paper', Brussels, CES.

Eyerman, R. and A. Jamison (1991). *Social Movements: a Cognitive Approach*, University Park, PA, Pennsylvania State University.

Favell, A. (1998). 'The Europeanisation of Immigration Politics', *European Integration Online Papers*, 2 (10), www.eiop.or.at/eiop/texte/1998-010a.htm.

Ferguson, J. (1990). *The Anti-Politics Machine*, Cambridge, Cambridge University Press.

Finnemore, M. and K. Sikkink (1998). 'International Norm Dynamics and Political Change', *International Organization*, 52 (4): 887–917.

Flynn, B. (2000). 'Postcards from the Edge of Integration? The Role of Committees in EU Environment Policy-Making', in T. Christiansen and E. Kirchner, *Committee Governance in the European Union*, Manchester, Manchester University Press: 79–97.

Ford, G. (1992). *Fascist Europe: the Rise of Racism and Xenophobia*, London, Pluto Press.

Fouloy, C. D. (1994). *European Lobbyists' Practical Guide*, Brussels, European Study Service.

Freeden, M. (1995). 'Green Ideology: Concepts and Structures', Oxford, OCEES, Mansfield College, Oxford University.

Freeden, M. (1996). *Ideologies and Political Theory: A Conceptual Approach*, Oxford, Clarendon Press.

Freeden, M. (1998). 'Is Nationalism a Distinct Ideology?', *Political Studies*, 46 (4): 748–765.

Gamson, W. A. (1975). *The Strategy of Social Protest.* Homewood, IL, Dorsey.

Gamson, W. A. (1988). 'Political Discourse and Collective Action', *ISR*, 1: 219–244.

Gamson, W. A. (1992). *Talking Politics*, London, Cambridge University Press.

Gamson, W. A., B. Fireman *et al.* (1982). *Encounters with Unjust Authority.* Homewood, IL, Dorsey.

Gamson, W. A. and A. N. Modigliani (1989). 'Media Discourse and Public Opinion on Nuclear Power: A Constructionist Approach', *American Journal of Sociology*, 95: 1–38.

Geddes, A. (1999). 'The Development of EU Immigration Policy: Supranationalism and the Politics of Belonging', in A. Geddes and A. Favell, *The Politics of Belonging: Migrants and Minorities in Contemporary Europe*, Aldershot, Ashgate.

Gellner, E. (1994). *Conditions of Liberty: Civil Society and its Rivals*, London, Hamish Hamilton.

Geyer, R. (2000a). 'Can Mainstreaming Save EU Social Policy? Mainstreaming Gender, Disability and Elderly Policy', *Current Policy & Economics in Europe*, 10 (2): 127–147.

Geyer, R. (2000b). *Exploring European Social Policy*, Cambridge, Polity Press.

Gilroy, P. (1987). *There Ain't No Black in the Union Jack*, London, Hutchinson.

Gilroy, P. (1990). 'The End of Anti-Racism', in W. Ball and J. Solomos, *Race and Local Politics*, London, Macmillan.

Giugni, M. (1999). 'Introduction', in M. Giugni, D. McAdam and C. Tilly, *How Social Movements Matter*, Minneapolis, University of Minnesota Press: xiii–xxiii.

Giugni, M. and F. Passy (1998a). 'Contentious Politics in Complex Societies: New Social Movements between Conflict and Cooperation', in M. Giugni, D. McAdam and C. Tilly, *From Contention to Democracy*, New York, Rowman & Littlefield.

Giugni, M. and F. Passy (1998b). 'Social Movements and Policy Change: Direct, Mediated, or Joint Effect?', American Sociological Association's Section on Collective Behavior and Social Movements – Working Paper Series, 1: 1–48.

Greenwood, J. (1997). *Representing Interests in the European Union*, London, Macmillan.

Greenwood, J. and K. Ronit (1994). 'Interest Groups in the European Community: Newly Emerging Dynamics and Forms', *West European Politics*, 17 (1): 31–52.

Haas, P. M. (1992). 'Introduction: Epistemic Communities and International Policy Coordination', *International Organization*, 46: 1–37, 367–390.

Haas, P. M. (1989). 'Do Regimes Matter? Epistemic Communities and Mediterranean Pollution Control', *International Organization*, 43: 377–403.

Habermas, J. (1992). *The Structural Tranformation of the Public Sphere*, Cambridge, MA, MIT Press.

Habermas, J. (1996). *Between Facts and Norms: Contributions to a Discourse Theory of Law and Democracy*, Cambridge, Polity Press.

Hall, P. (1986). *Governing the Economy : The Politics of State Intervention in Britain and France*, Cambridge, Polity Press.

Hanf, K. and A.-I. Jansen (eds) (1998). *Governance and Environment in Western Europe*, Harlow, Longman.

Hantrais, L. (1995). *Social Policy in the European Union*, London, Macmillan.

Harvie, C. (1994). *The Rise of Regional Europe*, London, Routledge.

Hasenclever, A., P. Mayer *et al.* (1997). *Theories of International Regimes*, Cambridge, Cambridge University Press.

Hechter, M. (1985). 'Internal Colonialism Revised', in E. A. Tiryakian, *New Nationalisms of the Developed West: Toward Explanation*, Boston, Allen & Unwin: 17–26.

Held, D. (1987). *Models of Democracy*, Stanford, CA, Stanford University Press.

Héritier, A. (1996). 'The Accommodation of Diversity in European Policy-Making and its Outcomes', *Journal of European Public Policy*, 3 (2): 149–168.

Herrmann, P. (1999). *European Integration between Institution Building and Social Process : Contributions to a Theory of Modernisation and NGOs in the Context of the Development of the EU*, Commack, NY, Nova Science Publishers.

Hildebrand, P. (1993). 'The European Community Environmental Policy, 1957 to 1992: From Incidental Measures to an International Regime?', in D. Judge, *A Green Dimension for the European Community*, London, Frank Cass: 13–44.

Hirst, P. Q. (1997). *From Statism to Pluralism*, London, UCL Press.

Hirst, P. Q. and S. Khilnani (1996). *Reinventing Democracy*, Cambridge, MA, Blackwell.

Hooghe, L. (1997). *Serving 'Europe' – Political Orientations of Senior Commission Officials*, European Integration Online Papers, 1 (8), http://eiop.or.at/eiop/texte/1997-008a.htm.

Hooghe, L. (2001). The European Commission and the Integration of Europe: Images of Governance, Cambridge, Cambridge University Press.

Hooghe, L. and G. Marks (1996). '"Europe with the Regions": Channels of Regional Representation in the European Union', *Publius: The Journal of Federalism*, 26 (1): 73–91.

Hoskyns, C. (1996). *Integrating Gender: Women, Law and Politics in the European Union*, London, Verso.

Hubert, A. (1998). *L'Europe et les Femmes: Identités en mouvement*, Paris, Editions Apogee.

Hudson, A. (2001). 'NGOs' Transnational Advocacy Networks: From "Legitimacy" to "Political Responsibility"?', *Global Networks*. 1 (3): 331–352.

Immergut, E. M. (1998). 'The Theoretical Core of New Institutionalism', *Politics & Society*, 26 (1): 5–34.

Johnson, S. P. and G. Corcelle (1989). *The Environmental Policy of the European Communities*, London, Graham & Trotman.

Judge, D. (1992). 'Predestined to Save the Earth: The Environmental Committee of the European Parliament', *Environmental Politics*, 1 (4): 186–212.

Judge, D. (ed.) (1993). *A Green Dimension for the European Community*, London, Frank Cass.

Kamrava, M. (1996). *Understanding Comparative Politics: A Framework for Analysis*. London, Routledge.

Keane, J. (ed.) (1988). *Civil Society and the State. New European Perspectives*, Bristol, Verso.

Keane, J. (1999). *Civil Society*, Stanford, CA, Stanford University Press.

Keating, M. (1998). *The New Regionalism in Western Europe: Territorial Restructuring and Political Change*, Cheltenham, Edward Elgar.

Keating, M. and J. McGarry (2001). *Minority Nationalism and the Changing International Order*, Oxford and New York, Oxford University Press.

Keck, M. E. and K. Sikkink (1998). *Activism Beyond Borders*, Ithaca, NY, Cornell University Press.

Kirchner, E. (1992). *Decision-Making in the European Community*, Manchester, Manchester University Press.

Klandermans, B. (1988). 'The Formation and Mobilization of Consensus', in B. Klandermans, H. Kriesi and S. Tarrow, *From Structure to Action: Comparing Social Movement Research Across Cultures*, Greenwich, CT, JAI Press: 173–196.

Klotz, A. (1995). 'Norms Reconstituting Interests: Global Racial Equality and US Sanctions against South Africa', *International Organization*, 49: 451–478.

Kohler-Koch, B. (2000). *Network Governance within and Beyond and Enlarged European Union*, Canadian European Studies Association, Quebec City.

Krasner, S. (1988). 'Sovereignty: An Institutional Perspective', *Comparative Political Studies*, 21 (1): 66–94.

Kriesi, H., R. Koopmans *et al.* (eds) (1995). *New Social Movements in Western Europe*, Minneapolis, Minnesota University Press.

Lehnbruch, G. and P. C. Schmitter (eds) (1982). *Patterns of Corporatist Policy-Making*, London, Sage.

Lentin, A. (1998). 'Effective Anti-Racist Strategies: New Social Movements as Potential Forces of Ethnic Mobilisation', unpublished MSc dissertation in Political Sociology, London, LSE.

Leonardi, R. (1992). 'The Role of Sub-National Institutions in European Integration', *Regional Politics and Policy*, 2 (1, 2): 1–13.

Leonardi, R. and S. Garmise (1992). 'Conclusions: Sub-National Elites and the European Community', *Regional Politics and Policy*, 2 (1, 2): 247–274.

Lloyd, C. (1994). 'Universalism and Difference: The Crisis of Anti-Racism in the UK and France', in A. Rattansi and S. Westwood, *Racism, Modernity and Identity*, Cambridge, Polity Press.

Loughlin, J. (1996). '"Europe of the Regions" and the Federalization of Europe', *Publius: The Journal of Federalism*, 26 (4): 141–162.

Loughlin, J. (2000). 'Regional Autonomy and State Paradigm Shifts in Western Europe', *Regional and Federal Studies*, 10 (2): 10–34.

Lynch, P. (1996). *Minority Nationalism and European Integration*, Cardiff, University of Wales Press.

Majone, G. (1989). *Evidence, Argument, and Persuasion in the Policy Process*, New Haven, Yale University Press.

Majone, G. (1993). 'When Does Policy Deliberation Matter?', *Politische Vierteljahresschrift*, Autumn, Special Issue on Policy Analysis: 97–115.

Majone, G. (ed.) (1996). *Regulating Europe*, London, Routledge.

Müller-Rommel, F. (1985). 'New Social Movements and Smaller Parties: A Comparative Analysis', *West European Politics*, 8: 41–54.

Müller-Rommel, F. (1990). 'New Political Movements and "New Politics". Parties in Western Europe', in F. Müller-Rommel, *Challenging the Political Order. New Social and Political Movements in Western Democracies*, Oxford, Polity Press.

March, J. (1988). *Decisions and Organizations*, Oxford, Oxford University Press.

Marks, G., F. W. Scharpf *et al.* (1996). *Governance in the European Union*, London, Sage.

Marsh, M. and P. Norris (1997). 'Political Representation in the European Parliament', *European Journal of Political Research*, 32 (2): 153–164.

Massinger, S. (1955). 'Organisational Transformation: A Case Study of a Declining Social Movement', *American Sociological Review*, 20: 3–10.

Mayer, C. S. (ed.) (1987). *The Changing Boundaries of the Political*, Cambridge, Cambridge University Press.

Mazey, S. (1998). 'The European Union and Women's Rights: From the Europeanization of National Agendas to the Nationalisation of a European Agenda?', *Journal of European Public Policy*, 5 (1): 131–152.

Mazey, S. (2001). *Gender Mainstreaming in the EU*, London, Kogan Page.

Mazey, S. and J. Richardson (eds) (1993). *Lobbying in the European Community*, Oxford, Oxford University Press.

Mazey, S. and J. Richardson (1994a). 'The Commission and the Lobby', in G. Edwards and D. Spence, *The European Commission*, Harlow, Longman.

Mazey, S. and J. Richardson (1994b). 'Interest Groups in the European Community', in S. Mazey and J. Richardson, *Pressure Groups*, Oxford, Oxford University Press: 191–213.

Mazey, S. and J, Richardson (1997). 'Policy Framing: Interest Groups and the Lead Up to the 1996 Inter-Governmental Conference', *West European Politics*, 20 (3): 111–133.

McAdam, D., J. D. McCarthy *et al.* (eds) (1996). *Comparative Perspectives on Social Movements*, Cambridge, Cambridge University Press.

McCarthy, J. D. and M. N. Zald (1982). 'Resource Mobilization and Social Movements: A Partial Theory', *American Journal of Sociology*, 6: 1213–1241.

Merkel, U. and W. Tokarski (eds) (1996). *Racism and Xenophobia in European Football*, Aachen, Meyer & Meyer Verlag.

Meyer, J. (1980). 'The World Polity and the Authority of the Nation State', in A. Berge-sen, *Studies of the Modern World System*, New York, Academic Press.

Meyer, J. and B. Rowan (1991). 'Institutionalized Organizations: Formal Structure as Myth and Ceremony', in W. W. Powell and P. J. DiMaggio, *The New Institutionalism in Organizational Analysis*, Chicago, Chicago University Press.

Meyer, J. W. and R. W. Scott (eds) (1983). *Organizational Environments: Ritual and Rationality*, Beverly Hills, CA, Sage.

Michelmann, H. J. (1978). *Organizational Effectiveness in a Multinational Bureaucracy*, Farnborough, Saxon House.

Modood, T. (1997). 'Difference, Cultural Racism and Anti-Racism', in P. Werbner and T. Modood, *Debating Cultural Hybridity: Multicultural Identities and the Politics of Anti-Racism*, London, Zed Books.

Modood, T. and P. Werbner (1997). *The Politics of Multiculturalism in the New Europe: Racism, Identity and Community*, London, Zed Books.

Morth, U. (2000). 'Competing Frames in the European Commission – The Case of the Defense Industry and Equipment Issue', *Journal of European Public Policy*, 7 (2): 173–189.

Neveso, M., K. Schoeters *et al.* (2001). 'Introducing Environmental NGOs: Their Role and Importance in European Union Decision-Making', Brussels, European Environ-mental NGOs.

O'Brian, R., A. Goetz *et al.* (2000). *Contesting Global Governance*. Cambridge, Cam-bridge University Press.

Offe, K. (1990). 'Reflections on the Institutional Self-Transformation of Movement Pol-itics: A Tentative Stage Model', in R. Dalton and M. Kuechler, *Challenging the Political Order: New Social and Political Movements in Western Democracies*, New York, Oxford University Press: 232–250.

Olson, M. (1965). *The Logic of Collective Action*, Cambridge, MA, Harvard University Press.

Pantel, M. (1999). 'Unity-in-Diversity: Cultural Policy and EU Legitimacy', in T. Ban-choff and M. P. Smith, *Legitimacy and the European Union: The Contested Polity*, London, Routledge.

Parliament, European (2000). 'Charter of Fundamental Rights of the European Union', *Official Journal of the European Communities*, Brussels.

Paterson, W. (1991). "Regulatory Change and Environmental Protection in the British and German Chemical Industries', *European Journal of Political Research*, 19: 307–326.

Patterson, O. (1991). *Freedom: Freedom in the Making of Western Culture*, New York, Basic Books.

Peters, G. (2000). *Institutional Theory in Political Science: The 'New Institutionalism' in Political Science*, London, Continuum International/Pinter.

Peterson, J. and E. Bomberg (1999). *Decision-Making in the European Union*, London, Response of the Platform of European Social NGOs to 'The Commission and Non-Governmental Organizations: Building a Stronger Partnership', *Platform*, Brussels, Platform of European Social NGOs.

Pollack, M. A. (1997). 'Representing Diffuse Interests in EC Policy-Making', *Journal of European Public Policy*, 4 (4): 572–590.

Powell, W. P. and P. DiMaggio (eds) (1991). *The New Institutionalism in Organizational Analysis*, Chicago, Chicago University Press.

Putnam, R. (2000). *Bowling Alone*, New York, Simon & Schuster.

Putnam, R., R. Leonardi *et al.* (1993). *Making Democracy Work*, Princeton, Princeton University Press.

Radaelli, C. M. (1995). 'The Role of Knowledge in the Policy Process', *Journal of European Public Policy*, 2 (2): 159–183.

Ramirez, F., Y. Soysal *et al.* (1997). 'The Changing Logic of Political Citizenship', *American Sociological Review*, 62: 735–745.

Redclift, M. (1992). *Sustainable Development: Exploring the Contradictions*, London, Routledge.

Rees, T. (1998). *Mainstreaming Equality in the European Union*, London, Routledge.

Regini, M. (2000). 'Dallo scambio politico ai nuovi patti sociali', in D. dellaPorta, M. Greco and A. Szakolczai, *Identità, Riconoscimento, Scambio: Saggi in Onore di Alessandro Pizzorno*, Bari, Laterza: 151–194.

Rein, M. and D. Schon (1994). *Frame Reflections*, New York, Basic Books.

Rein, M. and D. A. Schon (1977). Problem Setting in Policy Research', in C. H. Weiss, *Using Social Research in Public Policy-Making*, Lexington: MA, D. C. Heath: 235–251.

Risse-Kappen, T. (1994). 'Ideas Do Not Float Freely: Transnational Coalitions, Domestic Structures, and the End of the Cold War', *International Organization*, 48 (2): 185–214.

Risse-Kappen, T. (1995). *Bringing Transnational Relations Back In: Non-State Actors, Domestic Structures and International Institutions*, Cambridge and New York, Cambridge University Press.

Risse, T., S. Ropp *et al.* (eds) (1999). *The Power of Human Rights*, Cambridge, Cambridge University Press.

Rootes, C. (1997). *The Transformation of Environmental Activism: Activists, Organisations and Policy-Making*, European Sociological Association Conference, Essex University.

Rootes, C. (ed.) (1999). *Environmental Movements: Local, National and Global*, London, Frank Cass.

Rucht, D. (1997). 'Limits to Mobilization: Environmental Policy for the European Union', in J. Smith, C. Chatfield and R. Pagnucco, *Transnational Social Movements and Global Politics: Solidarity beyond the State*, Syracuse, NY, Syracuse University Press.

Ruzza, C. (1996). 'Inter-Organizational Negotiation in Political Decision-Making: EC Bureaucrats and the Environment', in N. South and C. Samson, *Policy Processes and Outcomes*, London, Macmillan: 210–223.

Ruzza, C. (1997). 'Institutionalization in the Italian Peace Movement', *Theory and Society*. 26: 1–41.

Ruzza, C. (2000a). 'Anti-Racism and EU Institutions', *Journal of European Integration*, 22 (1): 145–171.

Ruzza, C. (2000b). 'Sustainability and Tourism: EU Environmental Policy in Northern and Southern Europe', in K. Eder and M. Kousis, *The Europeanization of Environmental Politics: Sustainable Development in Southern Europe*, Boston, Kluwer: 101–126.

Ruzza, C. (2002). '"Frame Bridging", and the New Politics of Persuasion, Advocacy and Influence', in A. Warleigh and J. Fairbrass, *Influence and Interests in the European Union: the New Politics of Persuasion and Advocacy*, London, Europa Press.

Ruzza, C. and M. Adshead (1995). *A Comparison of Policy Communities in the Environment and Agriculture Sector in the EU*, 12th EGOS Colloquium, Istanbul.

Ruzza, C. and O. Schmidtke (1993). 'Roots of Success of the Lega Lombarda: Mobilization Dynamics and the Media', *West European Politics*, 16 (2): 1–23.

Sabatier, P. (1998). 'The Advocacy Coalition Framework: Revisions and Relevance for Europe', *Journal of European Public Policy*, 5 (1): 98–130.

Sabatier, P. and H. Jenkins-Smith (eds) (1993). *Policy Change and Learning: An Advocacy Coalition Framework*, Boulder, CO, Westview Press.

Santoro W.A. and G. M. McGuire (1997). 'Social Movement Insiders: The Impact of Institutional Activists on Affirmative Action and Comparable Worth Policies', *Social Problems*, 44 (4): 503–519.

Saurugger, S. (2002). 'L'expertis : une forme de participation des groupes d'intérêt au processus décisionnel communautaire', *Revue française de science politique*, 52 (4): 367–401.

Sbragia, A. (ed.) (1992). *Euro-Politics*, Washington, DC, Brookings Institution.

Scharpf, F. W. (1999). *Governing in Europe: Effective and Democratic?*, Oxford and New York, Oxford University Press.

Schlager, E. (1995). 'Policy Making and Collective Action: Defining Coalitions within the Advocacy Coalition Framework', *Policy Sciences*, 28: 243–270.

Schmitter, P. A. (1974). 'Still the Century of Corporatism?', *Review of Politics*, 36 (93): 85–93.

Schmitter, P. A. (2000). *How to Democratize the European Union and Why Bother?* Oxford, Rowman & Littlefield.

Schon, D. and M. Rein (1994). *Frame Reflection: Toward the Resolution of Intractable Policy Controversies*, New York, Basic Books.

Seippel, O. (2001). 'From Mobilization to Institutionalization? The Case of Norwegian Environmentalism', *Acta Sociologica*, 44 (2): 123–137.

Shore, C. (1993). 'Inventing the People's Europe – Critical Approaches to European-Community Cultural Policy', *Man*, 28 (4): 779–800.

Silverman, M. (ed.) (1991). *Race, Discourse and Power in France*, Research in Ethnic Relations, Aldershot, Avebury.

Sinnott, R. (1995). 'Policy, Subsidiarity and Legitimacy', in O. Niedermaker and R. Sinnott, *Public Opinion and Internationalized Governance*, Oxford, Oxford University Press: 246–276.

Sluiter, P. and L. Wattier (1999). *A Guide to European Union Funding for the Voluntary Sector*, London, Directory of Social Change.

Smismans, S. (2002). '"Civil Society" in European Institutional Discourses', *Cahiers Européens de Sciences Po*, Paris.

Smith, J., C. Chatfield *et al.* (eds) (1997). *Transnational Social Movements and Global Politics: Solidarity Beyond the State*, Syracuse, NY, Syracuse University Press.

Smith, M. (1993). *Pressure, Power and Policy*, Hemel Hempstead, Harvester.

Snow, D. A., E. B. Rochford, S. K. Worden and R. D. Benford (1986). 'Frame Alignment Processes, Micromobilization and Movements Participation', *American Sociological Review*, 51: 464–481.

Social Platform (2000). 'Response of the Platform of European Social NGOs to "The Commission and Non-Governmental Organisations: Building a Stronger Partnership"', Brussels, Platform of European Social NGOs.

Solomos, J. (1993). *Race and Racism in Britain*, London, Macmillan.

Soysal, Y. (1994). *Limits of Citizenship*, Chicago, University of Chicago Press.

Spencer, P. and H. Wollman (2002). *Nationalism: A Critical Introduction*, London, Sage.

Steinmo, S., K. Thelen *et al.* (eds) (1992). *Structuring Politics*, Cambridge, Cambridge University Press.

Stevens, A. and H. Stevens (2001). *Brussels Bureaucrats?: The Administration of the European Union*, Basingstoke and New York, Palgrave.

Streeck, W. and P. Schmitter (1991). 'From National Corporatism to Transnational Pluralism: Organized Interests and the Single European Market', *Politics and Society*, 19 (2): 133–164.

Swidler, A. (1993). 'Book Review: *Talking Politics* by William Gamson', *Contemporary Sociology – A Journal of Reviews*, 22 (6): 810–812.

Thalhammer, E., V. Zucha *et al.* (2001). 'Attitudes Towards Minority Groups in the European Union', Vienna, European Monitoring Centre on Racism and Xenophobia.

Tommel, I. (1998). 'Transformation of Governance: The European Commission's Strategy for Creating a "Europe of the Regions"', *Regional and Federal Studies*, 8 (2): 52–80.

Triandafyllidou, A. and A. Fotiou (1998). 'Sustainability and Modernity in the European Union: A Frame Theory Approach to Policy-Making', *Sociological Research Online*.

United Nations (2001). 'Reference Document on the Participation of Civil Society in United Nations Conferences and Special Sessions of The General Assembly during the 1990s', New York, Office of the President of the Millennium Assembly – 55th session of the United Nations General Assembly.

Van Dijk, T. A. (1992). 'Discourse and the Denial of Racism', *Discourse and Society*, 3: 87–118.

Walker, J. (1991). *Mobilizing Interest Groups in America: Patrons, Professions and Social Movements*, Ann Arbor, MI, University of Michigan Press.

Walzer, M.. (ed.) (1995). *Toward a Global Civil Society*, Providence and Oxford, Berghahn Books.

Warleigh, A. (2001). '"Europeanizing" Civil Society: NGOs as Agents of Political Socialization', *Journal of Common Market Studies*, 39 (4): 619–39.

Waters, M. (1989). 'Collegiality: Bureaucratization, and Professionalization: A Weberian Analysis', *American Journal of Sociology*, 94 (5): 945–972.

Weale, A. (1992). *The New Politics of Pollution*, Manchester, Manchester University Press.

Weale, A. and M. Nentwich (1998). *Political Theory and The European Union: Legitimacy, Constitutional Choice and Citizenship*, London, Routledge.

Weiler, J., U. Haltern *et al.* (1995). 'European Democracy and its Critique', *West European Politics*, 18 (3): 4–39.

Weir, M. (1992). 'Ideas and the Politics of Bounded Innovation', in S. Steinmo, K. Thelen and F. Longstreth, *Structuring Politics*, Cambridge, Cambridge University Press: 188–216.

Weiss, L. (1998). *The Myth of the Powerless State*, London, Polity Press.

Willetts, P. (ed.) (1982). *Pressure Groups in the Global System: The Transnational Relations of Issue-Oriented Non-Governmental Organizations*, London, Frances Pinter.

Wilson, F. R. L. (1990). 'Neo-Corporatism and the Rise of New Social Movements', in R. J. Dalton and M. Kuechler, *Challenging the Political Order. New Social and Political Movements in Western Democracies*, Oxford, Polity Press: 67–83.

Wilson, J. Q. (1983). *American Government: Institutions and Policies*, Lexington, MA, D. C. Heath.

Wincott, D. (1995). 'The Role of Law or the Rule of the Court of Justice? An "Institutional" Account of Judicial Politics in the European Community', *Journal of European Public Policy*, 2 (4): 583–602.

Wrench, J. and J. Solomos (eds) (1993). *Racism and Migration in Western Europe*, Oxford, Berg.

Zuo, J. and R. D. Benford (1995). 'Mobilization Processes and the 1989 Chinese Democracy Movement', *The Sociological Quarterly*, 36 (1): 131–155.

Index